FREUD'S EARLY PSYCHOANALYSIS, WITCH TRIALS AND THE INQUISITORIAL METHOD

In *Freud's Early Psychoanalysis, Witch Trials and the Inquisitorial Method: The Harsh Therapy*, author Kathleen Duffy asks why Freud compared his 'hysterical' patients to the accused women in the witch trials and his 'psychoanalytical' treatment to the inquisitorial method of their judges. He wrote in 1897 to Wilhelm Fliess, 'I . . . understand the harsh therapy of the witches' judges'. This book proves that Freud's view of his method as inquisitorial was both serious and accurate.

In this multidisciplinary and in-depth examination, Duffy demonstrates that Freud carefully studied the witch trial literature to develop the supposed parallels between his patients and the witches and between his own psychoanalytic method and the judges' inquisitorial extraction of 'confessions', by torture if necessary. She examines in meticulous detail both the witch trial literature that Freud studied and his own case studies, papers, letters and other writings. She shows that the various stages of his developing early psychoanalytic method, from the 'Katharina' case of 1893, through the so-called seduction theory of 1896 and its retraction, to the 'Dora' case of 1900, were indeed in many respects inquisitorial and that they invalidated his patients' experiences.

This book demonstrates with devastating effect the destructive consequences of Freud's nineteenth-century inquisitorial practice. This raises the question about the extent to which his mature practice and psychoanalysis and psychotherapy today, despite great achievements, remain at times inquisitorial and consequently untrustworthy. This book will therefore be invaluable not only to academics, practitioners and students of psychoanalysis, psychotherapy, literature, history and cultural studies, but also to those seeking professional psychoanalytic or psychotherapeutic help.

Kathleen Duffy graduated with a PhD from Regent's University, School of Psychotherapy and Psychology, London, and until her retirement, she was a consultant psychotherapist and was training and supervising junior psychiatrists within the Mental Health Services in Ireland. Her first career was as a head teacher in Ireland.

'A very interesting, cross-disciplinary book containing valuable material and with considerable original findings. The analysis of the development of Freud's thought and the disturbing implications of his change of mind regarding the seduction theory are particularly well made. Connections are clearly made, for example, that Freud continued, at times, to use harsh therapy on the basis of the influence of his study of the witch trials. The book is well written and is a pleasure to read'.

— **Professor Mary Grey**, author, ecofeminist liberation theologian; professor emeritus University of Wales, Lampeter; professorial research fellow at St. Mary's University, Twickenham, London, UK

'Whereas Jung looked for historical analogies in Renaissance alchemy, Freud found his parallels in witchcraft trials. So persuasively argues this stunning book by Kathleen Duffy. Deftly written, deeply researched and provocatively argued, *Freud's Early Psychoanalysis* reveals a contradictory and gendered history of sexuality, demonology and the imagination. Were Freud's early hysteria patients the victims of child abuse or of their fantasies? Were witches devil worshippers and enthusiasts for orgiastic rituals or dupes their own erotic longings? The harsh therapy is Freud's term for the inquisitorial method of examining suspected witches; one he both overtly and covertly adopted. This important work of psychosexual history is a must for all therapists, historians of medicine, gender theorists, theologians, psychoanalysts, clinicians and students. Duffy's meticulous and daring scholarship is essential reading for all those who care about how power is both stimulated and repressed within human desire'.

— **Susan Rowland**, PhD, is author of nine books on Jung, gender and the arts, her most recent being *Jungian Literary Criticism: the Essential Guide* (2019). Founding Chair of the International Association for Jungian Studies, she is co-Chair of MA Engaged Humanities and the Creative Life and faculty on the Jungian and Archetypal Studies PhD programmes at Pacifica Graduate Institute. She is working on Jung and Arts-Based Research, USA

'This is the most exciting – and thought-provoking – book in the field of psychoanalysis/-therapy I have read for many years: Kathleen Duffy underpins her initially almost unbelievable and shocking claim that Freud, in creating psychoanalysis, took sustained inspiration from the inquisitorial methods of the witch trials – the worst sustained excesses of violence against women in Western history – with a wealth of solidly researched historical evidence. Considering that all forms of psychotherapy are derived and/or influenced by Freud's work, Duffy's controversial work not only challenges conventional academic perspectives on psychoanalysis and its origins, but also urges clinicians of all modalities to seriously re-think the way we view and interact with the people we work with – and also with our colleagues. With the currently increasing awareness of the abuse of women in patriarchal society, the publication of this book could not possibly be more timely'.

— **Dr Gottfried M. Heuer**, psychoanalyst, independent scholar, author of *Freud's 'Outstanding' Colleague/Jung's 'Twin Brother': The Suppressed Psychoanalytic and Political Significance of Otto Gross*, UK

'In this carefully researched and well-written book, Kathleen Duffy lays out a deeply convincing and very disturbing argument that Freud's study of the witch trials and their underlying assumptions affected his thinking about women and hysteria in a profound way. First, it caused him to develop a more sceptical attitude towards the memories of his female patients, and second, it undergirded his shift from his original theory of hysteria – that it was caused by child sexual abuse – to his later theory that it was the consequence of his patients' fantasies or 'wish fulfilment'. The early history of psychoanalysis still affects our clinical thinking and this book makes an important contribution to clarifying many central assumptions. It is a vital contribution to our work with female patients in contemporary psychoanalytic settings'.

— **Polly Young-Eisendrath**, PhD; Jungian Psychoanalytic Association; Clinical Associate Professor of Psychiatry, University of Vermont, USA; Past President Vermont Association for Psychoanalytic Studies, USA; author of *Love Between Equals* and *Women and Desire*

FREUD'S EARLY PSYCHOANALYSIS, WITCH TRIALS AND THE INQUISITORIAL METHOD

The Harsh Therapy

Kathleen Duffy

Routledge
Taylor & Francis Group

LONDON AND NEW YORK

First published 2020
by Routledge
2 Park Square, Milton Park, Abingdon, Oxon OX14 4RN

and by Routledge
52 Vanderbilt Avenue, New York, NY 10017

Routledge is an imprint of the Taylor & Francis Group, an informa business

© 2020 Kathleen Duffy

British Library Cataloguing-in-Publication Data
A catalogue record for this book is available from the British Library

Library of Congress Cataloging-in-Publication Data
A catalog record has been requested for this book

ISBN: 978-0-367-36924-8 (hbk)
ISBN: 978-0-367-36925-5 (pbk)
ISBN: 978-0-429-35193-8 (ebk)

Typeset in Bembo
by Apex CoVantage, LLC

Printed in the United Kingdom
by Henry Ling Limited

Source: Dr Sigmund Freud & Dr Wilhelm Fliess (1890) Gettyimages

In memory of my parents, Patrick and Mary Jane,
whose love still sustains me.

CONTENTS

ACKNOWLEDGEMENTS

Writing is a solitary experience. Yet a writer depends on others for support and encouragement. Many people have been generous with their time in preparing this book for publication.

I acknowledge with gratitude the insightful comments of Enda Lyons, D.D., professional theologian, who critically read an early draft of Part One of my work. I thank Brigitte Leveque, who translated from the original French a chapter from Bodin (1580) not included in the English edition that I accessed through the University of London collection of rare books. I also thank the British Library and the Crawley Library staff, who gave me invaluable help by responding positively and promptly to my many requests for rare fifteenth- and sixteenth-century books.

I thank Pauline Duffy-Duncan and the younger members of the Duffy family, whose computing competency rescued me towards the end of my work when my own computer illiteracy hampered my progress. Friends and family exercised much patience during my preoccupation with this work. Their interest sustained me when the going was tough.

I am indebted to Anthony Stadlen, Freudian expert, who recognised my idea as a hypothesis worth pursuing, for his guidance in the original writing project and for his foreword to this book. I thank Professor Gottfried Heuer, whose enthusiasm and encouragement kept me committed to the publication of this project. Finally, I thank Susannah Frearson, Heather Evans and Lauren Ellis at Routledge for their assistance.

FOREWORD

On 21 April 1896, Freud announced to the Society for Psychiatry and Neurology in Vienna his new method (psychoanalysis) of unknotting (analysis) the soul (psyche). He claimed that it revealed sexual abuse in 100 per cent of his 'hysterical' patients. He called this a momentous discovery, like discovering the source of the Nile. He compared it to Koch's discovery, in the previous decade, of a bacillus as the specific aetiology of the illness tuberculosis. Freud hoped to become as famous as Koch by discovering and announcing, a fortnight before his 40th birthday, the specific aetiology of the so-called mental illness hysteria.

'Specific aetiology' means a factor in whose absence the illness *cannot* occur. Freud was staking his reputation on there *not* having been a single 'hysteric', male or female, since the beginning of time, who had *not* been sexually abused in childhood. This was his so-called seduction theory. It was an all-or-nothing claim. A single 'hysteric' who could somehow be shown never to have been sexually abused 'before the age of second dentition' would make his theory not just a little bit wrong but *wholly* wrong.

But only 17 months later, Freud admitted in a private letter to his friend Wilhelm Fliess that he lacked the evidence he had publicly announced that he had discovered for his dramatic claim. How had he come to make this claim? He acknowledged his motive: world fame before he was 40. But how had he deceived himself that he was *justified* in making it?

Kathleen Duffy's book can help answer this question. Moreover, it provides a method to clarify what is trustworthy and what is untrustworthy in the extraordinary proliferation of psychoanalysis and psychotherapy today. Dr Duffy focusses on one sentence from another letter that Freud wrote to Fliess, when Freud was still brooding on his seduction theory, nine months after having announced it and his avant-garde method, psychoanalysis, in Vienna. On 24 January 1897, Freud wrote to Fliess, 'I understand the harsh therapy of the witches' judges'.

Dr Duffy wonders 'how this rational and compassionate physician and therapist can have entertained this comparison'. How can he have compared his own well-intentioned healing efforts to what he called the 'squeezing out under torture' of the 'confessions' of the accused women in the early modern so-called witch trials? This book is her answer.

Her achievement is to show that while Freud no doubt relished the black humour of the situation (had not his fellow Jews been objects of the same annihilating religious persecution?), he was *entirely serious* in identifying the central methodology of the witch trials with that of his own psychoanalysis.

What they had in common was the *inquisitorial method*. The inquisitorial method in law entails the presumption of guilt. Our accusatorial or adversarial method, reached through centuries of struggle, entails the presumption of innocence. Yet Freud insists that his method is, precisely, inquisitorial. Dr Duffy shows, in meticulous detail, to devastating effect, that Freud is in earnest. And she shows that his comparison is accurate.

But what has psychoanalysis to do with guilt or innocence? The common feature is that the inquisitor seeks to establish a particular narrative about the person accused of being a witch or regarded as a mental patient. And the primary assumption is that the inquisitor's narrative is correct. If the accused witch or identified patient protests that the narrative is false, the onus is on them to prove it.

In practice, the attempted proofs and protests are all too often taken as further evidence that the inquisitor is right. For example, consider not just Freud's seduction theory but also his subsequent retraction of it. In the original theory, he stated that only under the 'strongest compulsion' of his new method, psychoanalysis, could his patients be induced to 'reproduce' the 'scenes' of sexual abuse that he admitted he was suggesting to them. And he reported that the patients insisted that these scenes, even if 'reproduced' with emotion, did not have the feeling of being memories. This, Freud pronounced, was the most decisive proof that they *were* in fact memories!

However, when he began to doubt the universality of his supposed specific aetiology, he had the problem of explaining to his colleagues how he had made such an error. His solution was to blame the patient. He now claimed that his original theory had been that the patients had come to him volunteering stories of sexual abuse, which he, by implication the enlightened and compassionate therapist, had at first believed but had now discovered in some cases to be fantasies.

What both his seduction theory and his retraction had in common was that he was right and the patient was wrong.

Freud loved to give detailed evidence, in the manner of a German *Novelle*, when he had it. But neither for the seduction theory nor for its retraction did he give a shred of evidence. This was his inquisitorial method at its height.

Not all psychoanalysis or psychotherapy is inquisitorial. Not all Freud is. Freud made brilliant hypotheses, from his patients' dreams about specific events in their childhood, and he encouraged the patients to test his hypotheses by asking relatives who could confirm or deny them. His patients Abram Kardiner and Maryse Choisy gave astonishing evidence of such testing. This is psychoanalysis at its best, though not even the best psychoanalysis has to include such virtuosity.

Thomas Szasz said in a seminar in 2007, 'I think psychotherapy is one of the most worthwhile things in the world'. Szasz, more than anyone, had exposed the parallels between the Inquisition and modern psychiatry. He knew what was wrong with psychotherapy. But he knew it from the perspective of one who thought it could be 'one of the most worthwhile things in the world'.

More than 40 years ago, one of my supervisors, Dr Robert L. Tyson, who was to become secretary of the International Psychoanalytic Association, suggested a rule that has been of incalculable value in my own practice of psychotherapy: 'Never tell anyone what they are feeling'. He also said, 'I regard it as an insult to the patient to make an interpretation without giving one's evidence for it'.

But not all psychoanalysts or psychotherapists talk, let alone act, like this. Many are the inquisitors and persecutors of their patients and clients. Anyone wanting to become a psychoanalyst, a psychotherapist, or a client should be alerted to this possibility by Kathleen Duffy's marvellous book. They should seek out their analyst, their therapist, their supervisor, their training institute with the same dispassionate discretion that Dr Duffy displays.

They should be aware that alongside the superb psychoanalysts and psychotherapists of the world, there are those whose method is, unfortunately, even *worse* than that of the inquisitorial judges of the witches. It was difficult, but not *impossible*, for a woman accused of being a witch to give evidence to disprove it to her inquisitors. Such was the case of the astronomer Kepler's mother, who was acquitted with the brilliant help of her son.

But *nobody* can disprove to a dogmatic psychoanalyst or psychotherapist that *they* have an Oedipus complex or that *they* hate and love their baby, nor can they disprove any of the other things certain analysts and therapists believe they know to be universal truths.

Kathleen Duffy's book will give invaluable scholarly assistance to specialists trying to make sense of Freud's conceptualisation of his practice in 1896. But I hope it will also serve as a guide, philosopher and friend to anyone seeking, or wanting to become, a trustworthy psychoanalyst or psychotherapist today.

Anthony Stadlen

PART I

INTRODUCTION

This book is about Dr Sigmund Freud (1856–1939) and his understanding of 'the harsh therapy of the witches' judges'. The subtitle of my book, 'The Harsh Therapy', is a direct quotation from Freud's letter on 24 January 1897 to his friend, Dr Wilhelm Fliess: 'I dream, therefore, of a primeval devil religion with rites that are carried on secretly and understand the harsh therapy of the witches' judges'. My task in this book is to try to make sense of that statement. There may be ambiguities in the statement but, at first glance, Freud, by using the word 'therapy', appears to be making a direct comparison between the procedures of the judges in the witch trials and his new method, psychoanalysis. He said that 'Connecting links abound'. How this rational and compassionate physician and therapist can have entertained this comparison is puzzling. It appears to be a serious comparison because Freud made a deep study of the literature on the witch trials. I am not writing a complete history of witches, witchcraft and witch trials, because my book is not about witches per se. I am confining my study of the literature on witches to the books that we know Freud read and the books that were available to him that he most likely read, in order to make sense of his statement 'I . . . understand the harsh therapy of the witches' judges'.

It is possible to see hints or implications of my work in a number of studies on Freud, such as Swales and Szasz, but no major detailed study has treated this subject thoroughly. My work posed particular difficulty because not all the primary texts on witch trials have been translated into English. I have been fortunate to have had access to primary sources written by judges who conducted the witch trials – for example, the recently translated English version of Bodin's *De la Demonomanie des Sorciérs* (1580), the first major work on the witch trials since the *Malleus Maleficarum* appeared in 1486. This was Freud's main source of information on the witch trials. He wrote to Fliess, 'I have ordered the *Malleus Maleficarum*, and . . . I shall study it diligently'. I have also had access to the works of Judges Remy and Boguet, who conducted the witch trials in the sixteenth century. These judges have given first-hand accounts of the trials of witches that they conducted. The *Malleus*, written by inquisitors during the late medieval period, lay on the bench of every judge who conducted witch trials in the centuries following its publication. It was accepted by them as the ultimate authority on how to extract confessions from witches. Witch trials were conducted in the late medieval period and reached their peak during the early modern period. However, Freud, who was mainly interested in how confessions were extracted from witches, referred to the trials as medieval. I have used both terms 'medieval' and 'early modern' to cover the periods of the witch trials in Europe.

I have examined the evidence of what Freud actually did, in all his published cases of hysteria, and subsequent research done on the cases. I drew on autobiographical accounts of those who were in analysis with Freud. I examined the inquisitorial element common in both the witch trials and Freud's cases and how both the judges and Freud justify and explain this inquisitorial approach to themselves. The attempt to relate and parallel the judges' procedures in the witch trials with Freud's procedures in treating his patients seemed to be a large undertaking. It seemed more rigorously scientific to make an initial presentation of the judges' procedures by drawing not on theory or speculation but on the actual case histories of the witches from the trials conducted by Judges Bodin, Remy and Boguet. I relate Freud's procedures to the judges' procedures throughout Part One and Part Two of my book.

To present Freud's procedures, I have again chosen examples drawn from his case histories of hysteria. These examples offer an opportunity for detailed treatment that no theory of his other works can offer. I highlight aspects of Freud's procedural approach that have largely been ignored, namely his inquisitorial method of drawing confessions out of his patients. I also examine his correspondence with Fliess, in which he discusses his search for the aetiology of hysteria in psychological factors. Thus, my study is firmly grounded in the concrete evidence from case histories of both Freud's patients and the judges' alleged witches.

I examine the case histories that describe what Freud was doing during the eight-year period between autumn 1892 and autumn 1900. I have limited my research to those years because it was within that period that he made the statement that is under investigation in my book: 'I ... understand the harsh therapy of the witches' judges'. I looked at the case histories immediately before and immediately after that statement. His early case histories or his later successful cases are too far removed from that statement to throw any light on it. I am trying to make sense of what was in Freud's mind when he wrote to Fliess that he understood the harsh therapy of the witches' judges. Other authors, notably Roazen and Lohser & Newton, have presented the later years of Freud's approach as told by the analysands. Even some of those analysands experienced the approach I am highlighting; for example, in the case of H.D. in *Unorthodox Freud* (1996) we read, 'The probing quality of his questioning had felt like "drilling" to her' (Lohser & Newton, 1996: 74).

In this book, I use the accepted term 'seduction theory' for Freud's claim that the specific aetiology of hysteria is sexual molestation in childhood. This claim, which was first put forward in his three papers in 1896, is examined in Chapter 4. However, even though everyone calls it the seduction theory, Freud never called it that, as far as is known.

In the beginning of the early modern period, which overlaps with the end of the medieval period in Europe, witches were believed to be possessed by the devil. Freud had compared his theory of hysteria with 'the medieval theory of possession held by the ecclesiastical courts'. He wrote to Fliess on 17 January 1897,

> my brand-new prehistory of hysteria is already known and was published a hundred times over, though several centuries ago. . . . I always said that the medieval theory of possession held by the ecclesiastical courts was identical with our theory of a foreign body and the splitting of consciousness.

Freud is saying that the theory of the witches' 'possession' by the devil is identical with his theory of hysteria. In Chapter 3, I examine what Freud means by 'a foreign body and the splitting of consciousness' in his cases of hysteria.

Freud asks, 'why did the devil who took possession of the poor things invariably abuse them sexually and in a loathsome manner'? In Chapter 1, I examine the history of the devil and the meaning of 'possession'. Freud's correspondence with his Berlin friend Wilhelm Fliess, on 17 and 24 January 1897, indicates his familiarity with the theory of possession and witchcraft. On the subject of hysteria, he wrote to Fliess, 'The idea of bringing in witches is gaining strength. I think it is also appropriate'. Reflecting on the witches he asks, 'why are their confessions under torture so like the communications made by my patients in psychic treatment? Sometime soon I must delve into the literature on this subject'.

Do we know what literature on witches Freud had accessed or when he became interested in witches? Between October 1885 and February 1886, Freud studied under the French neurologist Charcot, in Paris. This was when Charcot sought to demonstrate how all the physical symptoms of hysteria were identical to the various symptoms attributed to witchcraft and possession by the devil in the early modern period. In Freud's obituary to his great mentor, he noted that

> Charcot . . . drew copiously upon the surviving reports of witch trials and of possession, in order to show that the manifestations of the neurosis [hysteria] were the same in those days as they are now. He treated hysteria as just another topic in neuropathology.
>
> *(Freud, 1893: 20)*

In the year of Charcot's death, 1893, Freud and his colleague Breuer first published their joint theory of hysteria. Freud also noted in the obituary how their new theory of hysteria 'would only have been a matter of exchanging the religious terminology of that dark and superstitious age for the scientific language of today' (Freud, 1893: 20).

Freud had claimed that his new theory of hysteria was identical to 'the medieval theory of possession held by the ecclesiastical courts' (17 January 1897). Freud was the first to note the psychological relevance of the material in the case histories of the witches written by the judges in the fifteenth and sixteenth centuries. It was presumably Charcot who interested Freud in the witches. During Freud's stay in Paris from 3 October 1885 to 28 February 1886, he was exposed to a vast body of literature on the demonic possession of witches. Charcot had sponsored the republication of a number of books on demonology and witchcraft in a special series, the *Bibliothèque Diabolique*. In the series was *De Praestigiis Daemonum* (1563) by Jan Wier, which was translated into English for the first time in 1991. Other titles in the series included *The Sabbat of Witches*, *The Possession of Françoise Fontaine*, *The Possession of Jeanne Fery*, *The Possession of Jeanne of the Angels* and *The Criminal Trial of the Last Witch*, which took place in Geneva on 6 April 1652. *Discours des Sorciers* (1590) by Henri Boguet and *De la Demonomanie des Sorciers* (1580) by Jean Bodin were prepared for publication in the series, but as far as is known, they were not published in that series. These valuable primary sources were, however, published and it seems likely that Freud had access to them in Paris or, at least, was aware of them. Some of these works on witch trials are examined in Chapter 2 of this work. (Note on Wier: my spelling of Wier throughout this book, except within quotation marks, is the Dutch spelling because Wier was Dutch.)

Freud had in his library the *History of the Witch Trials* by Soldan that has copious references to the sixteenth-century works of Judges Bodin, Remy and Boguet. Freud writes, in his letter of the 24 January 1897, 'The story of the devil . . . now gaining significance for me'. In the same letter, he also writes, 'If only I knew why the devil's semen is always described as "cold" in the witches' confessions'. As if to find an answer, Freud continues, 'I have ordered the *Malleus Maleficarum*, and . . . I shall study it diligently'. Freud had written to Fliess that he must delve into the literature to find answers to his many questions on why the devil, who took possession of the witches, abused them sexually, and why their confessions under torture were so like the communications made by his patients under treatment. In Chapter 1 we examine the history of the devil and of witches in the medieval and early modern literature.

In 1907, when Freud was asked by the Viennese publisher Hugo Heller to name 'ten good books', he named Wier's magnum opus on the belief in witches as one of the 'ten most significant books' (Freud, 1906f: 245). If Freud turned to Wier, as his letter to Heller indicates, to find answers to his questions on witches, we can also expect that he turned to the works of Judges Bodin and Boguet, who wrote detailed histories of the witch trials that they conducted. In Chapter 2 I have outlined the procedures used by these judges. Freud says that his time spent in Paris under Charcot was critical to the development of psychoanalysis. He hints that the seeds of the new science were sown in Paris (Freud, 1914d: 13, 1925d: 13) As well as the direct influence of Charcot, it is arguable that Freud is also referring to the body of literature on the demonic possession of witches and 'the very interesting witch trials' that were being republished at that time under the sponsorship of the School of Charcot.

It was believed that the devil placed an invisible mark on the witch as a sign of ownership when the witch committed herself to the devil (Bodin, 1580: 112–113). In an obscure passage in his letter to Fliess on 17 January 1897, Freud refers to the inquisitors pricking the witch 'with needles to discover the devil's stigmata, and in a similar situation, the victims [his patients] think of the same old cruel story in fictionalized form'. Freud is here making a direct comparison between what the inquisitors were doing with the witches and what he was doing with his patients. He parallels this with the seduction stories of his patients and refers to Emma Eckstein's memory of a scene 'where the diabolus sticks needles into her fingers and then places a candy on each drop of blood'. Freud says, 'not only the victims but also the executioners recalled in this their earliest youth'. To clarify the meaning of this obscure passage, I have related it to a passage in 'Infantile Sexuality' and to a famous scene in *Screen Memories* (Freud, 1899a). This examination takes place in Chapter 5. The parallels between the judges' and inquisitors' procedures, examined in Chapter 2, and Freud's procedures become obvious. The judges or inquisitors press for evidence of the devil's invisible mark on the witch, which is a sign of shameful relations with the devil; Freud also presses for evidence that is believed to be hidden and repressed by the victim-patient.

Chapter 5 of the work examines Freud's developing understanding of the stories he is drawing out of his patients. He reflects: are they trying to deny the reality of seduction by inventing stories to cover up for the crimes of their seducers, or are they inventing stories of seductions to cover up their own memories of their own infantile perverse activities? Chapter 2 shows that similar questions were in the minds of the judges regarding the witches: did they 'invent' the stories of the Sabbats seductions by the devil, or were the sexual orgies at the Sabbats real happenings? Freud is asking, are the witches inventing these stories of seductions by the devil to cover up for real seductions committed against them, or are they fantasising scenes of seduction by the devil to cover up their own infantile perversions?

Continuing to make connections between witchcraft and hysteria, Freud writes, 'in the perversions, of which hysteria is the negative, we have before us a remnant of a primeval sexual cult, which once was – perhaps still is – a religion in the Semitic East (Moloch, Astarte)'. In Chapter 1, I examine the different understandings of the pagan worship of Moloch and Astatre and the arguments for and against the view that these so-called witches were members of a primeval devil religion. This helps us on the way to understanding the meaning of Freud's statement 'I dream, therefore, of a primeval devil religion with rites that are carried on secretly and understand the harsh therapy of the witches' judges. Connecting links abound' (24 January 1897).

In the beginning of the early modern period, which overlaps with the end of the medieval period in Europe, belief in witches and possession by the devil increased. Freud ordered a copy of the *Malleus Maleficarum* (1486) in order to search for answers to an age-old problem. The *Malleus* was used by every judge who conducted the trials of witches in the centuries after its publication. It acquired especial weight and dignity from the authoritative bull of Pope Innocent VIII (1484), which delegated authority to the authors to act as inquisitors of all those witches who 'have abandoned themselves to devils'. This main accusation made against witches was related to the other accusation: by their spells, they 'hinder men from performing the sexual act' (Kramer & Sprenger, 1486: xx).

The authors of the *Malleus*, Kramer & Sprenger, state that their 'principal subject' is the carnal act that incubi devils perform with witches who submit themselves willingly to these abominations (Kramer & Sprenger, 1486: 111). Regarding this principal accusation made by the inquisitors against so-called witches, they ask, 'How can these devils perform the human act of copulation, and how do witches bind themselves to and copulate with these devils?' (Kramer & Sprenger, 1486: 21). These inquisitors compare this problem to a similar situation in the Book of Genesis 6: 1–4, and they base their whole claim about witches on their misinterpretation of this biblical pericope. An in-depth exegesis of Genesis 6: 1–4 exposes a major fault in the foundational claim made by the inquisitors about witches. The literary form of this pericope is myth, and if the mythic is read literally, its true meaning is lost. The Yahwist writer uses this myth to demonstrate the evil of breaching the boundary of human existence through intercourse with supernatural beings. Demythologising this story leads to what Tillich refers to as the 'pathology of literalism' (Dourley, 1981: 31). The authors of the *Malleus* literalised this myth and so lost its true meaning. For a résumé of my exegesis of Gen. 6: 1–4 and for a detailed exploration of the arguments in the *Malleus*, I refer the reader to *Freud and Wier: Transitional Figures?* (Duffy, 1996: 6–17).

The authors of the *Malleus* (1486) describe seven ways that witches have of doing harm to men, including making the male organ disappear and causing impotence in men. These inquisitors claim that witches and the devil always work together (Kramer & Sprenger, 1486: 18). Impotence is recognised today as a serious problem for some men, but in the early modern period, witches were blamed for men's impotence. Witches were believed to be malicious, dangerous women who flew to Sabbats and copulated with demons. This second claim of the authors of the *Malleus* is related to their first claim, which is in turn based on their literal misinterpretation of Gen. 6: 1–4. Great fear of women's power is evident in the *Malleus*. This misogynist misconception of women is examined in Chapter 1 of this work.

The authors of the *Malleus* (1486) state that witchcraft affects 'also the powers of the imagination or fancy', which sometimes causes impotence in men. They acknowledge that

> the imagination of some men is so vivid that they think they see figures and appearances which are but the reflection of their own thoughts, and these are believed to be the spectres of witches, but they warn that because such things happen merely in the imagination, those who suppose that all the effects of witchcraft are mere illusion are very greatly deceived.
>
> *(Kramer & Sprenger, 1486: 3)*

Bodin (1580), Boguet (1590) and Remy (1595) make the same point, which is presented on Chapter 2 of this work. This is related to Freud's developing theory of hysteria, as can be seen in Chapter 5.

Chapter 2 of my work shows how the confessions of 'crimes' were extracted from these so-called wicked witches. They were punished not so much for what they were doing as for what others claimed they were doing. The judges claimed that these women deserved the heaviest punishment because they bewitched men's imagination. Although the inquisitors and judges describe most of the witches' activities as real, there is a current weaving through their accounts that indicates their doubts as to whether the witches' accounts of their copulating with demons were real or imaginary. The claim of the judges that the witches sometimes 'invent' stories of sexual seductions by the devil to cover up their own perverse sexuality is examined in Chapter 2. William of Paris is quoted by the authors of the *Malleus* (1486) as saying that impressionable women 'think that they have been made pregnant by an incubus' (Kramer & Sprenger, 1486: 167). Similarly, Freud alleges that Dora had an 'unconscious phantasy' of pregnancy, but he claims that Anna O., the first psychoanalytic patient, actually spoke of 'Dr Breuer's child coming'.

When we look at Part 2 as a whole, we see the same reasoning as the judges and the same methods as the judges in use in the apparently different world of Sigmund Freud. Chapter 5 of my work presents Freud's questioning his seduction theory: did his patients 'invent' stories of sexual seductions to cover up their own promiscuity, or did their motives derive from revenge? Freud discussed, through his correspondence with Fliess, his newly emerging insights into the origins of hysteria. In these letters, we can follow the shift in Freud's thinking when he began to look at the interaction between fantasy and reality in his patients' stories. I examine the possible influence of the fifteenth- and sixteenth-century literature on Freud's developing theories, from his abandonment of his seduction theory, which is presented in Chapter 6, to his claim in Chapter 7 that the aetiology of hysteria is to be found in the patient's own phantasies of seduction, which he claimed were attempts to fend off memories of their own infantile sexual activity. In summary, these widely different practices of Freud and the judges are shown to have the same methods in common.

Even though Part 1 mainly examines the judges' understanding of the witches' possession by the devil and the procedures used by the judges to effectively deal with that hysterical phenomena, throughout Part 1, I draw the reader's attention to similar processes at work in Freud's approach, which is examined in Part 2. Similarly in Part 2, I highlight the places in Freud's work where parallels can be drawn with the judges' procedures. Part 2 shows that Freud used an inquisitorial approach in much of his clinical work. This approach is a result of how he defined his primary task in the treatment, namely making the unconscious conscious and the struggle involved in that process. Freud described it as a struggle or contest with demons. He saw his task as uncovering the secrets of the patient. I show that Freud's powerful procedural tool, his pressure technique, is comparable with the techniques used by the witches' judges to uncover the devil's invisible mark on the witch, the sure sign of her secret alliance with the devil.

To uncover the secret of the witch, the judge used pressure to extract a confession; to uncover his patient's secret, Freud used his own pressure technique. Both the judges and Freud saw their task as fighting to overcome resistance. Harsh therapy was needed by the judges to overcome the demons, in order to secure victory, which was seen as saving the soul of the witch. Freud believed harsh therapy was necessary to overcome the patient's resistance to uncovering repressed memories. Freud called this 'a contest with demons', to secure a permanent cure of the neurosis.

This book raises theoretical questions about psychoanalysis. I have used the Conclusion to sketch out the broad range of those questions and their implications for all those seeking psychotherapy today and for psychotherapists themselves. My main work here, however, is to analyse or exegete, as thoroughly as I have been able, a single sentence from Freud's letter to Fliess on 24 January 1897: 'I understand the harsh therapy of the witches' judges'. By 'analyse' or 'exegete', I mean reconstruct, on the basis of as rigorous an examination as the available primary sources permit, what Freud meant by his prima facie odd, even bizarre, comparison. I hope my exploration will serve as a basis for further theoretical investigation of Freud's works.

CHAPTER 1

AN ANALYSIS OF THE IDEA OF DEVILS, WITCHES AND EVIL

1.1. Introduction

> What would you say, by the way, if I told you that all of my brand-new pre-history of hysteria is already known and was published a hundred times over, though several centuries ago? Do you remember that I always said? that the medieval theory of possession held by the ecclesiastical courts was identical with our theory of a foreign body and the splitting of consciousness? But why did the devil who took possession of the poor things invariably abuse them sexually and in a loathsome manner? Why are their confessions under torture so like the communications made by my patients in psychic treatment? Sometime soon I must delve into the literature on this subject'. [a week later] 'I have ordered the *Malleus Maleficarum*, and . . . I shall study it diligently. The story of the devil, . . . now gaining significance for me. Can you without trouble recommend to me some good reading from your excellent memory?
>
> (Freud's letters to Fliess, 17 and 24 January 1897)

Freud was clearly interested in delving into the story of the devil, his 'possession' of witches and his abusing them sexually 'in a loathsome manner'. He explains the reason for his interest: 'the cruelties make it possible to understand some symptoms of hysteria that until now have been obscure' (Letter to Fliess, 24 January 1897). At a meeting of the Vienna Psychoanalytic Society 12 years later, on 27 January 1909, Hugo Heller gave a presentation on the history of the devil. Heller explains that an incentive for the study of the devil was his interest in examining the theories of hysteria that Prof. Freud has evolved, 'whether unsuccessful repression, which can generate hysteria in the individual case, may not have played its part also in the mass hysterias of the Middle Ages, in the belief in the devil, witches, etc.'. Heller is draw-ing attention to the parallel that Freud has earlier drawn between the witches and his hysterical patients. He notes that the persecution of witches was connected with a belief in the devil, the one who brings about all evil. In relation to the procedures used by the judges for obtaining confessions, Heller also notes that 'not all of the confessions obtained by torture were merely forced admissions of what the person had been accused of: a great deal of such testimony was based on the delusions of the accused themselves' (Nunberg & Federn, 1967: 117–120). Heller here takes the view that some of the witches were forced to confess the accusations brought against them.

In the discussion after Heller's lecture, Freud takes a more extreme view: the witches' 'fantasies . . . were not created under torture but merely squeezed out by it' (Nunberg & Federn, 1967: 120). Freud is saying that the harsh therapy merely squeezed out of the witches those fantasies that were already there. Freud made a similar point about his own procedure in psychoanalysis when, on 21 April 1896, he presented his lecture *The Aetiology of Hysteria* at a meeting of the Vienna Psychoanalytic Society. He examined possible objections to his procedure: he refuted the idea that the doctor 'forces reminiscences' on the patient, that he 'influences . . . by suggestion to imagine and reproduce them'. His answer to that possible charge against psychoanalysis came by saying that he had 'never yet succeeded in forcing on a patient a scene I was expecting to find' (Freud, 1896c: 204–205). Not only is Freud comparing the confessions of the witches and his patients; he is also comparing his procedures in psychoanalysis with the judges' procedures in the witch trials.

My study of the devil, witches and evil in this chapter has the same aim as Heller's: a history of the devil is presented to highlight the similarities that Freud draws between his theories of hysteria and the fifteenth-century theories of possession by the devil, the father of evil. I analyse the understanding of evil in relation to views of women in general and witches in particular.

1.2. Misogynist misconceptions of women

One example of this concept of woman as evil is found in the Bible in the prophet Zechariah's vision of the woman in the basket. The angel said to the prophet, 'This woman represents wickedness'. Then he pushed her down into the basket and put the lid back down. The prophet tells us, 'I looked up, saw two women flying towards me with powerful wings like those of a stork. They picked up the basket and flew off with it' (Zech. 5: 5–9).

Even though scriptures or the early fathers of the Church did not invent the stereotype of woman as evil, they nonetheless perpetuated the notion. Tertullian, one of the first-century fathers of the Church called woman the devil's gateway. Jerome wrote of 'woman's seductive potential', and Augustine states that 'nothing so debases man as the fondling of a woman' (Keane, 1977: 21). Woman as temptation is often featured in monastic literature. As temptation, women's bodies played an indispensable role in the fantasy life of the male ascetic. One of these early Desert Fathers, the ascetic Jerome, wrote,

> Now, although in my fear of hell I had consigned myself to this prison where
> I had no companions but scorpions and wild beasts, I often found myself

amid bevies of girls. My face was pale, and my frame chilled with fasting; yet my mind was burning with desire and the fires of lust kept bubbling up before me when my flesh was as good as dead.

(Jerome, Epistle 22.7 NPN 6.25)

Male ascetics were repeatedly advised to consider all women without exception as threat, danger, and demonic from the perspective of male fears and fantasies (Miles, 1990: 50, 76).

Christine de Pizan (1405) was the first female author to raise her voice against the view of women as evil. In her *City of Ladies* (1405), she lifted up a catalogue of wise female rulers and of learned and virtuous women and argued that women's defects come not from their natures but from their subordinate status and lack of education. Ruether, in her book *Women and Redemption: A Theological History* (1998), says that this picture of women was continued in Protestant thinking, but Luther juxtaposes the witch not with virginal women but with the good wife. Luther inaugurates this view by depicting women as naturally weak and fearful and, therefore, turning to witchcraft for aid (Ruether, 1998: 128). The construction of the bad wife as witch seldom questioned its misogynist assumptions.

By the beginning of the early modern period, men had created representations of women out of their own fears and fantasies. They represented 'woman' as a frightening and fascinating creature whose anger and rejection could deprive them of gratification, delight and ultimately life and salvation. The damage of such unlimited male projection was felt by medieval and early modern women who were tortured and burned as witches (Miles, 1990: 169–170). It was about these witches that Freud asked, 'Why are their confessions under torture so like the communications made by my patients in psychic treatment? Sometime soon I must delve into the literature on this subject' (Letter to Fliess, 17 January 1897).

Andreski (1982) argued in *The Syphilitic Shock* that a wave of virulent misogyny coincided with the syphilis epidemic as men blamed prostitutes in particular and women in general for infecting them. 'The terror and abhorrence of syphilis', projected onto women, was, Andreski suggests, a fundamental underlying motive for the witch persecutions of the sixteenth century. This hypothesis needs further documentation, but it is a provocative suggestion (Andreski, 1982: 7–26). Freud, in his discussion on Heller's presentation on the history of the devil, referred to the 'transformation in the Devil's personality' as 'connected with the upsurge of repression in the Reformation (syphilis), which saved Italian Christendom from disintegrating during the early Renaissance' (Nunberg & Federn, 1967: 123).

In the Dora case, Freud mentioned that Dora's father had contracted syphilis before his marriage. Freud had concluded from his experience as a neuropathologist that 'syphilis in the male parent is a very relevant factor in the aetiology of the neuropathic constitution of children' (Freud, 1905e: 20). It was Dora's view that her father passed on his venereal disease to her mother and to herself. Freud assured Dora that in his view, 'the occurrence of leucorrhea in young girls pointed primarily to masturbation', but by 1923, Freud no longer maintained this view (Freud, 1905e: 76n.2). Freud claimed that Dora

> was now on the way to finding an answer to her own question of why it was that precisely she had fallen ill – by confessing that she had masturbated, probably in childhood. Dora denied flatly that she could remember any such thing.
>
> *(Freud, 1905e: 76)*

Freud persisted in furthering steps towards a confession of Dora's 'secrets' by pointing to Dora's symptomatic actions – playing with a reticule, concealing a letter she had been reading and 'her addiction to bed-wetting' – all of which Freud claimed amounted to 'circumstantial evidence of her having masturbated in childhood'. Echoing the words of the witches' judges, Freud proclaimed, 'When I set myself the task of bringing to light what human beings keep hidden within them . . . no mortal can keep a secret. . . . Betrayal oozes out of him at every pore' (Freud, 1905e: 76–78). We shall see in the next chapter how the judges also used circumstantial evidence to draw a confession of guilt out of the witches.

Most of the people accused of being witches in the medieval and early modern periods in Europe were women. The European Continent was dominated by the fear of female witches. Parrinder (1958) writes, 'There is to this day numerous African secret societies which seek to keep women in subjection to the males, and the witchcraft belief serves that end'. Women who are imagined to be seeking escape from male domination by joining witch associations are quickly put back in their place by witch-hunts (Parrinder, 1958: 60). The fevered imagination of the inquisitors Sprenger and Kramer and the judges Bodin, Boguet and Remy, who conducted the trials of witches, give the impression that these women were engaged in an organised, concerted plot to overthrow the male-dominated Church and society, but in fact, most of the accused were decrepit old women whose powers were far below the possibility of performing the evil deeds ascribed to them. The explanation that the judges and inquisitors gave for the feebleness of the accused women is that the devil deserts them once they are made prisoners and fall into the hands of justice (Boguet, 1590: 132).

The authors of the *Malleus Maleficarum* (1486) say that there are more women than men addicted to witchcraft because women are more carnal than men. They mention Delilah (OT Judg. 16: 4–18) and other wayward women in support of their argument (Kramer & Sprenger, 1486: 43). The inquisitors' lurid descriptions of the sexual orgies at the Sabbat and the part played by the devil, who knows that the women love carnal pleasures, is in stark contrast to the ascetic teaching of the Church on sexual morality. Is it possible that these celibate authors were reacting against their own repressed sexuality by projecting their sexual phantasies onto women? The succubus whom they describe was believed to be a female demon who had intercourse with sleeping men; the incubus was believed to be a male demon who preyed on sleeping women. Witches were those who practised coition with these demons.

The authors of the *Malleus Maleficarum* (1486) spend much time debating the passage in Gen. 6: 1–4 that asks whether offspring can be created from such coition. The fact that women were accused of witchcraft, mainly or exclusively, shows a deep-rooted sexual antagonism. The inquisitors or witch finders were men, mostly celibates. Their morbid preoccupation with the subject of copulation with the devil, of which they accused the witch and about which they themselves wrote in lurid detail in the *Malleus Maleficarum*, is an interesting point in their psychology. The subjection of women, who were believed to have pacts with the devil, was one aim of the witch-hunting. In return for their commitment to the devil, it was believed that the devil gave them power to harm men. Witches were accused of causing male impotence and depriving men of their virile member. Witches were believed to receive power from the devil to do many other evil deeds (Duffy, 1996: 6–16).

1.3. 'The story of the devil . . . now gaining significance for me'

Heller presented his review of Roskoff's *History of the Devil* to a meeting of the Vienna Psychoanalytic Society on 27 January 1909 because of Freud's interest in 'the belief in devils' and to 'stimulate a thorough discussion of the topic'. After the presentation, Freud expressed his appreciation of the importance of the problem and added that 'the highly complex personality of the Devil – his prehistory – is an interesting subject for research'. He says, 'the Middle Ages uses the Devil – to exculpate itself: it shoves onto him the impulses that it does not want to acknowledge'. Heller had pointed out that the medieval 'persecution of witches' was 'connected with' the belief in the devil, who 'brings about all evil'.

Dr Paul Carus (1852–1911), a contemporary of Freud, presents the universality of the idea of evil and the devil in his book, *The History of the Devil and the Idea of Evil* (1900). Carus was a philosopher of science. As a youth he fled from an intolerant Germany to publish his liberal thoughts on science and religion. While scientists were writing against religion with passion Carus was devoting his energies to paving a middle road on which both science and religion could progress. Carus described the devil as symbolic of a real part of human experience. The devil is personified as evil. Carus believed in the devil in the sense that evil is an actual presence in the world. He confronted the problem of evil and interpreted the devil as the universe's resistance to human efforts to progress (Carus, 1900: 6–7). Carus claimed that devil-worship preceded the worship of a benign deity and that fear is always the first incentive to religious worship. People worshipped thunder because it had known and obvious dangers outside human control. We fear the dangerous and the bad, not the good, so the worship of an angry deity or devil was the first stage in the evolution of religion.

1.3.1. Devil-worship: 'a religion in the Semitic East (Moloch, Astarte)'

Most civilised nations still preserve stories of having, at an early period of their religious development, immolated human beings in propitiation of angry deities. Human sacrifices are frequently mentioned in the Bible. In 2 Kings 4:27, we hear of the King of Moab, who 'took his eldest son who should have reigned in his stead and offered him as a burnt offering'. The prophets were constantly preaching against the pagan practice of those Israelites who, in imitation of the religion of their neighbours, sought to 'sacrifice their sons and daughters to devils' or let them 'pass through the fire of Moloch to devour them'.

In Freud's letter of the 24 January 1897, he also writes about the worship of Moloch in the context of his discussion on hysteria. He says,

> it is as though in the perversions, of which hysteria is the negative, we have before us a remnant of a primeval sexual cult, which once was – perhaps still is – a religion in the Semitic East (Moloch, Astarte). . . . I dream, therefore, of a primeval devil religion with rites that are carried on secretly and understand the harsh therapy of the witches' judges.

Freud is saying that he understands the harsh therapy in the same sentence where he says that he dreams of a primeval devil religion. This is immediately after he has referred to the pagan worship of Moloch and Astarte. The arguments of various authors on the theory of witchcraft as a remnant of a primeval cult are examined later in this chapter. The witches' judges used the biblical references to the worship of Moloch and Astarte to justify their harsh therapy. This will be examined later in the chapter.

Human sacrifice was one of the principal characteristics of devil-worship (Carus, 1900: 50). Primitive religion, which began with fear, may be defined as 'the fear of evil and the various efforts made to escape evil'. At an early stage almost all worship was to propitiate the powers of evil. Now the power of evil is no longer worshipped but rather the struggle is against evil (Carus, 1900: 13–14). Freud wrote to Fliess on 24 January 1897, 'I dream of a primeval devil religion', when he was considering the so-called witches' Sabbat. Is Freud saying that the judges' harsh therapy was an understandable response to perverse evil practices of sacrificing children to devils? But were the witches engaged in devil-worship?

The inquisitors and judges in the witch trials drew on the accounts of witches in the Old Testament to justify their treatment of witches. They claimed that the laws of Exodus demand capital punishment for witchcraft (Ex. 22: 18). But the word 'witch' in Exodus means 'sorceress', not 'devil-worshipper'. King Saul, when in greatest anxiety, called on the witch of Endor, who could be better described as a medium (1 Samuel 28: 3–15). The authors of the *Malleus Maleficarum* (1486), the first handbook for the punishment of witches, based their claim for the need for the punishment of witches on a passage from the first book of the Bible, Gen.

6:1–4. This pericope, which the authors of the *Malleus* take literally, is a mythical presentation of the meaning of evil.

Assyrian pictures represent evil spirits in the shape of goats. The Hebrews are warned that they must 'no longer be unfaithful to Yahweh by killing animals in the fields as sacrifices to the goat-demons' (Lev. 17:7). Carus questions whether these goat demons (Seirim) and night demons (Lilith) were a residue of an earlier religious stage preceding the period of monotheistic Yahwism or were they a mere superstition 'which haunted the imagination of the uncultured' (Carus, 1900: 69).

Nothing is more common in history than the change of the deities of hostile nations into demons of evil. For the Hebrews, Beelzebub – the Phoenician God – became another name for Satan. Hinnom or Gehenna, the place where Moloch had been worshipped, became the Hebrew name for hell in place of the word 'Sheol'. The idol of Moloch, the Ammonite deity, to whom Freud refers in his letter to Fliess on 24 January 1897, was made of brass, and its stomach was a furnace. Children were placed in the monster's arms to be consumed by the heat of the idol. The cries of the victims were drowned by drums. Even King Manasseh made his son pass through the fire of Moloch (2 Kings 21). In the context of the harsh therapy of the witches' judges, Freud refers to the sacrifice of children implicit in the worship of Moloch.

King Josiah tried to put an end to this terrible practice of pagan worship. He tore down the altars dedicated to the goat demons. He desecrated the place of worship of Moloch so that no one could sacrifice his son or daughter as a burnt offering to the god Moloch. He desecrated the altars for the worship of idols – Astarte, the goddess of Sidon, and Moloch, the god of Ammon (2 Kings 23). These severe measures taken by King Josiah to put an end to the worship of Moloch and Astarte is foreshadowing the severe inquisitorial measures taken by the witches' judges to end the witches' supposed worship of the devil.

I again refer the reader to Freud's letter to Fliess on 24 January 1897, in which he states that 'in the perversions, of which hysteria is the negative, we have before us a remnant of a primeval sexual cult, which once was – perhaps still is – a religion in the Semitic East (Moloch, Astarte)'. This is an important point to which we shall return because it is immediately after his reference to the worship of Moloch that Freud says he understands 'the harsh therapy of the witches' judges'. Freud is drawing comparisons between the worship of Moloch, witchcraft and hysteria. By implication, he is also drawing comparisons between what he was doing with his patients and what the judges were doing with the witches, because he calls the judges' procedures therapy.

1.3.2. 'The gold the devil gives his victims' – the price of 'possession'?

The witches were believed to have sold their souls to the devil, who then possessed them. Freud writes, 'I read one day that the gold the devil gives his victims regularly turns into excrement. . . . So, in the witch stories it is merely transformed back into the substance from which it arose' (Letter to Fliess, 24 Jan. 1897). Guazzo (1608) claimed that during the ceremony of profession of witchcraft, the witch gave the devil a piece of her clothing as a sign that she belonged to him, and she vowed to fly to the Sabbat (Guazzo, 1608: 13ff). The devil then placed his mark on her body, especially on the private parts. An Essex woman who was accused of being a witch said that she had learned the art of witchcraft from her grandmother, who taught her to give her blood to Satan (Parrinder, 1958: 63–64). Freud has a similar story from one of his patients: 'Eckstein has a scene (that is, remembers) where the diabolus sticks needles into her fingers and then places a candy on each drop of blood' (Letter to Fliess, 17 Jan. 1897).

1.4. 'The highly complex personality of the devil'

What was the witches' judges' understanding of the devil? What was Freud's understanding of the devil? He referred to the devil's 'highly complex personality' in his discussion after Heller's talk on the devil. Satan and his demons, as they were known to the early Christians, were already products of a long and complex evolution, and they continued to change during the following centuries. Satan was regarded by the early Christians as the prince of this world, and this belief dominated in the Church as long as pagan authorities remained in power. When Christianity became established as the state religion of the Roman empire, Satan was dethroned and God reinstated in the government of the world.

By medieval times, demons had once again become powerful and menacing, and they were also far more closely involved in the lives of individual Christians (Cohn, 1975: 68). It was not until the period of the Black Death, in the fourteenth century and later during the Reformation, that we see a new explosion in the idea of evil, especially of the devil. When the Black Death ravaged Europe with its plagues, caused by fleas and lice on humans, the Jews in specific were accused of causing the plague, and most of the German Jews were exterminated, as happened again in the twentieth century when scapegoats were needed again (Parrinder, 1958: 21).

In Freud's letter to Fliess of 24 January 1897, he wrote, 'we have before us a remnant of a primeval sexual cult'. Is he postulating the theory of witchcraft as a primitive sexual cult or as sexual phantasies or both? Judge Boguet's chief accused witch, Françoise Secretain, had Christian rosary beads that she used most devoutly in saying her prayers. She, therefore, was not a member of any primeval cult. Her case is presented in Chapter 2 of this work.

It was believed in the medieval period that demons retained their capacity to take on a bodily form at will; the form that became standard was pitch-black, naked and covered with wrinkled skin. Demons were believed to operate through the moral weakness of humans but were subject to an omnipotent god. A German monk wrote stories of the devil to be used in sermons. One story shows a demon in the guise of a smartly dressed fellow or a handsome soldier when he is set on seducing a woman. The stress shifted since the days of the early Christians onto the resourcefulness of demons and the relative helplessness of human beings. One monk, Caesarius, claims that a demon can enter a person's body and take up residence in its bowels where the excrement is. Another monk tells that in each monastery, a staff of demons is employed, and several demons pursue the same individual. One demon provoked an attack of giddiness to prevent the abbot from celebrating Mass. Demons tempt monks to sleep at unsuitable times, but the monk hastens to assure the novice that the snores that come from him are really the work of demons (Cohn, 1975: 69–72).

All this is a far cry from the faith of the early Christians. Now the demons have come to represent desires that individual Christians have but that they dare not acknowledge as belonging to themselves. The psychic tension and conflict that they generate express themselves often, as we saw, in such physical symptoms as giddiness and sleepiness. It was because Christians, particularly monks, were so obsessed with the power of Satan and his demons that they were so ready to see devil-worship in the most unlikely quarters. Cohn (1975) claims that the fantasy of a secret society of devil-worshipping witches was created by the anxieties that haunted the minds of Christians (Cohn, 1975: 73–74).

From Charlemagne's founding of the Holy Roman Empire around 800 CE, for one thousand years, Christianity was officially recognised as the religion of the Empire, and as a result Christianity had an impact on the private and public affairs of the people. With the conversion of the warlike Teutonic nations of North West Europe – Germans, Anglo-Saxons, Norse people – a warlike spirit entered Christianity. The chief god of the Teutons was a god of war. Teutonic legends frequently mention the devil (Carus, 1900: 241). The evil powers of this Teutonic part of Europe were transferred onto the devil. However, the barbarous practice of human sacrifice to the devil was abandoned (Carus, 1900: 191–195).

The conception of the devil's abode, hell, as depicted by Dante (1314) in *The Divine Comedy* is the product of a Northern European imagination. The deepest hell of Dante's Inferno is the wintry desolation of an ice palace. Dante reproduced in his description of Satan and hell the mythological views of northern Europe so popular in his day. In the last Canto, Dante describes the residence of the sovereign of hell, an ice palace that is almost inaccessible through the cold blizzards that blow about it; there the ruler of hell and his most cursed fellows stand with their bodies partly frozen in the transparent ice (Carus, 1900: 247). Dante writes,

> I stood (with fear I write it) where at last
> The shades, quite covered by the frozen sheet,
> Gleamed through the ice like straws in crystal glassed;
> Some lie at length and others stand in it. . . .
> The emperor of the sorrowful realm was there,
> Out of the gliding ice he stood breast high.
> (Dante, 1314: 1 Canto 34: 10–13, 28–29)

On 24 January 1897, Freud wrote to Fliess,

> If only I knew why the devil's semen is always described as "cold" in the witches' confessions. I have ordered the *Malleus Maleficarum*, and . . . I shall study it diligently. The story of the devil, the vocabulary of popular swear words, the songs and customs of the nursery – all these are now gaining significance for me. Can you without trouble recommend to me some good reading from your excellent memory?

Freud acquired a copy of *The Divine Comedy* at a later stage. Could this Northern European view of Satan standing 'breast high' in ice account for the stories of the devil's cold semen in the witches' confessions? In the next chapter of this work, we will find in the witches' confessions recorded by Bodin, Remy and Boguet frequent references to the devil's cold semen, a matter that was of interest to Freud.

1.5. The Protestant understanding of the devil

The Reformation brought a change in belief in the devil to a tendency to interpret him in psychological terms. Instead of expecting him in the horrors of nature and in the surroundings, he is to be found in our own hearts, where he appears as temptation in all forms, as allurements, ambition, vanity or the vain pursuit of power, pleasure and possessions. The idea of understanding Satan as temptation is not new, but temptation begins to be better understood as a psychological condition of subjective states. However, Luther was a child of his time and he saw the devil everywhere. He regarded the pope as the Antichrist. The devil was, for Luther, a real, living, concrete personality. Luther believed in the devil's power to assist witches in their evil designs, and he declared that witches should suffer death (Carus, 1900: 338–343). Protestant as well as Catholic churches hounded the so-called witches and administered harsh therapy.

1.6. The devil: myth or reality?

The Catechism of the Catholic Church (1994) says that the devil and the other demons were created good by God, but they became evil by their own doing (CCC, 1994: 88). The *Catechism* again says that for liberation from demonic 'possession', an exorcism is performed, but first, it is important to ascertain that one is dealing with the presence of the evil one and not an illness (CCC, 1994: 374). In popular literature, the devil plays a most important role. Without him, there would be no plot, and the story would lose interest. He is the mischief maker and the incarnation of all physical and moral evil in the world. Literature of devil stories is extensive. The most famous legend of contracts with the devil is the saga of Dr Johannes Faustus. The original form of the Faust legend represents the Catholic viewpoint. The oldest Faust book (1587) tells of Faust, the son of a farmer, who studied theology at

Wittenberg. Failing to make sufficient progress, Faust conjured up the devil and forced him to become his servant.

Faust made a compact with the devil, who consented to serve him for 24 years, and Faust would allow him to deal with him as he pleased at the end of the 24 years. The contract was sealed by Faust with his blood, which he drew with a penknife from his left arm. Sealing contracts with blood was an ancient custom. The covenant between the Israelites and Yahweh was sealed by blood (Ex. 24: 1–8). When the time of his contract had almost elapsed for Faust, he grew melancholic, but the devil mocked him. At midnight on the last day, a frightful noise was heard. Next morning Faust was found torn to pieces. In Goethe's Protestant version, Faust's soul is saved. In his letter of response to Hugo Heller's request to name 'ten good books', Freud names Goethe's version of Faust as one of 'the ten most magnificent works (of world literature)' (Freud, 1906f: 245).

The figure of the evil one began slowly to lose the awe that it exercised on the imagination of the people during the medieval period. The idea of evil has been personified by all nations. The serpent or the dragon as a picture of the devil appears not only in the Bible (Gen. 3: 1) but also in Babylonian literature. Even the splendid description of Leviathan (Job 41) as a monster of the deep is a reproduction of Chaldean mythology. The pedigree of the evil one antedates the Bible. There is no religion in the world that has not its demons or evil monsters who represent destruction and misery. During the medieval period, the nefarious activity of the devil was believed to be done through his agents, the witches.

1.7. Who was selected for the role of witch?

Women, mainly between the ages of 50 and 70, were the ones accused of witchcraft. Daughters of accused witches were also suspect because witchcraft was believed to run in families. Family jealousies or neighbours' quarrels sometimes provided fertile ground for witchcraft accusations. It is worth recalling Freud's words about dream life:

> Hatred, too, rages without restraint; wishes for revenge and death, directed against those who are nearest and dearest in waking life, against the dreamer's parents, brothers and sisters, husband or wife, and his own children, are nothing unusually uncommon.
>
> *(Freud, 1916:157)*

Also suspect were eccentrics, bad-tempered or solitary women, women with a sharp tongue who were quick to scold and threaten, frightening to look at, ugly and squinty or who had pocked skin and a deformed figure that bent and bowed with age. One suspected old woman is described as having dirty clothes, outlandish gear, long teeth and cloven feet. The kind of imagination that could create such beings was also capable of transforming old women, weighed down by their infirmities, into embodiments of malevolent power (Cohn, 1975:248–249).

According to Cohn (1975), two distinct notions pervaded in the fifteenth and sixteenth centuries of what witches were:

> (a) One notion came from the popular imagination: witches were women who harmed their neighbours by occult means. The accused was almost always an old woman who was the enemy of new life, who killed the young and caused impotence in men and sterility in women.

> (b) The other notion of the witch came from the inquisitors and judges. Their primary complaint was that witches attended the Sabbat, collectively worshipped the devil in bodily form and engaged in sexual orgies involving mating with Satan and communal feasting on the flesh of babies.
>
> *(Cohn, 1975: 251–252)*

The division that Cohn makes is useful, but the categories overlap and are more complex than Cohn claims. All witches were believed to have a pact with the devil, who in turn empowered them to do harm to men. It would be more helpful to say that the Sabbat orgies were of most concern to the inquisitors and judges, and the evil deeds of witches were most feared by the general population. Witches were believed to cast spells and work magic through the power of the devil.

1.8. Miracles or magic: a dualistic approach?

People condone their own faults while condemning those of others. The virtues of the pagans were, to Augustine, only 'polished vices' while the heroism of Christian martyrs was mere obstinacy in the opinion of Roman praetors. A major comparison is seen if we compare the story of Elijah with the story of the witches. The story in the Bible is read with great edification in how the prophet Elijah, a man of God, told the king that 'there will be no dew or rain for the next two or three years until I say so'. And at the end of the period of drought, Elijah said to the king, 'I hear the roar of rain approaching'. In a little while, the sky was covered with dark clouds, the wind began to blow and heavy rain began to fall (1 Kings 17–18). The so-called witches, who posed as rainmakers, were looked upon with contempt and punished because they were said to have performed the same feat as the prophet Elijah, but they were believed to have accomplished their feat through the power of the devil. The witches' art was believed to be practised to injure humans and was therefore feared.

1.9. 'Their "flying" is explained'

The magic of flight is an ancient folklore theme found in literature throughout the world. The belief in night flying is ancient and widespread. In Hindu superstitions, witches were believed to use spells to enable themselves to fly through the night to places of meeting. Medieval Jewish belief spoke of women flying with unbound hair to nocturnal assemblies. In Africa it is still believed that witches fly to their meetings as bats or owls (Parrinder, 1958: 44). In popular European belief, the witch flew to the Sabbat on a broomstick.

Christianity, at first, condemned the belief in night flying as erroneous. One of the oldest documents denying the existence of witches is the Canon Episcopi. It is an important document because of its early origins. It was first published by a Benedictine monk in 906 CE, but the original document was probably written between 350 CE and 550 CE. It condemns belief in witchcraft as delusional, and it dismisses the stories of night flying as fantasies. It decreed that some wicked women, reverting to Satan, and seduced by the illusions and phantasms of demons, believe and profess that they ride at night with Diana on certain beasts. Therefore, priests everywhere should preach that such phantasms are sent by the evil spirit, who deludes them in dreams. In the twelfth century, the Canon Episcopi was incorporated into Canon Law by the canon lawyer, Gratian. The Decretum of Gratian (1144) was absorbed as Canon XXVI into the decisions of the Third Lateran Council in 1179. The Canon Episcopi attributes the night rides of witches to dreams and branded all claims of night flying as illusory. Until the thirteenth century, the Church officially considered the traditional powers of witches as imaginary, bred of insanity or dreams. It was therefore heretical to express belief in the reality of witches. But in the ensuing centuries, other beliefs came to be associated with the illusion of night flying; for example, the witches were believed to be flying to secret meetings with the devil.

Freud also refers to the belief in the 'night flying' of witches. He wrote to Fliess on 24 January 1897, 'The idea of bringing in witches is gaining strength. I think it is also appropriate. Details are beginning to abound. Their "flying" is explained; the broomstick they ride probably is the great Lord Penis'. He added, 'The secret gatherings, with dancing and entertainment, can be seen any day in the streets where children play. . . . The story of the devil, . . . the songs and customs of the nursery – all these are now gaining significance for me'. We will return to this parallel with the witches, in Part Two, when we examine Freud's *Screen Memories* (1899a) on the theme of children playing. One can also think of the nursery rhyme "Mother Goose Riding on Her Gander" as reflecting the theme of riding referred to by Freud in his letter. I am suggesting in this book that Freud was influenced by his reading of the literature on witches to consider the possibility that his own patients were phantasising seduction.

Medieval theologians had great difficulty with the Canon Episcopi, which had declared night flying illusory. The Canon Episcopi denied the reality of the night-ride with Diana and declared that those women who believed that they rode with her were the victims of a devilish delusion.

1.9.1. Witches: fly-by-nights?

A new generation of theologians, including Thomas Aquinas (1225–1274), denied the Canon Episcopi and sought to convince people that night flying with

Diana to Sabbats and copulation with demons were not imaginings or phanta-sies but facts. The authors of *Malleus Maleficarum* (1486), followers of Aquinas, declared that the witchcraft that they, as inquisitors, were fighting was a different thing, connected only in name with the witchcraft condemned as imaginary by the Canon Episcopi. The inclusion of the devil in the European witchcraft in medieval times added a new element to witchcraft. This addition of Hebrew-Christian demonology distinguishes the witchcraft of that time from that of former periods. It is the inclusion of the element of demonology in witchcraft that makes the understanding of the medieval and early modern witch trials more complex. In the witch assemblies or Sabbats, the chief figure was said to be a man, a devil, or a male animal. Most of the witches were women. Boguet (1590) says that they

> first worship Satan, who appears to them now in the shape of a big black man and now as a goat; and to do him greater homage they offer him can-dles, which burn with a blue flame; then they kiss him on the shameful parts behind,
>
> *(Boguet, 1590: 55)*

The authors of the *Malleus* (1486) were followers of Aquinas, and they asserted that the witches' flying was not imaginary; it was 'proved by their own confessions'. They record the account of a woman who when asked whether she could be transported only in imagination or actually in body answered that 'it was possible in both ways' (Kramer & Sprenger, 1486: 108). The two Dominican authors of the *Malleus* claimed that the night was the proper time for nefarious activities and thought it a suitable time for witches to hold meetings. They held that the noc-turnal Sabbat took place while ordinary people were asleep. According to ancient belief, for example, in the Canon Episcopi, this would have been explained by the dream activity of the witch herself. But the authors of the *Malleus* had other thoughts. They declared that even if existing in the imagination only, such beliefs were dangerous, justifying torture and death. In the next chapter of this work, we shall return to the significance of this belief in relation to Freud's theories of seduc-tion and his drawing of parallels between the witches' confessions and his patients' stories.

1.10. Witchcraft in France: the case of Françoise Fontaine

Trevor-Roper (1988) tells of the confession of a servant girl, Françoise Fontaine, made at Louviers to Loys Morel. Morel says that her story was 'elicited by patience, not pressure'. It is the standard story: the visit of the devil in the guise of a man dressed in black, the lack of pleasure in copulating with the demon and the ice-cold semen. In his introduction to the case of Françoise Fontaine, the Viscount de Moray has shown, from the evidence of the Salpetriere hospital in Paris, that 'every detail of Françoise Fontaine's experience has its parallel today: the diabolic incubus is only the sixteenth century form of a kind of sexual hysteria familiar to every twentieth century psychiatrist' (Trevor-Roper, 1988: 50). The case of the possession of Françoise Fontaine was republished under the title, *Procès-verbal fait pour délivrer une Fille Possédée par le Malin Esprit* in 1883 in the Bourneville series, under the sponsorship of Charcot. This case would have been accessible for Freud during his stay in Paris in 1885–1886. He wrote to Fliess on 17 January 1897: 'my brand-new prehistory of hysteria is already known and was published a hundred times over, though several centuries ago … I always said that the medieval theory of possession … was identical with our theory'.

1.10.1. Three French 'significant books' on 'the very interesting witch trials'

While the crime of witchcraft was taking shape in the minds of inquisitors and judges, many books were being written to instruct the uninitiated in the evil mysteries of the new heresy: witchcraft. Three of the most famous books on witchcraft and on witch trials were written by French authors who were also judges in the witch trials: *An Examen of Witches* (1590) by Boguet, *On the Demon-Mania of Witches* (1580) by Bodin and *Demonolatry* (1595) by Remy. When the reality of the witches' Sabbat became the accepted belief of these authors, the problem of dreams had to be faced. We shall see in the account of the witch trials that, in their forced confessions, the witches did confuse their dreams with reality. But was most of the confusion between fantasy and reality in the minds of the *inquisitors* who extracted the confessions? Mention has already been made in this work of the varying views of Freud and Hugo Heller regarding the fantasies squeezed out of the witches by the harsh therapy when they were discussing the matter at a meeting of the Vienna Psychoanalytic Society on 27 January 1909.

1.11. 'I must delve into the literature on the subject'

While Freud was studying under Charcot in Paris between October 1885 and February 1886, Charcot was trying to demonstrate the precise correspondence between hysteria and witchcraft. Charcot wanted to demonstrate how all the physical symptoms of hysteria were identical to the various symptoms attributed in the medieval period to witchcraft and possession. He sponsored the publication of a number of books on demonology and witchcraft in a special series, the *Bibliothèque Diabolique*, under the editorship of Bourneville. The case of the possession of Françoise Fontaine was published in this series in 1883. Modern French translations of Bodin's *Demon-Mania* (1580) and Boguet's *An Examen of Witches* (1590) were also prepared for publication in this series, but they were not published at that time. A list of books in the series can be found in Appendix 2.

The French translation of Wier's main opus, *De Praestigiis Daemonum, et incantationibus ac veneficiis*, was also published in the same series while Freud was studying under Charcot. The first English translation appeared in 1991. This book by Wier must have made a profound impression on Freud. He refers to it in an undated letter to Hugo Heller, editor of *Neue Blätter für Litteratur und Kunst*, Vienna. Freud is writing in response to a request from the Viennese publisher to name 'ten good books'. Freud replies that if he were asked to name the 'ten most significant books', he should have to mention such 'scientific achievements like those of Copernicus, of the old physician Johann Weier on the belief in witches, of Darwin's *Descent of Man*, and then others would have found a place' (Freud, 1906f: 245). It was presumably in the series on witchcraft and demonology in the *Bibliothèque Diabolique* that Freud read Wier's classic. He presumably also had access to the works of Bodin (1580) and Boguet (1590), which were in preparation for publication in the same series.

The Irish historian Lecky in his book *History of the Rise and Influence of the Spirit of Rationalism in Europe* (1865) discusses Wier's major opus *De Praestigiis* (1563). On the 30th of October 1927, Freud wrote to the widow of the political theorist, Heinrich Braun-Vogelstein (1854–1927), in which he recalls how her late husband, Heinrich, had directed his attention to Lecky's work. The Irish historian Lecky also discusses Bodin's *On the Demon-Mania of Witches* (1580). Stadlen (1999) directed my attention to a book by Binz (1885), which has an account of Bodin's *On the Demon-Mania of Witches* (1580). Binz's work on Wier was published in 1885 and republished in 1896. Freud would have been aware of all these publications on witches and witch trials when in January 1897 he expressed his interest in studying literature on witches. We can presume that he studied Bodin's *Demon-Mania*. Bodin's work is an attempt to refute Wier's argument in *De Praestigiis* (1563). Bodin refers to Wier as 'The Protector of Witches' (Bodin, 1580: 66).

Freud also had in his library the 1911 revised version of Soldan's *Geschichte der Hexenprozesse*, translated as *A History of Witch Trials*. This book in two volumes contains copious material from Bodin, Boguet and Remy on witch trials. Soldan claimed that the witch cult was a legacy of Greco-Roman antiquity (Trevor-Roper, 1988: 18). Freud expressed the same idea in his letter to Fliess on the witches when he wrote, 'we have before us a remnant of a primeval sexual cult'. The imaginary evils that these books were describing were called sorcery, devil-worship or witchcraft. The word most commonly used for the devil's agents, for whose extermination the books were written, was witches. The growth of the witch persecutions was ascribed by the inquisitors and judges to the increased activity of the devil. It was, in fact, due to the increased activity of these witch-hunters. Witches were held responsible for every misfortune, most especially every form of sexual dysfunction that was suffered by men. Judges faced with the task of proving an impossible crime turned for instruction on the procedures at witch trials to the books by Bodin, Remy and Boguet. The next chapter gives a detailed account of the witch trials conducted by these three judges and the harsh therapy they prescribe.

1.12. Legal procedures in witch trials: inquisitorial or accusatory?

Freud had studied the 'very interesting witch trials' and was therefore familiar with the procedures that the judges used. He drew parallels between the witches' confession and his patients' stories. He asked, 'Why are their confessions under torture so like the communications made by my patients in psychic treatment?' He also said in the next paragraph of that letter to Fliess on 17 January 1897, 'the inquisitors prick with needles to discover the devil's stigmata, and in a similar situation, the victims [his patients] think of the same old cruel story in fictionalized form'. Freud seems to be comparing his procedure by pressure in psychoanalysis with the procedures of the inquisitors. He is also implicitly comparing the two procedures when he calls the judges' procedures therapy. The inquisitors and judges used an inquisitorial procedure in the witch trials. In his case histories, Freud reveals, at times, the forced nature of his procedure: he wrote that Dora 'was on the point of having her secret torn from her by the doctor' (Freud, 1905e: 78). Freud also wrote that 'patients must really have experienced what they reproduce under the compulsion of analysis', and 'Only the strongest compulsion of the treatment can induce them to embark on a reproduction' of the scenes of their childhood (Freud, 1896c: 204, 205). These examples from Freud's writings show that he saw his task as similar to that of the judges, a contest with demons, and therefore force was needed. The medieval and early modern judges saw the need to use force to extract confessions of maleficium out of the witches.

The offence of maleficium, whether real or imagined, an offence of which witches were accused, was difficult to prove. It was unlikely to find eyewitnesses to an act of maleficium so the accused had a good chance of establishing their innocence. Therefore, to accuse anyone of maleficium was to take a great risk indeed. At Strasbourg in 1451, a man who had accused a witch of maleficium and failed to make his case was arrested, tried for calumny and drowned in the river Ill. The authors of the *Malleus* (1486) deplored the fact that even in the late fifteenth century, the accusatory procedure was still in force at Coblenz. Much had to change before mass witch-hunts could begin. The accusatory procedure had to be replaced by the inquisitorial procedure (Cohn, 1975: 160–163).

1.12.1. Accusatory procedure

Almost throughout the medieval period – until the thirteenth century – the accusatory form of the criminal procedure obtained. Under the accusatory procedure, the initiative in bringing a charge lay with a private individual; under the inquisitorial procedure, it lay with the authorities. The accusatory procedure favoured the accused. The accuser was obliged to conduct the case without the assistance of a counsel. The accuser who failed to convince the judge would almost certainly be penalised by imprisonment and by paying compensation for the infamy brought on the accused. To condemn the accused, the judge required either a spontaneous confession or else an array of proofs that should be 'clearer than the noonday sun'. The result of the accusatory system was that nobody would become an accuser unless impelled by the most powerful motives.

1.12.2. Inquisitorial procedure

The inquisitorial procedure stood in marked contrast to the accusatory procedure. In the inquisitorial procedure, the judge initiated the investigation or 'inquisition' of the suspect. Early in the thirteenth century, Pope Innocent III had established it as the normal way of proceeding against clerics. The Inquisition took its name from the inquisitorial procedure. These official enquiries were extremely unfair to the accused. If they were allowed a lawyer, it was in order to urge the accused to confess. While a confession was required from the accused, torture could be used to extract it. The accused who confessed under torture would be called on to confirm the confession three days later and would be expected to explicitly state that the confession was freely made and not as a result of torture or the fear of torture. If the accused withdrew the confession on the grounds that it had been extracted by torture, the accused was then handed over to the secular arm of the law to be burned alive.

It was admitted by some lawyers that 'not one in a thousand witches would be convicted if regular legal procedures were followed' (Peel & Southern, 1969: 113). As witchcraft was believed to be such an exceptional crime, and as witches could supposedly count on the invisible help of the devil, many normal processes of law were put to one side. Rumour or gossip and a confession forced out by torture or by a false promise of pardon were all accepted as evidence of guilt. Trials were designed to display the details of the crime for which the accused was already assumed to be guilty rather than to establish their guilt or innocence (Peel & Southern, 1969: 113). An inquisitorial approach started from the premise that people are guilty until proved innocent (Peel & Southern, 1969: 115).

The inquisitors and judges, fighting against the so-called enemies of the faith, divided the world into light and darkness. To penetrate the secrets of the kingdom of darkness, it was necessary to capture members of Satan's intelligence service – witches. The inquisitors set to work. Trevor-Roper explains it thus: 'Since a system was presupposed, a system was found; the confessions extracted under torture were seen as the visible projections of a vast and complex invisible organization, and so, every new confession supplied fresh evidence for deductive minds' (Trevor-Roper, 1988: 42).

Judicial torture, which had not been used in Roman law for many centuries, was once again used by the inquisitors where confessions were difficult to extract. In 1468, when the pope declared witchcraft a *crimen exceptum*, he thereby justified the use of torture to obtain confessions. It was not as yet introduced by the secular courts. The obscene details of the witches' confessions do not, at first, appear in secular tribunals, but only before the tribunals of the Inquisition. In other words, they were obtained only by tribunals that used torture. Trevor-Roper also claims that it was the torture that produced absurd confessions (Trevor-Roper, 1988: 43–44). It was not until the sixteenth century that secular courts introduced torture to extract the required confessions from the witches, as we shall see in the next chapter of this work, where we examine the trials conducted by Bodin, Remy and Boguet. It was sufficient to discover a wart or an insensitive spot that did not bleed when pricked or an incapacity to shed tears in order to convict a so-called witch.

From the similarity of many confessions, it seems that a set form of questioning was used and that in some cases the accused had only to answer yes to the suggestions. These were then written down in the first person and read out to the crowd at the execution. If, when the torment was eased, the victim went back on her admission, she was again taken to the torture chamber to be tortured. The stereotypical questions usually elucidated the length of time the accused had been a witch; the details of the witches' meetings that she had attended and how she had travelled to them; the harm that she had done; the number of times that she had sexual intercourse with the devil or minor demons and details of this intercourse (Peel & Southern, 1969: 118). Reverend William Perkins has another explanation for the similarity of many of the confessions. He claims that the fact that the witches' confessions were almost identical points to a central organisation of witches (Trevor-Roper, 1988: 49).

The inquisitorial procedure used to convict the many women who confessed under torture was far from ideal. Guilt was assumed from the outset. The accused was plied with questions that were repeated to try to trap the accused into contradicting themselves. Questions were prepared that demanded a single yes. Hopkins, who conducted witch trials in England, was accused of putting this type of question forward: 'You have four Imps, have you not? . . . Are not their names so and so?' (Parrinder, 1958: 80). Words were obviously put into their mouths. That many of the confessions were fabrications becomes clearer than ever in the cases of torture.

Some witches confessed freely, even too anxiously, in order to put an end to their torture. Many others remained silent. Their very stubbornness in refusing to confess was taken as a sign of possession by the devil, who is known to be taciturn. Few brave spirits resisted under torture or refused to admit the crimes with which they were charged. Some were anxious to put themselves right with the Church, in time for eternity to escape eternal damnation, which was threatened (Parrinder, 1958: 83). Many were so deranged by prolonged torture that they half believed to be true what was said about them, by so many witnesses, inquisitors and judges. For example, Thomas Ady (1655) wrote,

> Let any man that is wise, and free from prejudice, go and hear but the Confessions that are so commonly alleged, and he may see with what catching and cavilling, what thwarting and lying, what flat and plain knavery these confessions are wrung from poor innocent people, and what monstrous additions

and multiplications are afterwards invented to make the matter seem true, which yet is most damnably false.

(Ady, 1655: 126)

The inquisitors and judges freely admitted that there could be no external witnesses to the Sabbats or to the flights to the Sabbats. It was therefore a secret crime that had to be extracted from the witch herself by a freely made confession. Other evidence to be looked for was the devil's mark of ownership. The terms 'witch's mark' and 'devil's mark' are often interchanged. The witch's mark was supposed to be the visible place on the witch's body from which her 'familiar' or devil drew his sustenance. The devil's mark was the invisible stigmata acquired by the witch when she bound herself to Satan (Peel & Southern, 1969: 23). Freud referred to the devil's mark as evidence of guilt sought by the inquisitors when he wrote to Fliess on 17 January 1897: 'The inquisitors prick with needles to discover the devil's stigmata'. Importantly, Freud compared this with what he was doing with his patients, whom he called 'victims', when he says, 'in a similar situation the victims think of the same old cruel story in fictionalized form'.

Parrinder says that 'it is hard to think that the whole extensive system of belief in witches' meetings is pure delusion – until one hears modern African witches confessing freely and with detail to the most impossible things' (Parrinder, 1958: 42). Wier (1563) had spent some years in Africa before he wrote his main opus on witches, in which one of his condemnations of the judges and inquisitors was for their belief in night flying. Freud referred to the significance of Wier's work in a letter to Heller (Freud, 1906f: 245).

1.13. Witchcraft, a new heresy: a conspiracy?

Witchcraft belief was created by the Church's belief in a personal devil. People possessed of a lively imagination began to dream that they and/or other people had relations with this personal devil. Such people, mostly women who imagined themselves witches voluntarily surrendered themselves to the harsh therapy of the inquisitorial approach (Peel & Southern, 1969: 14) This is an important point to keep in mind when Freud was comparing his patients to the witches. Most patients came to Freud voluntarily. We know that Anna O., whom Freud calls the first psychoanalytic patient, was forced into treatment. Dora did not go to psychoanalysis completely voluntarily; her father brought her.

In 1486 the authors of the *Malleus Maleficarum* pleaded for 'the application of the "si aliquis" canon to the "witch-midwives", so as to punish them with death' (Ranke-Heinemann, 1988: 215). The 'si aliquis' canon in Church law was a thirteenth-century anti-contraceptive text that stated that whoever administers sterilising poisons is a murderer. Was Freud aware of this church text at the time of writing his Aliquis analysis, which dealt with the similar theme of reproduction? Part Two of this work examines Freud's Aliquis analysis.

1.14. Witchcraft in England

The first of the modern English laws against witchcraft was passed in 1542, towards the end of the reign of Henry VIII. This act made witchcraft a criminal offence. Before this, it had been dealt with by ecclesiastical courts. The main area of persecution in England was the South East. Like the European courts, special measures were taken in dealing with people in league with supernatural powers of evil. No accused witch was given a chance to prepare a defence. She would not even know before the trial the actual charges against her. The chief witnesses were usually children (Peel & Southern, 1969: 57).

At the time of the trials of the Lancashire Witches in 1612, the judges had a powerful reason for seeking the conviction of the accused: the known opinion and writings of King James, a fierce witch opponent, who had it in his power to dismiss them. The first witch to face Judge Bromley was Chattox, an 80-year-old widow who is described by Potts as 'a very old, withered, decrepit creature, her sight almost gone'. Her palsied chattering may have accounted for her nickname. Her landlord's son had tried to rape her young married daughter in her own home. Chattox confessed that following this attempt to seduce her daughter, she called her 'familiar' or devil and bade him take revenge on the young man. Both Chattox and her daughter were convicted of witchcraft and hanged (Peel & Southern, 1969: 58–59). In her confession, Chattox could not even be consistent about the place where she had supposedly given her soul to the devil, but the judges were in no way concerned by the manifest contradictions in her 'voluntary confession' (Peel & Southern, 1969: 90). Peel and Southern claim that by questions and suggestions, the judges turned whatever story she told into the tale they wanted to hear (Peel & Southern, 1969: 28). We shall examine in Part Two of this work the procedures that Freud used with his patients to find what 'we are in search of' (Freud, 1937d: 265).

Demdike, another old woman who was imprisoned with Chattox, described the speediest way to take a man's life away (Peel & Southern, 1969: 28).

> Make a picture of clay, like unto the shape of the person whom they mean to kill and dry it thoroughly, . . . then take a thorn or pin and prick it in that part of the picture you would so have to be ill; and when you would have any part of the body to consume away, then take that part of the picture and burn it. And when you would have the whole body to consume away, then take the remnant of the said picture and burn it; and so thereupon by that means, the body shall die.

The technique that Demdike described is ancient. Mention of it is found in the histories of ancient Chaldea, Egypt, Greece and Rome. In Egypt the images of wax or clay were often cursed, bound as if dead or stuck with pins or miniature weapons. These figures may at one time have been the means of concentrating hypnotic power, but according to Peel and Southern, as the witches used them, they were probably straightforward magic: harm to the image to harm the person. Following this confession of her own depravity, Demdike died in prison before her certain conviction (Peel & Southern, 1969: 29).

Peel and Southern claim that the original idea of a witch was a person with magical powers, usually evil. From early times, it had been believed that there were women with the ability to fly through the air on sticks. Added to this, in the mind of the Church, the new witches joined forces with the devil, the father of evil, and held assemblies to do him homage. Like Parrinder (1958), Peel and Southern claim that the witches were tortured until they confessed to all the activities their accusers fantasised. These forced confessions were then regarded both as evidence of the guilt of the witches and as confirmation of the reality of their crimes (Peel & Southern, 1969: 107).

1.15. Different theories on witches

An examination of the theories on witches is important because they help us to know how Freud understood witches. This will enable us to answer our question, what did he mean when he said that he understood the harsh therapy they received? Freud wrote two letters to Fliess in January 1897, about witches. He described the various understandings of witches as 'possessed'; as marked by the devil as a sign of their pact with him, and pricked by inquisitors to discover the invisible mark or stigmata; as "flying" to the Sabbat and as sexually abused by the devil; and as members of a 'primeval devil religion with rites that are carried on secretly'. Freud also spoke at a meeting of the Vienna Psychoanalytic Society on 'the very interesting witch trials' and said that the witches' confessions were 'fantasies that were not created under torture but merely squeezed out by it' (Nunberg & Federn, 1967: 123).

To understand Freud's position on witches, the following pages will examine two theories on witchcraft:

(a) Witchcraft is 'a remnant of a primeval devil religion' or an old pagan cult, which was finally suppressed only by the witch-hunts of the fifteenth and sixteenth centuries.
(b) A challenge to that theory is that witchcraft is a 'hysterical phenomenon', an imaginary offence because it is impossible. Both of these theories reflect Freud's statements on witches.

In the eighteenth and nineteenth centuries, no educated person believed that there had ever been a sect of witches. According to Cohn (1975), it is only since 1830 that this has gradually ceased to be taken for granted. Some scholars who maintained that a sect of witches did exist have argued strongly that witches were organised in groups under recognised leaders; that they adhered to an anti-Christian cult; and that they assembled under cover of night at remote spots to perform their rituals. Because this view has been propounded by academics at leading universities in Europe and North America, it has been taken on trust by multitudes of educated people. The next pages review the various theories of witches.

1.15.1. Arguments in favour of witches as members of 'a primeval devil religion'

What was the true nature of European witchcraft, and what influence did it have on the formulation of Freud's theory of hysteria? Jarcke was the first of many modern scholars to advance the view that the great witch-hunt was directed against an anti-Christian sect. In 1828, when Karl Ernst Jarcke was a young professor of criminal law at the University of Berlin, he edited the records of a seventeenth-century German witch trial for a legal journal and appended some brief comments of his own. He argued that witchcraft was above all a nature religion that had once been the religion of the pagan Germans. After the establishment of Christianity, this religion survived with its ceremonies and sacraments, as a living tradition among the common people, but it took on a new significance. The Church condemned it as devil-worship. At the core of this old pagan religion were secret arts for influencing the course of nature.

In 1839 another writer, Franz Josef Mone, who was director of the archives of Baden, saw witchcraft as a cult deriving from pre-Christian times. He claims that its origin lay not in the religion of the ancient Germans but some Germanic people who sojourned on the north coast of the Black Sea. These people had come in contact with the cult of Hecate and the cult of Dionysos. The slave element in the population adopted these cults and fused them into a religion of their own. This religion was characterised by the worship of a goat-like god, by the celebration of nocturnal orgies and by the practice of magic and poison. Because it was regarded with contempt by freeborn people, the slaves had to practise it in secret. This underground religion, according to Mone, was witchcraft. The witches were therefore members of 'a fully organized secret society', and the devil who presided over the Sabbat was a distorted version of Dionysos (Cohn, 1975: 104).

Neither Jarcke's nor Mone's theories are convincing to Cohn. Jules Michelet takes the opposite view in his book *La Sorcière* (1862). He portrays witchcraft as a justified protest against the social order that was crushing the lower class. Michelet claims that the Sabbat became a defiance of the existing social order. It was led by a woman, the priestess who mates with Satan. Michelet refers to the fact that Satan's seed, when received by the witches, felt cold. Innumerable contemporary accounts refer to the devil's semen as 'cold'. Michelet gives as explanation that the mating must have been followed by an icy 'purification' to prevent conception. Michelet also suggests that the Sabbat was a celebration of a fertility cult, aimed at securing an abundance of crops and to encourage the breeding of animals (Cohn, 1975: 106–107).

Dr Margaret Murray's theory of witchcraft is that it is a relic of an ancient pagan cult. She bases practically the whole of her theory of witchcraft on the place of the devil as god of the cult. She says, 'It is impossible to understand the witch-cult without first understanding the position of the chief personage of that cult' (Murray, 1921: 28ff). But this argument is not convincing, because if the medieval witch cult had been a relic of an ancient pagan cult, why is there no mention of ancient European gods' names given to devils or deities in the witches' confessions? We never find the old pagan gods' names – Thor, Woden, Loki or Grendel – in the witches' confessions. Instead, we find biblical, ecclesiastical or mere fanciful names: Devil, Demon, Satan, Lucifer, Fancy and Tibb. These names would have been more familiar to the inquisitors and judges than to the witches. Were these names being suggested to the witches while confessions were being extracted under torture?

Murray's theory, put forward since 1921, that European witchcraft was the remnant of ancient pagan cults that survived long after the adoption of Christianity, had widespread influence. She was asked to write the article 'Witchcraft' in the fourteenth edition of Encyclopaedia Britannica, in which she says,

> When dealing with the records of the medieval witches, we are dealing with the remains of a pagan religion which survived, at least in England, till the eighteenth century, two thousand years after the introduction of Christianity. . . . The number of witches put to death in the sixteenth and seventeenth centuries is a proof of the obstinate paganism of Europe.

Murray (1921) claims that the use of force was needed to overcome the old religion. She quotes verbatim from innumerable confessions of witches to prove her theory, but she ignores *how* these confessions were obtained and the fact that the accounts of the trials were written by the judges. Murray also ignores the significant writings of the sceptics: Wier, Scot and Webster. Her basic assumption is that the devil is a real person. Cohn (1975) dismisses Murray's writings on witchcraft because she was not an historian but an Egyptologist, archaeologist and folklorist, and he says that her grasp of the historical method was nonexistent (Cohn, 1975: 109). Many other writers like Runeberg used Murray's writings as their primary source. One therefore cannot assume from their arguments that Sabbats took place, during which fertility rites were performed. Cohn (1975) argues that there is no evidence that there ever was a secret society of witches.

If the so-called witch cult was a remnant of a primeval devil religion, as Murray suggests and as Freud asks in one of his letters on witches, why did it not receive serious attention by the Church for over a thousand years of Christianity's existence? Christianity was not a new religion in the fifteenth century, when the witch trials began in earnest. Parrinder asks, 'is it true that the Church had only gained sufficient strength to combat this pagan cult by the sixteenth to the eighteenth centuries'? In fact, the Church was never more powerful than in the early medieval times, yet it did not undertake any large-scale action against witchcraft (Parrinder, 1958: 106–107).

Murray's theory gained a considerable following. The Rev. Montague Summers, who wrote the introductions to the English version of the *Malleus*, to Boguet's *Examen* and to *Remy's Demonolatry* and to his own two books on witchcraft, follows

Murray's lead. From the records of the trials of accused witches, no evidence can be found of Sabbats except in the wishes of inquisitors, judges and some authors who came to believe in them. Summers is obsessed by thoughts of the devil. For Summers, witches were what the witch-hunters of the fifteenth, sixteenth and seventeenth centuries said they were: members of a conspiracy, organised and controlled by Satan to bring about the destruction of Christianity. The confessions given in witchcraft trials and the stories in the manuals of witch-hunting magistrates are accepted as true unquestioningly by Summers.

According to Elliot Rose in *A Razor for a Goat* (1989), the libidinous aspects of the Sabbat are all-important: the dancing and the copulation of the leader with his followers. This led Rose to imagine a cult especially attractive to women. In this view, the witch cult becomes a successor, on Christianised Europe, of the Dionysian religion of ancient Greece: The 'flying ointments' used by the witches were ecstasy-producing drugs. The leader of the cult possessed the secret knowledge of herbs that temporarily released human beings from the limitations of humanity. This book was published just as the craze for psychedelic experiences was building up. Elliot Rose's source is Margaret Murray's writings, which when examined turn out to be, according to Cohn, full of the wildest fantasies (Cohn, 1975: 118).

Professor Jeffrey Burton Russell, in his book *Witchcraft in the Middle Ages* (1972), is of the same school of thought as Murray and Summers. His book is the best learned attempt to show witchcraft as an organised anti-Christian religion. Russell claims that witchcraft was a protest against the dominant religion and this meant also a form of social rebellion: 'The witch was a rebel against Church and society at a time when the two were wholly identified'. Russell (1972) believes that the victims of Conrad of Marburg in Germany in 1231–1233 did in all probability worship the devil and hold sexual orgies. He regards the Waldensians, Cathars and Templars as organisations of witches.

For Russell, the participants of the sex orgies were mostly women who worshipped the devil and copulated with him. This latter was not pleasurable, he notes, because a woman could not be wholly relaxed with the devil. Russell (1972) claims that the sect of witches was the product of a Christian society that insisted on religious conformity. But he also believes that witchcraft was partly rooted in folk practices and beliefs connected with fertility. These fertility rites, with dancing and eroticism, were transformed by the pressures of a hostile Christian society into the witches' Sabbat. Russell writes, 'what people thought happened is as interesting as what "objectively did happen" and much more certain' (Cohn, 1975: 122–124).

Freud had two volumes in German of *A History of the Witch Processes* (1911) by W. Soldan in his library. Trevor-Roper (1988) stated, 'To the German, Wilhelm Gottlieb-Soldan, the first historian of the craze, the witch cult was a legacy of Greco-Roman antiquity, naturally developed and artificially preserved. To him, its gradual conquest was one aspect of the rise of "rationalism" in Europe' (Trevor-Roper, 1988: 20). Trevor-Roper says that W.G. Soldan's pioneering work, *Geschichte der Hexenprozesse* (Stuttgart, 1843), has been twice reprinted (Trevor-Roper, 1988: 123n.9). It is the last edition (1911), edited by Max Bauer, that is in Freud's library.

Soldan argued that, in so far as witch beliefs were the relics of a pagan religion, these beliefs could be traced to Roman and so to Greek and Oriental paganism and not to Germanic paganism (Soldan, 1911: 494 in Trevor-Roper, 1988: 40).

Freud looked at the possibility of the witch cult in the medieval period as a remnant of an ancient religion. He wrote to Fliess on 24 January 1897: 'I dream, therefore, of a primeval devil religion with rites that are carried on secretly and understand the harsh therapy of the witches' judges'. Trevor-Roper (1988) does not believe that witchcraft is a relic of a pagan religion but is instead a scholastic and medieval creation. He says that 'the fancies of the late Margaret Murray were *justly*, if irritably, dismissed by a real scholar as "vapid balderdash"' (Ewen, 1938 in Trevor-Roper, 1988: 40).

1.15.2. Arguments against the belief in witchcraft as a 'remnant of a devil religion'

Cohn (1975) rejects the argument of the fertility cults as mere dreaming. He says that the prevalence of such beliefs facilitated the destruction of millions of human beings (Cohn, 1975: 122–124). He does not accept the existence of a sect of orgiastic, infanticidal, cannibalistic, devil-worshipping, heretical witches. He claims that stereotyped accusations that contain manifestly impossible elements ought not to be accepted as evidence of physical events. To back up his claim, he points to the view in 'primitive' societies of bands of destructive witches who kill human beings, especially children; who travel at night by supernatural means; and who foregather in remote spots to devour their victims. All these notions crop up again and again in anthropological literature. But anthropologists agree that these bands exist in imagination only; nobody has ever come across such a society of witches. And that indeed is the nub: the tradition has suffered from the defect of grossly underestimating the capacities of human imagination. Cohn claims that it was the dread of secret societies that created the nonexistent society of witches (Cohn, 1975: 124–125).

Trevor-Roper (1988) also refutes 'the prophets of progress', who claim that witchcraft was 'a lingering ancient superstition' (Trevor-Roper, 1988: 12). He claims that it was the judges, inquisitors, lawyers and clergy who mobilised the dark forces and organised the systematic 'demonological' witch craze of the sixteenth and seventeenth centuries. He refers to the Canon Episcopi, which in the ninth century forbade belief in night flying with Diana as hallucinatory. He quotes from Lea (1911): 'In the twelfth century John of Salisbury dismissed the idea of a witches' Sabbat as a fabulous dream' (Trevor-Roper, 1988: 13).

Because of the seeds sown by monks of the medieval period, melancholic old women were believed to be anointing themselves every night with 'devil's grease, made out of the fat of murdered infants, and, thus lubricated, were slipping up chimneys, mounting on broomsticks or airborne goats, and flying off to the witches' Sabbat' (Trevor-Roper, 1988: 15). Trevor-Roper says that 'the intellectual fantasies of the clergy seem more bizarre than the psychopathic delusions of the madhouse' (Trevor-Roper, 1988: 18). We shall examine in the next chapter the books by three sixteenth-century judges, Bodin, Remy and Boguet, which incorporated all the information on how to recognise, accuse, torture, extract confessions from and convict a witch. Bodin strongly condemned his contemporary Wier whom he described as a dangerous 'patron of witches', but it was easier for the judges to deal with the powerless, poor witches than with their influential patrons.

In the face of the horrible accusations of evil deeds performed with the power of the devil, inquisitors and judges felt justified in burning witches alive. But the witches' 'confessions' do not establish their stories as fact. Other explanations can be found. Parrinder (1958) tells us that African women today make the same sort of confession without clear proof that they have done these wicked things. In medieval Europe, child mortality was high. The explanation of cot deaths was unknown, and many mothers might well imagine that they had been responsible for the mysterious deaths of their children, feel guilty and think that they deserved punishment for their neglect. Angry fathers might accuse them of murder. The fact is also that old women would often act as midwives and would therefore be liable to suspicion if children died during childbirth (Parrinder, 1958: 53). Blame was also laid at the door of the witch if a man was impotent.

The evidence for these secret crimes committed by the witches rests mainly on the accusations made against them and the confessions extracted under torture. Those who believe that witchcraft in Europe was a survival of an ancient cult rely on the witches' confessions, extracted under torture, for the details of the Sabbat and witches' sexual orgies with devils. The witches' confessions fitted in perfectly with the tales about heretical sects that had been circulating for centuries.

Carus (1900) presents the case of a deluded witch. He recounts the story of an old spinster in Hanover who declared herself a witch and warned the villagers to avoid her lest she injure them by her glance. She tried to drown herself during an attack of melancholy. Her physician said she suffered from confusion of mind, but she would not submit to treatment, because she said that the devil could not be driven out by medicine. She said, 'It is in vain to try to cure a witch. I deserve death and shall gladly die, but please do not burn me, have me dispatched with the sword'. The physician

> persuaded her that her neck was sword-proof and succeeded in inducing her to take medicine to make her neck soft again for decapitation. She was then treated according to the prescriptions of her physician, with bodily exercise and regular diet and sleep until her mind improved, and she forgot all about witchcraft and her sword-proof neck.
>
> *(Carus, 1900: 292–293)*

In the fifteenth and sixteenth centuries, inquisitors and judges began to combine these fantasies with the stereotype of a devil-worshipping, orgiastic, infanticidal sect (Cohn, 1975: 228). Because the notion of nocturnal travels for purposes of cannibalism not only fitted in with the existing stereotype but made it much more credible, it appealed strongly to those concerned with tracking down heretics. Tales that a few deluded ones told spontaneously had to be confirmed by the rest. Torture was applied to ensure that this happened. Now heretics who allegedly worshipped the devil, in addition to perpetrating the horrors traditionally attributed to heretics, flew at night to their assemblies. A new crime had been invented, 'crimen magiae'. The inquisitors believed that Christendom was full of witches. In most regions, witches were tried by judges who were already convinced that witches belonged to a satanic conspiracy against Christendom (Cohn, 1975: 239).

Parrinder (1958) claims that the origin of the belief in a devil-worshipping sect lay in the fantasies of the judges and inquisitors who extracted confessions of pacts with the devil from these accused women. Parrinder states that

> it is strange that there is absolutely no written material of any kind originating from these diabolical rites and pacts. . . . But just as the Sabbats could never be witnessed, neither could the pacts ever be seen by a non-witch. The literature of witchcraft is wholly the product of the persecutors. So, there is no material or objective evidence whatever of the witches meetings or contracts with the Devil.
>
> *(Parrinder, 1958: 72–73)*

Parrinder believed that the confessions extracted from the witches originated in the fantasies of the judges.

Parrinder (1958) maintains that the inquisitors and witch finders put false statements into their victims' mouths. Bacon (1857) says that 'The witches themselves are imaginative and believe oft-times they do that which they do not; and people are credulous in that point and ready to impute accidents and natural operations to witchcraft' (Bacon, 1857: 642k. in Parrinder, 1958: 104). A Spanish inquisitor who checked the persecution in his own country by careful and firsthand investigations of charges against witches, after examining hundreds of cases, concluded that 'there were neither witches nor bewitched until they were talked about and written about' (Lea, 1907: 233f in Parrinder, 1958: 104). So many impossible things were attributed to witches that eventually reason revolted against the persecutions.

Freud had a different understanding of the witches' confessions. He said in 1909 that the witches' fantasies 'were not created under torture but merely squeezed out by it' (Nunberg & Federn, 1967: 123). Freud was claiming that he understood the necessity for the harsh therapy in order to squeeze out the witches' phantasies. Between these two extreme views, Heller took up a more balanced position, closer to Freud's. Heller said, 'not all of the confessions obtained by torture were merely forced admissions of what the person had been accused of; a great deal of such testimony was based on the delusions of the accused themselves' (Nunberg & Federn, 1967: 120). Heller is admitting that some witches were merely agreeing with the accusations because of the forced nature of the treatment. This is a view similar to Cohn's.

Cohn (1975) claims that the origin of the new stereotype of the witch lay not in literature but in the evidence extracted during the trials. The grain of truth in the evidence lay in the fact that some women really believed that they flew at night; some women really believed that they copulated with incubi. But much came from the imagination of certain inquisitors and judges who used and abused the inquisitorial procedure to obtain all the confirmation they needed (Cohn, 1975: 238). The problem is to disentangle what was in the minds of the witches from what was in the minds of the judges.

Peel and Southern (1969) give as explanations of the ridiculous confessions the unendurable pain that sooner or later forced the supposed agents of the devil to assent to anything suggested to them. One woman, before she died, told her confessor that she never dreamt that suffering could force a person to tell such lies as she had told; she confided to her confessor that she was not a witch and had never seen the devil. She had been eventually forced to plead guilty and accuse others (Peel & Southern, 1969: 117).

Field (1960) has made available the results of the first psychiatric study ever made of Africans accused of witchcraft. She affirms that while witches are commonly thought to have secret cults, 'no such cult in fact exists'. But she emphasises that her patients with mental illness were people who would be liable to witchcraft accusations. Childlessness or lack of success in business added to the mental anxiety. In her study of African women accused of witchcraft, Field (1960) emphasises the great importance of belief in 'possession', the compulsion to act at the dictate of the evil spirit. While women confessed to impossible things, some believed in the reality of their confessions, and such confessions brought relief of mind. Field says that a woman frequently confesses to sexual orgies and feasting when she 'has been demonstrably asleep on her mat throughout the night that she is supposed to have spent in feasting'. This, says Field, is a symptom of mental illness, or the product of a disordered imagination, and it reproduces the ideology of society (Field, 1960 in Parrinder, 1958: 199).

Because the confessions of these disturbed women seem to relieve their minds and even provide a means of reconciliation with family or the powerful in society, this does not excuse the cruelty of the witch-hunts. But society suffers from neuroses just as individuals do. To clear itself from guilt, society looks for scapegoats on which to lay its faults. Witches were the scapegoats in sixteenth-century and seventeenth-century Europe, at whose door society laid the blame for high child mortality, impotence, storms and all the 'dis-eases' of society that favoured the growth of fear and superstition. Is the harsh therapy of the inquisitors and judges, that Freud seems to have approved of and practised himself, still the practice of some psychoanalysts and psychotherapists today, or is it no longer used to settle intrapsychic and interpersonal conflicts in people and society?

In *A Seventeenth-Century Demonological Neurosis* (1923d), Freud says that 'the neuroses of those early times emerge in demonological trappings. . . . The demonological theory of those dark times has won, in the end, against all the somatic views of the period of "exact science"'. Freud explains the demons as 'bad and reprehensible wishes, derivatives of instinctual impulses that have been repudiated and repressed' (Freud, 1923d: 72). In 1893 Freud had called this explanation the theory of a splitting of consciousness, which he claimed was 'a solution to the riddle of hysteria'. He said, 'by pronouncing possession by a demon to be the cause of hysterical phenomena, the Middle Ages in fact chose this solution; it would only have been a matter of exchanging the religious terminology . . . for the scientific language of today'. In the same context, Freud wrote that Charcot, in explaining hysteria, 'drew copiously upon the surviving reports of witch trials and of possession' (Freud, 1893f: 20). We shall be examining in the next chapter the judges' accounts of the witch trials that they conducted.

1.16. Why the harsh therapy?

Carus (1900) asks, was it because of the superstition of their accusers; serving the interests of the powerful; sheer ignorance; the purest intention of doing the right thing in the interest of the eternal salvation of the witch; or the pious desire to obey the word of God, 'Thou shalt not suffer a witch to live' that witches were tortured and burned? The highest authorities of both Catholic and Protestant Christianity not only upheld the idea of witch prosecution but enforced it. Under Pope Alexander III, the title of inquisitor, in the sense of judge in matters of faith, was used for the first time at the Council of Tours in 1163.

Under Pope Innocent III (1198–1216), the new Order of Dominicans was founded, which became the working force of the Inquisition. Pope Gregory IX appointed the Dominicans as papal inquisitors and had his policy on witches codified in 45 articles by the Council of Toulouse in 1229. Gregory IX also sent the infamous Conrad of Marburg to Germany and gave him unlimited power to bring before his tribunal all people suspected of witchcraft (Carus, 1900: 308–309). The authors of the first and most famous handbook on witch persecution, *Malleus Maleficarum* (1486), were two Dominican theologians who had absorbed the teachings of their order's predecessors, Albert the Great and Aquinas.

Abbot Tritemius (1442–1516) believed that there was 'no other way of protecting the commonwealth against the obnoxious influence of the Devil-worshipping malefactors than by extirpating them, but best by burning them alive'. He complained that 'Men and animals die through the infamy of these women, and none considers that it is due to the malignity of witchcraft. There are many who suffer from serious diseases and do not even know that they are bewitched' (Carus, 1900: 326). Boguet states that 'Satan forms a league with his followers against Heaven and plots the ruin of the human race' (Boguet, 1590: 59). It was believed in the fifteenth and sixteenth centuries that the devil used witches to help him plot the ruin of the human race.

Cohn (1975) argues that the misogynist diatribes against women as inherently evil gave the judges the right to torture and burn them as witches. The purpose of the torture was to break the grip of the devil. Each trial was a battle between the forces of God and the forces of the devil. The battle was fought for the witch's soul. A witch who confessed and perished in the flames had at least a chance of purging her guilt and achieving her salvation (Cohn, 1975: 253–255).

The great dangers of witchcraft seemed to demand extraordinary means for combating its evils, and thus, torture was used in a barbaric way. Some of the instruments of torture were tongs to tear out fingernails or to be used red hot for pinching; boards and rollers covered with sharp spikes were frequently used. Witch prosecution was a convenient weapon in the hands of unscrupulous people for satisfying some private vengeance (Carus, 1900: 328–333).

Thousands of so-called witches were condemned to the cruellest tortures and the most dreadful death for the sake of their own salvation and for the glory of God. But what an image of God was being presented: a fearsome monster worse than Moloch of ancient Phoenicia. Carus decides that 'the horrors of the Inquisition are ultimately due not to ill will or even to the desire for power but to error which had assumed the shape of a deep-seated religious conviction' (Carus, 1900: 403).

It is easier to document the facts of the witch trials and to speculate on the origins of witchcraft than to find an explanation of the meaning of the witch craze. The mind of one age is not necessarily subject to the same rules as the mind of another age. One needs to hold superstition and reason and religion in dialogical tension. Murderous fantasies were formulated into a new mythology in the *Malleus Maleficarum* (1486), which contained inquisitorial procedures later adopted and expanded by Bodin (1580), Remy (1595) and Boguet (1590) in their policy of exterminating witches. That mythology, which the inquisitors and judges manufactured, acquired a reality of its own. Social tensions could then be explained according to this new mythology.

A second stage in the witch craze developed when the helpless victims of society, the witches, clutched at the new mythology of Satan's kingdom as a theme for their own delusions. In a climate of fear, deviants were connected to a central pattern. Society's fears of certain women who were nonconformists led to their trial as witches. The same thing happened with McCarthyism in the United States in the 1950s: fear was given intellectual form as a heresy, and suspected individuals were then persecuted, by referring to that heresy. In the same way, the hatred felt in the fifteenth, sixteenth and seventeenth centuries for the witches as nonconformists was intellectualised as a heresy, and the suspected witches were brought to judgement in the witch trials.

Once a stereotype has been built up, it can last for centuries. The fables of poisoned wells and ritual murder of Catholic children during the crusades, the Black Death, the Thirty Years' War and Nazism sum up the bizarre mythology of anti-Semitism. The Burning of London in 1666 and the Gunpowder Plots represent the mythology of Papist Aggression. All these stereotypes are built on fears. Fears became crystallised. Medieval society articulated their fears and their obsession with the devil, and they found a scapegoat for their fears in the imagined agent of the devil: the witch. They projected their personal fears onto an objective fantasy – that is, the devil and the witch.

The pressures on the witch and on the other groups just mentioned were social. These groups were seen as social nonconformists. Trevor-Roper (1988) claims that the real reasons for persecuting them differs from the reasons given. In the Church's periods of introversion and intolerance, it looked for scapegoats. In the sixteenth century, the witch replaced the Jew as scapegoat. Trevor-Roper (1988) states that witches and Jews were persecuted as types of social nonconformity rather than for doctrinal or other given reasons. Witchcraft was one of the charges often made against Jews, who according to Pierre de l'Ancre, writing in 1622, behave just like witches (Trevor-Roper, 1988: 34–36).

In general, Trevor-Roper says, the Church was opposed to the persecution of witches. The two Dominican authors of the *Malleus Maleficarum* (1486), whom Trevor-Roper accuses of monkish phantasmagoria, found themselves obstructed by Church leaders in Germany. The pressure to persecute witches came, according to Trevor-Roper, from the religious orders of men seeking a scapegoat for social frustration. If the Dominican authors of the *Malleus* created hatred of witches, they created it in a favourable social context. They detected the social pressure and mobilised it. They provided the mythology without which the witch craze would never have become a movement (Trevor-Roper, 1988: 38–39, 55). But no one questioned the substance of the myth of witches copulating with demons.

1.17. Conclusion

Carus (1900) claims that the alleged horrors of devil-worship and the resulting witch persecution were the consequences of a misconception of the nature of evil and of the nature of woman as evil. Science began to shed light on the superstitious character of the belief that created the crime of witchcraft. It was pointed out by jurists Alciatus and Ponzinibius that bodily excursions of witches to Sabbats were pure imagination but the objection by inquisitors to that statement was that jurists could not understand the case of witchcraft (Carus, 1900: 370). The authors of the *Malleus* declared that the secular judges were not qualified to judge heresy, and they declared medieval witchcraft a heresy.

From our analysis of the theories on witches, it appears that the weight of the more enlightened opinion is in favour of the idea that medieval witchcraft, with its pact with Satan, its witches' Sabbats and its copulating with demons, is not a product of a primeval devil religion. Those who make this claim present different theories of the hysterical phenomena. Some see it as wholly the product of the inquisitors and judges themselves. Some see it as wholly the product of deluded women. Trevor-Roper sums up by saying that the 'Hammerers of Witches built up their systematic mythology of Satan's kingdom and Satan's accomplices, [the witches], out of the mental rubbish of peasant credulity and feminine hysteria' (Trevor-Roper, 1988: 40–41). Freud claimed that the witches' 'fantasies were not created under torture but merely squeezed out by it'. But he does not exonerate the judges. He says, 'The entire proceedings in the witch trials calls to mind children's games in a meadow, which often enough degenerate into sexual orgies' (Nunberg & Federn, 1967: 123). What did Freud mean by comparing the proceedings to children's games in a meadow? The next chapter will answer that question and will examine the proceedings in the witch trials from accounts written by the judges who conducted the trials. The voices of dissent that were raised against the harsh therapy will also be heard. The judges who have left us accounts of how they administered the harsh therapy were Bodin, Remy and Boguet; some of the men who put in writing their objections to the harsh therapy were Wier, Scot and Spee.

CHAPTER 2

THE JUDGES AND INQUISITORS IN THE WITCH TRIALS

2.1. Introduction

This book explores the parallels that Freud appears to be drawing between his procedures in his work with his patients and the procedure of the judges in the witch trials. To make sense of Freud's allusions to witches and to the harsh therapy of the witches' judges, it is necessary to consider in some detail what the judges in the witch trials were doing and how they conceptualised what they were doing. This chapter of the work will, therefore, address the question of the harsh therapy used by the witches' judges to extract a confession of guilt from the witch.

What did Freud mean when he said in his letter to Fliess on 24 January 1897, 'I . . . understand the harsh therapy of the witches' judges'? In the second paragraph of his letter in which he made this puzzling statement, Freud seems to be comparing what the inquisitors and judges were doing with what he was doing with his patients. He calls his patients 'victims' in a 'similar way' as the witches were victims. From his days in Paris studying under Charcot, Freud was seeking 'a solution to the riddle of hysteria' in the literature on the witch trials. In his obituary to Charcot in 1893, he said that Charcot 'drew copiously upon the surviving reports of witch trials and of possession, in order to show that the manifestations of the neurosis were the same in those days as they are now' (Freud, 1893f: 20). Charcot had tried to demonstrate the precise correspondence between hysteria and witchcraft. Freud's interest in witches, which was sparked off by Charcot, continued. He again refers to the witches in 1909 at a meeting of the Vienna Psychoanalytic Society on 27 January 1909, when he commented on 'the very interesting witch trials'. As late as 1923, Freud again wrote that Charcot 'identified the manifestations of hysteria in the portrayals of possession and ecstasy that have been preserved for us'. He regretted that more attention had not been paid 'to the histories of such cases'. He said, 'The states of possession correspond to our neuroses. . . . We merely eliminate the projection of these mental entities into the external world which the Middle Ages carried out' (Freud, 1923d: 72).

In his letter to Fliess on 17 January 1897, Freud compares his brand-new theory of hysteria to the medieval theory of possession. He poses two questions about witches: 'why did the devil who took possession of the poor things invariably abuse them sexually and in a loathsome manner' and 'why are their confessions under torture so like the communications made by my patients in psychic treatment?' It is because of Freud's interest in the witch trials, his identification of witchcraft with hysteria and his understanding of 'the harsh therapy of the witches' judges' that this part of the work examines at length the witches' confessions in which they report the devil's abuse.

The accounts of the witch trials that I examine are mainly primary sources because they were written by those who conducted the trials in the sixteenth century. The three most famous sixteenth-century judges who gave accounts of witch trials are Bodin, Remy and Boguet. Their accounts of witch trials are of particular importance because these men presided over the secular courts where the trials were held. It was their writings on the manner of the procedure of a judge in the witch trials, based on the medieval book the *Malleus Maleficarum* (1486), which were used by the authorities to deal drastically with witches. We know from his letter to Fliess on 24 January 1897 that Freud 'ordered the *Malleus Maleficarum*', and he said, 'I shall study it diligently'. While Freud was studying in Paris, Charcot sponsored the publication of a series of books on witch trials. Boguet's *Discours des Sorciers* (1590) and Bodin's *De la Demonomanie* (1580) were prepared for publication as part of that series (cf. Appendix 2). Freud did not refer to these authors in his writings, but he did refer to another author, Wier, whose main opus on witchcraft was published in the same series, the *Bibliotèque Diabolique*. The writings of Bodin, Remy and Boguet are quoted in Lecky's *History of the Rise and Influence of the Spirit of Rationalism in Europe* (1865), which Freud read, and in a book by Soldan in Freud's library in the Freud Museum, London, so we know that Freud was familiar with these authors.

Judge Boguet, who wrote *An Examen of Witches* (1590), states that the contents of his book are drawn from 'trials which I have myself conducted, during the last two years, of several members of this sect, whom I have seen and heard and probed as carefully as I possibly could in order to draw the truth from them' (Boguet, 1590: vi). Judge Remy claims that the contents of his book *Demonolatry* (1595) are drawn from nine hundred witch trials that he conducted (Remy, 1595: vii). Judge Bodin was the first of the three French authors to publish works on the witch trials. His book *On the Demon-Mania of Witches* was first published in French in 1580. He claims to have written it to 'assist judges who do not have the leisure to research' the traps and snares of witches (Bodin, 1580: 44).

In the introduction to the English version (1995) of Bodin's book, Pearl says that *Demon-Mania* (1580) was held responsible for the large-scale prosecution of witches in the four or five decades following its appearance. Bodin (1529–1596) was born in Angers and studied law in Paris around 1562. He believed in the existence of angels and demons. He saw demonism as a crime against God. Bodin believed that the state was responsible for enforcing God's commands and should therefore suppress demon-worship and punish those who participated in that forbidden practice. He saw witchcraft as a demonic activity. During his adult life, France was torn by a civil war related to religious issues. Calvinism had taken root in France, and the extreme elements of the Catholic population were upset and resorted to violence. Each group accused its enemies of being in league with the devil and of committing the worst crimes against God, the state and the Church (Bodin, 1580: 9–14).

Nicolas Remy, who was also a judge in the witch trials, was born in Lorraine in 1530. On 24 August 1591, he was named lord high justice with supreme power and jurisdiction in the duchy of Lorraine. In 1596 he journeyed up and down the province examining suspect witches and inquiring into all cases with the most indefatigable energy and perseverance. He retired from this post of lord high justice in 1606 (Remy, 1595: xxviii). In the introduction to Remy's book *Demonolatry* (1595), Summers claims that 'No historical record could be more valuable, no record could be more interesting than this graphic account from firsthand knowledge and experience over many years which Remy has given us' (Remy, 1595: xxxii).

In Demonolatry (1595), Remy gives his credentials: 'I was for nearly fifteen years continuously conducting the trials of criminals in Lorraine, all the while my head was filled with considering the monstrous assemblies of witches who were very frequently among those who came up before me for trial, with thoughts of their banquetings, dancings, charms and spells, their journeyings through the air, the horrid practices of their carnal relations with the Demon' (Remy, 1595: ix). The contents of *Demonolatry* (1595) are 'drawn from the capital trials of 900 people, more or less who within the last 15 years have in Lorraine paid the penalty of death for the crime of witchcraft'. His aim was to 'publish the truth of all the prodigious tales that are told of this sort of witchcraft particularly such as have come within my own experience in my examination of cases' (Remy, 1595: vii). He claims that no writer has 'so great a number of cases as I have been able to bring forward and at first hand' (Remy, 1595: xi). The following are among the themes on witches that Remy selected to write: how witches journey to the Sabbat; the plots they weave there; their eating, dancing and lying with demons; whether they repent when they are brought to trial; or whether they are so hardened in their obstinacy that they defeat the sagacity of even the wisest judge. Judges, according to Boguet, 'probed' as carefully as they could 'in order to draw the truth' from the witch (Boguet, 1590: vi). We shall see in Part Two how this parallels what Freud was doing with his patients.

While the judges Boguet and Remy give firsthand accounts in their books of the witch trials that they conducted, it is clear from reading Bodin's book that his accounts are mainly drawn not from his own experience but from stories told to him and from accounts of witches from earlier authors, particularly Sprenger & Kramer (1486) and Wier (1563). In the light of this, it is worth noting, Bodin's work rather than Boguet's or Remy's that has created most interest in recent years. Conferences have been held to discuss his work. Bodin, in his *Demon-Mania* (1580), draws heavily on the stories in Wier's *De Praestigiis Daemonum* (1563), which he sets out to refute, but he sometimes distorts Wier's account – for example, Wier's story on pages 302–303 (Bodin, 1580: 139). Jan Wier, an eminent physician, was the first serious opponent of the witch-hunts that were set in motion by the *Malleus Maleficarum* (1486), the first handbook for the persecution of witches. Wier's attack on witch-hunters was followed by Bodin's attempt to refute Wier's argument.

Bodin saw the need for harsh therapy in order to protect society from witches. Witches were evil-doers, and society therefore needed to be protected from their evil spells. Bodin was critical of Wier's work, specifically *De Praestigiis*, labelling him 'Protector of witches' and labelling his teacher Agrippa (1486–1535) 'The Master Sorcerer' and 'the greatest witch of his age' (Bodin, 1580: 66–70). Bodin condemned Wier for defending Agrippa's name against his detractors. Wier's opinions on witchcraft sharply differed from Bodin's. Wier saw witches as foolish old women suffering melancholia, which made them easy prey for the devil, who tricked them into thinking that they could do evil deeds. According to Wier, the 'therapy' for their delusion was physical healing and religious instruction, not corporal or capital punishment. He held that the demonic pact was a fantasy. Bodin was concerned that Wier's views would lead judges to regard accused witches as ill and permit them to go unpunished.

Zilboorg (1941) states that, after Wier, Dr Felix Plater (1536–1614) went into the dungeons where so-called psychotics were kept, which he did to try to understand them. He, like Wier, came to the conclusion that their affliction must be the handiwork of the devil. Zilboorg also says that 'From a thing of good and evil spirits, mental disease gradually evolved into a thing of the spirit, of the soul' (Zilboorg, 1941: 23, 24). Freud contributed to the evolution of that understanding of mental processes in his interpreting dreams as 'the royal road to the knowledge of the unconscious in the life of the soul'.

The third of the three French writers, Henry Boguet, was chief judge in the district of Saint Claude in the county of Burgundy. In 1590 Henry Boguet published *Discours des Sorciers*. The 1602 edition was translated into English as *An Examen of Witches* (1929). Boguet states that the contents of his book are drawn from 'trials which I have myself conducted'. It also includes the procedure necessary for a judge in trials of witchcraft. The editor, Summers, says that 'these instructions were long held as supremely authoritative, and they were used as the official handbook and directory in trials of witchcraft by many local Parliaments and other Courts of Justice' (Boguet, 1590: 328). Summers states that the *An Examen of Witches* (1590) has been called 'a book precious as gold' (Boguet, 1590: vii). However, wealthy members of Boguet's family did not share this view. They bought up every copy of *An Examen of Witches* (1590), as it came from the printing press, and promptly consigned the copies to the flames so that it is now one of the scarcest of the witchcraft manuals. Summers tells us that Boguet's own family spread scandalous stories about him that he must have been a sorcerer himself to have such knowledge. Summers claims that after the *Malleus Maleficarum* (1486), 'there is perhaps no treatise more authoritative, and certainly no treatise more revelatory of the human side of trials for witchcraft and of the psychology of those involved in such trials than *An Examen of Witches*' (Boguet, 1590: vi).

Summers, who wrote the introduction to *An Examen of Witches* (1590) by Boguet describes it as one of the most valuable documents in the whole library of demonology. He says that Boguet had to deal with a particularly noxious, well-organised and essentially dangerous coven. He reflects, 'When we consider the zeal of Jean Bodin, Henry Boguet, Nicolas Remy and Pierre de Lancre we must always remember the difficulties and hazards these brave men had to face. . . . Their contest with the evil one was hard and long' (Boguet, 1590: xxiv). Freud also saw himself in a similar contest. He says, 'No one who, like me, conjures up the most evil of those half-tamed demons that inhabit the human breast, and seeks to wrestle with them, can expect to come through the struggle unscathed' (Freud,1905e: 108). Freud expressed this contest in intrapsychic terms as a contest with repressed wishes: 'the demons are bad and reprehensible wishes, derivatives of instinctual impulses that have been repudiated and repressed' (Freud, 1923d: 72).

Boguet (1590) wrote to the vicar general:

> there are witches by the thousand everywhere, multiplying on the earth as worms in a garden. . . . If effect could be given to my wish, the earth would be immediately cleared of them. . . . . I shall use every endeavour to make war on them, both by bringing them to justice and by my humble writings.

And again, he says, 'our aim is not to allow Satan to enlarge his kingdom further'. Boguet admits that the stories told of witches are astounding, beyond comprehension – for example, causing hail or the death of a man or sending the devil into a man's body or changing themselves into wolves. Boguet, in his preface, attributes to Satan the works performed by witches. But he says that at other times, 'Satan has worked purely by means of illusion' by troubling and confusing the witches' eyes or fantasy (Boguet, 1590: xlii–xliii). We shall see the relevance of Boguet's belief when we examine Freud's developing theories on hysteria.

Boguet says that witches learn from Satan how to compound a poison that they pour into the broth of their enemies and that they have ten thousand ways of harming men with the help of the devil, including cutting a man's throat in his bed. He says that witches have only the intent to harm; it is Satan who actually performs the deed. But the witch as author of the crime is worthy of punishment. Witches, he claims, are more difficult than others to convict because they have a cunning advocate: Satan. And he concludes his preface with 'I am a sworn enemy of witches', and 'I shall never spare them'. Harsh therapy, indeed.

2.2. Background to the witch-hunt in Europe

Under Charlemagne in the eight century, a law was passed that prohibited any consultations with fortune tellers or any inquiry from such folk as to the meaning of dreams. Charlemagne died in 814 CE. Part Two of this work gives an account of

Freud's interest in *The Judge* by Meyer, a story of seduction that is set in the reign of Charlemagne. In 829 CE a church council was held in Paris that appealed to Charlemagne's son to assist, by the secular arm, the Holy Church in the crusade against witchcraft (Remy, 1595: xix). In the introduction to Remy's book, Summers states that the legislation of Charles le Chauve, who died in 877 CE, was as drastic as that of the sixteenth and seventeenth centuries. Witches were made to pay the death penalty 'in order that the very memory of so heinous a crime may be utterly abolished and uprooted from the land' (Remy, 1595: xx).

Although Pope Gregory XI in 1374 authorised the inquisitors to prosecute all cases of sorcery, while excluding lay judges, we saw in Chapter 1 how the local Parlements in France gradually weaned this offence from ecclesiastical jurisdiction. Bodin says that by decree of Parlement in 1390, authority was granted to civil magistrates while excluding clergy from bringing witches under their jurisdiction. When this jurisdiction was transferred to the civil courts, the accused were treated with far greater severity, and even the innocent had little chance of escape, according to Summers (Remy, 1595: xxiv).

The vast majority of Christians in Europe during this period were peasants who often had only a thin veneer of Christianity over more primitive beliefs. Their world was inhabited by magical forces and beings. People were afraid of giants, dwarfs and werewolves, which were thought to be able to harm people. People thought that spells could be cast on humans, on livestock, on crops through reciting secret words or concocting evil recipes. Some took advantage of these fears of spells in order to get from others what they might not otherwise receive. These spells were a weapon of the weak against stronger people who, because of their power, had no need to resort to these manipulations. We shall see in Part Two that Freud believed that Dora used her 'illness' as a weapon against her father (Freud, 1905e: 98).

The literate upper class who studied the ancient Latin and Greek classics and fifteenth- and sixteenth-century Italian Renaissance works were elitist Renaissance thinkers (Bodin, 1580: 14–15). People today are familiar with Renaissance art and architecture but less familiar with the magical and occult philosophies, developed by the ancients, which were important components of Renaissance culture. Learned occult conjuring and magical literature flourished in the early sixteenth century, along with such pseudosciences as alchemy and astrology. Therefore, the educated elite were as concerned with occult magic as were the common people. While the peasants cast spells that they had acquired through oral tradition, the elite spellcasters tried to control the occult forces of the universe according to the wisdom of the ancients that they read in learned books (Bodin, 1580: 16). Jan Wier had studied medicine in Bonn under the physician and alchemist Cornelius Agrippa. It was Agrippa who decisively influenced Wier in his open challenge of many of the premises of the witch-hunters.

Another crucial development in the consciousness of the upper classes during medieval times was the explosion in the idea of evil, especially of the devil. In the art and literature of the late fourteenth, the fifteenth and early sixteenth centuries there was an almost obsessive concern with grotesque images of hell and the demons who inhabited it. Perhaps this heightening of dark fears is attributable to the Black Death (1347–1349), which killed over one-third of the entire population of Europe. The fear of the presence of the devil and the powers of evil in the world was heightened by the coming of the Reformation. Luther identified the pope with the Antichrist, and the Protestants considered much of Catholic tradition as diabolical superstition. Catholics called Protestants heretics who deserved extermination on earth and damnation in hell.

It was in this atmosphere that demonology developed. Almost one hundred years before Bodin's *Demon-Mania* (1580), the authors of *Malleus Maleficarum* (1486) had argued that the devil existed and that humans could be allies of his if they were inclined to evil. These human allies, they said, were witches, who deserved death. It was believed that the devil could take possession of a person. Demonic possession was an especially important aspect of witchcraft beliefs in France, where several highly publicised cases occurred (Bodin, 1580: 17–18). We know from Freud's writings that Charcot 'drew copiously upon the surviving reports of witch trials and of possession' in his lectures on hysteria in the Salpêtrière (Freud, 1893f: 20).

2.3. The view of women in the medieval and early modern periods

In the sixteenth century and through long tradition, women were held to be both lustful in their sexuality and weak in their religious faith. Formal education was reserved for males, and few women were educated outside the home. Bodin (1580) did not expound explicitly on the inferiority of women or their inclination to evil because he could assume, correctly for the most part, that his readers shared this opinion of women. Generally speaking, when people discussed witches, they thought of women. The stereotype of women as witches was widely held. Bodin, like most people of his day, believed that the majority of witches were women (Bodin, 1580: 187n.21). If men were accused, it was usually because of their connection with an accused woman (Bodin, 1580: 19).

Remy says that female witches far exceeded male ones in number since it is much easier for the demon to impose his deceits on the female sex. Remy shows his prejudice in stating that it is not unreasonable that 'this scum of humanity should be drawn chiefly from the feminine sex' (Remy, 1595: 56). In the case of female witnesses of the crime of witchcraft, Bodin says that women must be given credence even though they are de facto 'disreputable' and 'ignominious', as a shameless woman would be (Bodin, 1580: 186). Hysteria, which was Freud's interest, had this in common with witchcraft: hysteria, as its name implied, was a woman's 'dis-ease'.

Remy says that Satan knows that 'the filthy rabble of witches is commonly desirous of revenge', so Satan deceives them by promising them a means of avenging themselves when they have been angered by a received hurt (Remy, 1595: 4). Freud also describes some of his so-called hysterical patients as 'under the influence of a morbid craving for revenge' (Freud, 1905e: 134). Remy says that the devil provides the witch with diabolical powders and ointments that infallibly cause sickness or the death of those against whom it is used. The drugs owe their potency to the demon, not to any inherent properties of their own. Remy says that 'there have been cases of witches who, as soon as the judge gave them permission to rub or anoint themselves with the unguent, have at once been carried aloft and have disappeared' (Remy, 1595: 6). However, even though he conducted 'the capital trial of 900 persons' accused of witchcraft, he does not tell us that he witnessed the phenomenon.

The demon deceives the witch by promising riches. Remy records the confession of Catharine of Metingow, whom he tried at Dieuze on 4 November 1586. She received as she thought a gift of money from a demon, but when she shook out the purse, she found nothing but swine's dung (Remy, 1595: 8). In a similar vein, Freud wrote to Fliess on 24 January 1897,

> I read one day that the gold the devil gives his victims regularly turns into excrement; and the next day Mr. E., who reports that his nurse had money deliria, suddenly told me . . . that Louise's money always was excrement. So, in the witch stories it is merely transformed back into the substance from which it arose.

Sinister and grotesque powers were associated with women in medieval and early modern times. Witches were believed to possess the capability of poisoning people on whom they wanted to take revenge. Miles (1990) claims that because medieval women had not enjoyed the conditions necessary for formulating self-representations that could have informed collective male views of women, men created representations of women out of their own fears and fantasies. Medieval men figured 'woman' as a frightening and fascinating creature whose anger and rejection could deprive men of gratification, delight and ultimately life and salvation. Miles claims that the 'damage of such unlimited projection' has been felt by medieval woman who was seen as witch (Miles, 1990: 169, 170).

Hans Baldung-Grien (1484/85–1545), a Southern German artist who worked in Strasbourg in the first half of the sixteenth century during the emerging witch craze, created grotesque images of women. His artistic work on the front cover of this book, *The Witches Sabbat* (1510) depicts the naked female body of witches, which bears a striking resemblance to his naked Eves, thus emphasising the seductive evil of witchcraft. The background can also be seen as an extension of the dark side of the forest of Adam and Eve, painted by his teacher, Dürer. Baldung did not provide a critique of the witch trials but rather aligned his visual force with the psychical and physical forces used in the trials to condemn witches.

2.4. Where witches were put on trial

Thousands of trials of witchcraft in Europe in the sixteenth and seventeenth centuries took place in secular courts. Witchcraft was regarded as a secular crime and was dealt with in criminal courts along with murder, theft, arson and assault.

Ecclesiastical courts, or inquisitions, dealt with the crime of witchcraft only in Spain and Italy. It was in the north of Europe, where the secular court system looked after this offence, that the heaviest persecution of witches took place.

Torture was used to obtain confessions in the witch trials. It was also used by the courts in other criminal procedures, and many crimes like murder, theft, treason, heresy and blasphemy were punished by death. The judge's own beliefs in the area of witchcraft were crucial in determining how severely the court dealt with the accused. Several large-scale persecutions of particular brutality can be attributed to particular judges. The French courts, where Bodin, Remy and Boguet worked, were more severe than the Spanish and Italian inquisitions but less severe than the German and Scottish courts and equally severe with the English courts (Bodin, 1580: 20).

2.5. A specific evil deed caused by witches: male impotence

The first major witch persecution manual, *Malleus Maleficarum* (1486) lists first among the evil powers of witches the ability to cause male impotence. The *Malleus* acquired especial weight and dignity from the authoritative bull of Pope Innocent VIII (1484), in which he empowers the authors to imprison and punish all those who 'have abandoned themselves to devils' and who, by their spells, 'hinder men from performing the sexual act' (Kramer & Sprenger, 1486: xix–xx). They describe in detail the harm witches do to men by making the male organ disappear and causing impotence. However, they say that if a man is obstructed from copulating, he is 'deluded by devils' (Kramer & Sprenger, 1486: 7, 168). The blame is placed on the witch because in order 'to bring about these evils ... witches and the devil work together' (Kramer & Sprenger, 1486: 18).

Bodin (1580) quotes both the 'Si per sortiarias' canon, from which he concludes that 'copulation can be prevented by maleficent art', and Thomas Aquinas' statement that 'one can be tied with respect to one woman and not to others'. Bodin warns that the most pernicious filth of witches is 'the impediment given to those who marry, which is called tying the codpiece-string' – that is, causing male impotence. This was a widely feared spell, reputedly cast by a witch who uttered it while tying knots in a string. It was thought to cause impotence in men. Bodin relates that after presiding over trials in Poitiers in 1567, his hostess with whom he was staying recounted 'more than fifty ways to tie the codpiece-string', in order to impede sexual fulfilment (Bodin, 1580: 99). However, it is worth noting that his hostess said that there are some people whom it is impossible to tie, indicating that the witch's power to cause impotence was a delusory fear.

In 1560 one witch was imprisoned because a newlywed bride accused her of having bound her husband – that is, preventing sexual relations between them. The bride threatened the witch that she would never get out of prison if she did not release her husband from his impotence. As soon as the judge was informed that the husband was no longer impotent, the imprisoned woman was released. Bodin claims that it is the devil who guides and directs all this malice of the witch in order to exterminate the human race. Bodin states that witches 'do not have the power to remove a single member from a man except the virile organs ... causing the shameful parts to be hidden and withdrawn into the abdomen' (Bodin, 1580: 100–101). Bodin is accusing so-called witches of causing a man's impotence and blaming the devil for preventing the procreation of the human race (Bodin, 1580: 101).

Remy examined the case of a young wife who was accused of depriving her old husband of his masculinity by putting herbs into his food because he was unfaithful to her. Remy says, 'it is perfectly clear that there was no actual loss of the man's generative organ' but rather that a false glamour was drawn over his eyes which made him imagine that his member had disappeared (Remy, 1595: 112). An illusion of the eyes can be caused by spells, while in truth everything remains exactly as it was (Remy, 1595: 114).

2.6. Whether witches copulate with demons

This important question was debated before the Emperor Sigismund. How do devils perform the human act of copulation with witches? This was discussed by all the witches' judges, who resolved that such copulation is possible. They compare this problem to a similar one in the Book of Genesis 6:1–4, which states that the sons of God had intercourse with the daughters of humans. The witches' judges base their decision on Thomas Aquinas' literal interpretation of Gen. 6:1–4. But a detailed exegesis of this biblical pericope, examining it in its context, reveals that the pericope is not meant to be taken literally but instead carries a message concerning the problem of evil.

Following the opinion of Aquinas, the authors of *Malleus Maleficarum* literalised this myth. They strengthen their claim by quoting Augustine, who says that 'it is not outside belief that the Giants of whom scripture speaks were begotten not by men but by angels or certain devils who lust after women'. But the demythologising of this story leads to the 'pathology of literalism'. This myth is presenting the problem of evil, but when it is read literally, its true meaning is lost (Duffy, 1996: 7–9). The erroneous belief of the inquisitors and judges about witches' copulating with demons is based on the literalising of this myth. This in turn leads to a belief in the witches' pact with the devil and their subsequent power to do harm to men. Extracting a confession of copulating with the devil was a necessary part of the witch trials. Freud showed an interest in this aspect of the witches' confessions. In a letter to Fliess on 24 January 1879, Freud wrote, 'If only I knew why the devil's semen is always described as "cold" in the witches' confessions'.

2.7. The judges' need for harsh therapy?

Why the harsh therapy? Bodin lists the benefits that accrue from the harsh therapy: it prevents the ruin of the state by appeasing the anger of God; it brings the blessing of God on the whole country; it strikes fear and terror into other witches, because 'others having seen the punishment are afraid to commit the offence' (Deut. 13:11; 17: 13; 19: 20; 20; 21); it reduces the number of the wicked in society; it enables the good to live in security; and it punishes the wicked. Bodin continues,

> there is no penalty cruel enough to punish the evil of witches, since all their wickedness and blasphemies rise up against God to vex and offend Him in a thousand ways. . . . Against which, one must seek vengeance with the greatest diligence and utmost rigour, in order to bring an end to the wrath of God and His vengeance upon us.
>
> *(Bodin, 1580: 203–204)*

Bodin then lists the crimes of witches: treason against God by their 'foul connection' with the devil; cursing and blaspheming God; doing homage to the devil; promising their children to the devil; sacrificing infants to the devil before they have been baptised; dedicating their unborn children to the devil; making an oath to lure others into his service; swearing by the name of the devil; engaging in incest; eating human flesh, especially of small children and drinking their blood; killing with poisons or spells; and lastly, copulating with the devil, a wickedness they all confess. Bodin is convinced that all witches who have a formal compact with the devil are normally guilty of all or most of these evil deeds (Bodin, 1580: 204–207). Bodin's book listing all the crimes of witches was being prepared for publication by the School of Charcot while Freud was studying there.

Bodin greatly emphasised the need for judges to be well trained, competent and sound in judgement. In advising judges on how to proceed against witches, he demanded solid proof of guilt in order to find the accused guilty. One firm proof was a freely made confession of guilt by the accused. If the accused refused to confess, the court could order her 'to be put to the question' – that is, tortured in order to produce a confession. For a confession extracted by torture to stand as proof, it had to be freely repeated after the torture. We shall see in Part Two how Freud's patients, 'under the influence of the technical procedure which I used at that time', produced confessions that he later was obliged to admit that he 'had perhaps forced on them' (Freud, 1925d: 33–34). Freud is here admitting that some of the confessions that he extracted from his so-called hysterical patients were perhaps forced out of them.

To prove the point about the reality of witches, their evil deeds and the need for harsh therapy, Bodin refers to many biblical passages: 'Put to death any woman who practises magic' (Ex. 22:18); 'Do not give any of your children to be used in the worship of Moloch' (Lev. 20:1); Isaiah reminds the idolatrous Israelites, 'you are no better than sorcerers, adulterers, prostitutes. . . . You worship the fertility gods by having sex under those sacred trees of yours. You offer your children as sacrifices. . . . You go to the high mountains to offer sacrifices and have sex. . . . You forsake me . . . You put on your perfumes and ointments and go to worship the god Molech' (Isaiah 57:3–10) (Bodin, 1580: 39); 'Cursed be he who gives his seed to Molech'

(Lev. 20:2) (Bodin, 1580: 133); and Solomon says that the seed of the Canaanites who acted thus was 'cursed by God' (Wis. 12:11) (Bodin, 1580: 50).

To justify his stand on harsh therapy for witches, Bodin also recalls that God exterminated the Amorites who committed lewd acts, who practised sorcery and worshipped the devil with sacrifices of their children (Deut. 18:9–14) (Bodin, 1580: 64, 102). Bodin reminds us of the unlawful diabolical means that King Saul used when he turned to the witch of Endor to learn the outcome of his affair (Bodin, 1580: 89). We shall see the importance of these scriptural references to the sacrifice of children to Moloch when we come to examine Freud's Aliquis analysis and his reference to a primeval sexual cult of Moloch in the context of his understanding of 'the harsh therapy of the witches' judges'.

Bodin explores the relationship between witches and the devil. He refers to Augustine's book *The City of God*, written in the early fifth century, which says that one would be impudent to try to deny that demons have carnal relations with women. He defines 'witch' as one who knowingly tries to accomplish something by diabolical means. 'Diabolical means' are the superstitions taught by Satan to witches to destroy the human race (Bodin, 1580: 45, 90). Bodin searches scripture and the writings of the ancient philosophers to find words to describe this enemy of the human race: Satan, Demon, Evil Spirit, Dragon, the Destroyer, Leviathan.

Bodin points out that God, in speaking to the Hebrew people about the vengeance that he will take on Egypt, refers to the pharaoh as the great Leviathan (Bodin, 1580: 48). Some take Leviathan to be the monster crocodile controlled by magicians (Job.3: 8). The monster lives in the river Nile. Ezekiel speaks the words of the Lord to Leviathan: 'I am your enemy, you monster crocodile, lying in the river. You say that the Nile is yours and that you made it. . . . I will pull you up out of the Nile. . . . I will get men to attack you with swords' (Ezek. 29:3, 4, 8). Bodin draws on commentators who agree that the river [Nile] means 'that torrent of fluid nature which always flows on to corruption, which is characteristic of the Destroyer'. And he says, 'The devils of this elemental torrent . . . extinguish the light of reason' (Bodin, 1580: 48–49). We shall see, when we come to Part Two, that Freud refers to his 'important finding' on hysteria as 'the discovery of a caput Nili [the source of the Nile] in neuropathology'.

The prophet Isaiah says that 'the Lord will use his powerful and deadly sword to punish Leviathan, that wriggling, twisting dragon, and to kill the monster that lives in the sea' (Isaiah 27: 1). Bodin comments,

> By the sea he means the fluid and elemental matter which Plato and Aristotle, searching for the origin of evil, said was the cause of all ills, and which Solomon in his allegories and parables calls woman, when he said that there is no malice which approaches the malice of woman.
>
> *(Bodin, 1580: 48–49)*

Solomon, in the Book of Proverbs, describes woman as the seducer of man. This is an image of woman that Freud later came to accept. Bodin states that association with evil spirits ought not to seem strange, since good spirits have a partnership with humans. However, it is 'usually only the greatest simpletons and women' who, according to Bodin, were snared 'into making formal partnerships with Satan' (Bodin, 1580: 62–63).

Bodin points to the condemnation of witchcraft in ancient societies as his central argument for the need for harsh therapy for witches (Bodin, 1580: 143). He writes disparagingly of so-called witches: 'Not that it is possible to drive witches away completely without there always being some, who are just like toads and grass-snakes on the ground, spiders in houses, caterpillars and flies in the air. . . . If one lets the vermin multiply, it engenders corruption in everything' (Bodin, 1580: 145–146). Bodin continues, 'witches are stupid and ignorant scoundrels scorned by everyone. . . . witches are foul smelling, which comes from copulation with devils'. They thus become 'hideous, doleful, ugly, stinking'.

If witches cannot be instructed in the law of God and led into his service, Bodin prescribes applying cauteries and hot irons and cutting off the putrefied parts (Bodin, 1580: 173). Decker claims that the application of hot irons and clitorectomies were still being performed on hysterical girls into the late nineteenth century, when Freud came on the scene, because physicians had nothing else to offer hysterics except an admission of ignorance (Decker, 1986: 102). Bodin claims that roasting and slowly burning is not nearly as great a pain as what Satan makes them suffer in this world, not to mention the eternal pains that are prepared for them. It was seen to be in the interest of the eternal salvation of the witch that the judge tried to extract a confession from her (Bodin, 1580: 174). Similarly, it was in the interest of curing his patients that Freud tried to extract a confession out of them.

The aim of the harsh therapy, according to Bodin, is not to make them suffer more than they are suffering but

> to bring an end to the wrath of God on the whole people; also, in part, to bring them to repentance and to cure them or at least, if they will not change their ways, to reduce their number. It is, therefore, very salutary for the state to search out and severely punish witches.
>
> *(Bodin, 1580: 174)*

Bodin calls the punishment of witches a 'holy task'.

2.8. Evidence required to convict a witch during the witch trials

Bodin lists three requirements to prove the crime of witchcraft: (1) the truth of the fact that witches were in league with the devil, attended Sabbats and, with the devil's power, committed evil deeds; (2) the testimony of several sound witnesses; and (3) a voluntary confession.

2.8.1. Four 'concrete facts' that prove the accused is a witch

2.8.1.1. Spells?

If spells are found on the witch who is arrested; if a pact between the witch and the devil, signed by him, is found in her chest; if the witch cuts off a man's virile member and then rejoins the member: these are evidence to prove the crime of witchcraft (Bodin, 1580: 181–183). Bodin does not say how the investigation of these crimes is made.

2.8.1.2. The devil's mark?

If the devil's mark is found it is concrete evidence of a pact with the devil. Bodin says that if the devil distrusts those who agree to give themselves to him forever, he also marks them. This mark was sometimes called the devil's stigmata. Freud was aware of the belief in the devil's stigmata because he tells Fliess on 17 January 1897 that 'the inquisitors prick with needles to discover the devil's stigmata', and he also compares the witches confessions with parallel stories told by his patients; for example, 'Eckstein has a scene where the diabolus sticks needles into her fingers and then places a candy on each drop of blood'.

Bodin says that the most detestable witches are those who renounce God to give themselves to the devil, by express agreement. This agreement is sometimes made verbally, but sometimes he makes them sign it with their blood, in the manner of the ancients. Therefore, the mark is a sure sign, which judges use. Trois-eschelles du Maine, having been condemned by the city provost in 1571, obtained immunity in order to persuade him to reveal his accomplices, and having done so, he said

> that they were marked, and that one would find the mark by undressing them. It was found that they bore a mark like the paw or track of a hare, which had no feeling, so that witches do not feel the punctures when they are pierced right to the bone in the location of the mark.
>
> *(Bodin, 1580: 112–113)*

Remy describes two kinds of marks, one invisible and the other visible. Pricking was necessary to discover the invisible one, and it bled, though it was an insensitive spot. The visible one usually was as big as a wart and if pricking was used 'no pain is felt and not a drop of blood is shed'. This fact was held to be so certain a proof of capital guilt that it was often made the base of examination and torture. Remy gives as an example Claude Bogart, who was about to be put to the torture, and when her head was shaved, a scar was discovered on top of her forehead. The judge ordered a pin to be thrust deeply into it. It was seen that she felt no pain. Yet, Remy complains, she persisted in denying the truth. But after she was brought to the torture, she not only acknowledged that the mark had been made by a demon but recounted several other cruel injuries that she had received from the demon.

On another woman, Mugette, the sergeant who stripped her found, on her left thigh, a mark 'as big as a wart', and Remy declares, 'it seems to me that they are very far from the truth who ascribe this matter to natural causes' (Remy, 1595: 9–10). The mark was believed to be a sign of a pact with the devil. Sometimes the pact was signed in blood. Freud wrote in *A Seventeenth-Century Demonological Neurosis* (1923d) about a pact made with the devil by a seventeenth-century painter suffering from melancholia. In investigating 'the painter's demonological illness' psychoanalytically, Freud considers the 'painter's bond with the Devil as a neurotic phantasy' and points out 'many striking analogies' and 'a number of subtle connections which we are able to demonstrate in this case' (Freud, 1923d: 84). Freud is comparing the seventeenth-century painter's 'demonological illness' with his neurotic patients' illnesses.

2.8.1.3. Transported to the Sabbat?

If the witch is transported to the Sabbat, is this a 'concrete fact'? Freud refers to the witches' transport in the context of his writing to Fliess on 24 January 1897 about two of his patients, Mr. E. and Emma Eckstein. He explains that 'the broomstick they ride is probably the great Lord Penis'. Bodin learned from his reading that transport to the Sabbat takes place after the witch has applied ointment to her body, but sometimes, he says, it takes place without applying ointment. The witches are transported sometimes on a billy goat, sometimes on a flying horse, sometimes on a broom, sometimes on a pole. Some go naked, others dressed, some at night, others by day. Bodin says that in the region of Maine, no less than 30 witches denounced each other through mutual envy, and their confessions agreed on the transporting, the worship of the devil, the dances and the renunciation of all religion. At the trial of the witches of Valery in Savoy, conducted in 1574, witches confessed

> bodily transport on just a pole without ointment, then the abjuration of God, the worship of the Devil, the dances, feasts, and the kissing of the shameful parts of Satan in the guise of a beast, then the obligation to commit a thousand evils, and the powders given to everyone.
>
> *(Bodin, 1580: 117)*

Boguet examined the possibility of witches being conveyed to the Sabbat. He says that Wier (1563) denies that witches are conveyed from one place to another in the manner that they allege, but Boguet has always been well persuaded that they are conveyed because of the authority of Sprenger & Kramer (1486) and others who maintain this view and also because of the confession of nearly all witches that they have been conveyed to the Sabbat. Françoise Secretain confessed to Boguet that she placed a white staff between her legs and uttered certain words and that she was then conveyed through the air to the witches' assembly.

Remy discusses whether witches do in fact fly to and are bodily present in 'their nocturnal synagogues' or whether they are only 'possessed by some fantastic delusion, and, as happens when the empty mind is filled with dreams at night, merely imagine that they are present' (Remy, 1595: 47). This is an important question, which Freud refers to in his comments 'on the very interesting witch trials' at the meeting of the Vienna Psychoanalytic Society on 27 January 1909. Freud says, 'We find unmistakably infantile elements in those fantasies that were not created under torture but merely squeezed out by it' (Nunberg & Federn, 1967: 123). Freud seems to be saying what Remy was saying: the flights to the Sabbat were fantasies of the witches. Bodin, Remy and Boguet question whether the witches' flights to and presence at the Sabbats were real or only fantasies. We shall see in Part Two that Freud, at the time of studying the literature on witches, was having grave doubts about his seduction theory and was looking at the possibility of phantasies of seduction.

It was claimed that the witches anointed themselves with ointments before they flew to the Sabbat (Bodin, 1580: 114–117). Boguet claims that the ointments used by witches 'are for the most part made of the fat of little children who, under the Devil's instigation, were murdered by witches'. Boguet believed that these ointments can have no other effect but 'to deaden and stupefy the witches' senses so that Satan may the more easily have his will of them' (Boguet, 1590: 69). At other times, Satan mixes some ingredient with it that causes deep sleep. Boguet cites Cardan, who says that the ointment sends these old hags to sleep and afterwards makes them dream marvellous dreams.

Although Sprenger & Kramer (1486) claim that witches can corrupt and soften the hearts of their judges by merely looking at them, Boguet is not willing to admit that power. Jeanne Platet confessed that to cause the death of people or cattle, she used to rub them by hand with an ointment given her by the devil. Boguet says, 'the ointments may be veritable poison which on being applied to the skin penetrates it and passes into the inner parts of the person or beast which is thus killed or made ill by the witch'. Boguet does not explain how the witch, who applies the poisonous ointment, is not poisoned herself.

2.8.1.4. Presence at the witches' Sabbat?

A proof that a witch was present at the Sabbat constitutes evidence of guilt. Remy says, 'I am quite willing to agree with those who think that such Sabbat meetings at times exist only in dreams'. Witches often are

> merely visited in their sleep by an empty and vain imagination. For the Demons are equally ready either to transport them whither they wish when they are awake, or to impress the image of such a happening upon their minds while they are sleeping and influenced by a brief mania.
>
> *(Remy, 1595: 51)*

Remy says that demons imbue and fill the soul with a vision of things from farthest lands; they often insinuate themselves into people's minds and mark them with whatever thoughts they please. Remy refers to Cardan, who thinks that witches, during their sleep, imagine that they are visiting various distant lands where they see kings, theatres, dances and fountains and even imagine that they have slept and taken their pleasure with the most comely young men (Remy, 1595: 52). This belief of the witches' judges that these copulations with the devil at the Sabbat exist only at times in the imagination of the witch is a crucial point that we shall return to in our investigation of Freud's retraction of the seduction theory.

Having accepted the fact that witches' journeyings to the Sabbat are at times but 'an empty imagination begotten of dreams', Remy resumes his discussion of witches often in fact travelling to their nocturnal synagogues (Remy, 1595: 47). As positive evidence, he points to the masks that they have in their homes for wearing to assemblies. He says, 'it is no idle rumour that witches do in person attend these assemblies' (Remy, 1595: 63). He believes that witches fly up mainly through the chimney because nearly all of those convicted of this crime have, by their free confessions, bore witness to the truth of this fact. Some rode on a pig, a bull, a forked stick or a black dog (Remy, 1595: 53).

Remy says, 'In Lorraine, during the sixteen years in which I have judged prisoners charged with this crime, no less than eight hundred have been clearly proved guilty and condemned to death'. And again, he says,

> In my capacity as judge I remember having sentenced to the stake for the crime of witchcraft some two hundred persons, more or less, who have in free and open confession asserted that on certain days it was their custom to meet together by the bank of some pool or river, preferably one well hidden from the eyes of passers-by; and that there with a wand given them by the Demon, they used to stir the water until there arose a dense vapour and smoke, in the midst of which they were borne up on high.

Remy says that they scattered some 'drugged' powder into the water and beat it in order to bring down rain upon the earth (Remy, 1595: 74). One must remember that in the days before washing machines and water on tap in homes, the women gathered by the bank of the river to do the family washing. They beat the clothes and possibly would have scattered powder on them. It was believed that at the Sabbat the devil furnished them with powders to bury beneath the entrances to stables, sheepfolds and houses in order to kill or injure.

> Also present was a great black billy goat which spoke like a person to them, and they danced around the goat. Then each kissed his rear while holding a burning candle. After that the billy goat was consumed in fire and each one took some of the ash or powder to kill a steer or cow. . . . Finally, the Devil said to them with a terrible voice these words, 'Take revenge or you will die!'
>
> *(Bodin, 1580: 118–119)*

Boguet was aware that witches who confessed that they were at the Sabbat were there only in spirit while remaining in their houses 'as dead' for the space of two or three hours. Boguet tells the story of a man of the village of Unau in the district of Orgelet who brought his wife before the magistrates and accused her of being a witch, saying that when they were in bed together one Thursday night, he noticed her absolutely still without even breathing; he shook her but could not waken her. He became so frightened that he could not move from his bed or even cry out. When his wife awoke, she said she felt nothing of what her husband had done to her, because she was so tired from the work that she had done the day before. Her husband supposed she had been to the Sabbat, since he had already some suspicions of her. Boguet is of the opinion that this woman had been to the Sabbat in spirit. His reasons are that her 'seizure' came on a Thursday night, the customary night for the Sabbat; that she woke at cockcrow and the Sabbat ends at cockcrow; that the excuse of tiredness 'proves that there was deceit on her part'; and that the husband was unable to move or cry out. The magistrates who adjudicated this case said that the woman was descended from parents who had been suspected of witchcraft (Boguet, 1590: 48). In this case, the husband's phantasy seems to have been enough to convict his wife of being a witch.

Referring to those witches who remain unconscious and as it were dead, Boguet says that 'it is probable that Satan sends them to sleep . . . and reveals to them in their sleep what happens at the Sabbat so vividly that they think they have been there; and therefore they can give a marvellously accurate account of it' (Boguet, 1590: 51). But Boguet asserts that this only happens to those who have been there in person and have already enlisted beneath Satan's standard. We shall return to Boguet's belief, in our examination of the first stage of Freud's retraction of his seduction theory.

2.8.2. The testimony of several 'sound witnesses'

If a witch is accused by accomplices, they should at once be brought face to face because there is nothing that so confounds a witch as to be confronted with a companion from the Sabbat (Boguet, 1590: 215). Infamous and notorious characters, personal enemies and children who have not yet reached the age of puberty may legally give evidence in a case of witchcraft (Boguet, 1590: 230). Evidence from such witnesses is considered by judges to be sufficient proof to convict a witch. In the crime of witchcraft, according to Boguet, all sorts of people are accepted as witnesses, including accomplices, because it is an exceptional crime and committed at night and always in secret. It is mainly other witches who attend the Sabbat who are best fitted to give evidence (Boguet, 1590: 229). The judge should commit the accused witch to prison on the accusation of a single accomplice. The same applies for common rumour, which is 'almost infallible' in the matter of witchcraft (Boguet, 1590: 212).

Remy records evidence given by Nicolette Lang-Bernhard, who was returning from an old mill on 25 July 1590 at high noon, when she saw in a field nearby a band of people dancing round in a ring, with their backs turned towards each other. Some of the feet were like those of a goat or oxen. Frightened, she called on the name of Jesus, and 'all the dancers seemed to vanish at once except one named Petter Gross-Petter, who rose quickly into the air.' Nicolette spread the story through all the village. In spite of protestations that this was a false allegation, Petter was 'induced to confess his crime, and finally to name and make known others who had been his partners in it' (Remy, 1595: 50). Remy says,

> the final and incontrovertible proof of the truth of this occurrence was the fact that the place where this dancing had been enacted was found, on the day after the matter was reported by Nicolette, trodden into a ring such as is found in a circus where horses run round in a circle; and among the other tracks were the recent marks of the hoofs of goats and oxen. . . . Here is an actual fact, not a visionary dream. . . . If this is not proof enough to convince anyone. . . . I would have him know that I have not imagined or invented any part of the story.
>
> *(Remy, 1595: 50–51)*

Remy does not say that the tracks of human feet were found, nor does he seem to know that such tracks of animals' feet in a circle are often visible in fields where animals are fed. Freud writes to Fliess on 24 January 1897, drawing comparisons between his patients' stories and the dancing in the witches' confessions, 'E'.s Louise was such a dancing witch; he was first . . . reminded of her at the ballet. Hence his theater anxiety'. Regarding the significance of the witches' dances in which they worship the demon at the Sabbat, Remy recalls that the Israelites turned aside from the true worship of Yahweh to idolatry and danced in a ring around the golden calf. He says that this dancing is 'the begetter of sin' and leads to fanatical frenzies and madness (Remy, 1595: 61). He says, it 'always opens no small window to vice. . . . And just as their banquets are attended by hunger and bulimy, their copulations by pain and disgust, . . . so also those dancings and caperings, . . . never fail to cause weariness and fatigue and the greatest distress' (Remy, 1595: 60).

Bodin records that according to the confession of the witches of Longny, no Sabbat is carried on where they do not dance, which makes the men frenzied and the women abort. Bodin claims that 'This is a matter of the highest consequence for a state, and something one should prevent in the most rigorous way'. Concerning the frenzy, Bodin says that 'all frenzied and deranged people engage in such dances and violent leaps' (Bodin, 1580: 120). In the letter to Fliess on the 24 January 1897, Freud writes, 'In connection with the dancing in witches' confessions, remember the dance epidemics in the Middle Ages. E'.s Louise was such a dancing witch. . . . Gymnastic feats in the hysterical attacks of boys and the like belong in the category of flying and floating'.

2.8.3. Confessions of being abused by the devil at the Sabbat?

Freud asks in a letter to Fliess on 17 January 1897, 'why did the devil who took possession of the poor things invariably abuse them sexually and in a loathsome manner?' Remy says that witches must render an account to the devil of the evils they did with the powders he had given to them at the Sabbat, and if one is discovered who has done nothing since the last assembly, she gets several raps with a cudgel on the soles of her feet. Remy says that to avert blows, the wealthier witches offer a gift to the demon. Poorer witches give black cocks or hens. These gifts are accepted by the demon, 'but if any of them refuses or omits to make some payment, she immediately incurs threats, blows, sickness, the death of children, household loss or some signal disaster' (Remy, 1595: 40–41).

Witches complain that Satan never fails to invent reasons for blaming and severely punishing them, such as if they are late in attendance at the Sabbat. Remy records stories told by witches from the trials he conducted. At Nicole Morele's trial at Serre in January 1587, she confessed that 'the Demon had hands of iron with which he pounded her head'. Rosa Gerardine, at her trial in November 1586, made manifest to the judge the scars that she had received. Catherine Praevote confessed at her trial in September 1589 that the demon imposed a compulsion on her to kill her own offspring. Agnes Eyswitz confessed that she was constrained to poison her 20-year-old son, Peter, under pain of death at the hands of the demon. At Jean le Ban's trial in January 1586, moved by fear of threatened torture she confessed to the judge all her crimes of witchcraft. She said that for this confession, the demon so pounded and kicked her that she thought her last day had come. Remy concludes from these confessions of ill treatment that witches are forever the victims of evil impulses and misery (Remy, 1595: 44–46).

Bodin claims that witches on their own confessions 'were displeased when they found some sort of very cold semen', and they were tormented day and night 'unless they continued in the service of their master'. Bodin read in the confessions of innumerable witches that they suffer 'when they are forced to worship Satan in the guise of a stinking billy goat, and to kiss it on the part one does not dare write or frankly say' (Bodin, 1580: 152–156). He says that many witches confessed to being 'beaten by the Devil if they did not do his commandments' (Bodin, 1580: 164). Freud noted in *A Seventeenth-Century Demonological Neurosis* (1923d) that 'If we are bold enough to apply this idea of the Devil as a father-substitute to cultural history, we may also be able to see the witch trials of the Middle Ages in a new light' (Freud, 1923d: 87n.1). It might also have been informative to look at the idea of the devil as a husband substitute in some cases in the medieval witch trials.

2.8.3.1. 'Voluntary or open' confessions

Remy says that to escape from the tyranny of the devil, many witches desire death. He states that all the witches confess that the demon is 'so harsh and unjust a taskmaster to them that they often wish to throw off his yoke and return to their former freedom'. When through weariness of his tyranny and feelings of guilt and fear of heavier punishment they decide to die by suicide, some hang themselves, others stab themselves and yet others throw themselves into a river or well (Remy, 1595: 163). Jeanne le Ban, in an open confession to Remy, bore witness about the demon having tried to persuade her to drown herself or to hang herself: 'The Demon who certainly has a hand in it urgently hastens the business' (Remy, 1595: 161). Remy says that the demon urges witches to die by suicide if there is imminent danger of their being suspected (Remy, 1595: 163).

Remy claimed that 'these poor wretches do not always have to put an end to their lives' by suicide because 'the Divine Shepherd in his ineffable goodness and mercy often calls back to the fold the sheep that have been led away by the wolf, and again feeds them on His celestial pastures' (Remy, 1595: 162). Therefore, 'many witches do not defer the confession of their crimes until it is wrung from them by torture, but of their own accord and with the greatest joy of spirit lay bare their sins', so that they can preserve themselves from eternal unhappiness.

Remy records that Catharine Latomia (1587) did not deny that for her great wickedness she was deserving of the extreme penalty as well as of the judge's utmost wrath. She asked that her death no longer be deferred, because her soul was a very heavy burden to her. Idatia of Miremont (1588) 'passionately entreated the Judge to deliver her up to death as soon as possible' in order to escape from the demon. Apollonia a Friessen (1589) 'said that nothing more welcome could happen to her than death' because 'she could not free herself of her Demon's tyranny except by death' (Remy, 1595: 162).

Even when the witch is 'under the protection of the judge', the demon retains his hold on the witch and thus prevents her from confessing even when being tortured. Quirina Xallaea, at her trial in February 1587, recalled that her demon visited her in prison and told her that 'if only she could bear in silence a brief period of pain she would certainly gain her liberty afterwards' (Remy, 1595: 164). Remy says that if by chance the judge signed to the torturer to relax the pressure a little, the demon anticipated this and foretold it to her as if it were his doing. Françoise Fellet (1584) said that 'silence was imposed upon her by the Demon' (Remy, 1595: 165).

Many have been put on the fire and have not been burned, for the demon within them has blown back the fire; or if they have been burned, they have not felt it, neither have they felt any prickings, scratches or tortures. As Alexee Belheure, at her trial in January 1587, was preparing to make a free and open confession, she said,

> Can you not see him lying under the couch? . . . See how he is threatening me with his looks and trying all he can to frighten me from saying a word! This is not the first time he has tried to keep me from telling the truth.
>
> *(Remy, 1595: 165)*

Witches confessed to Boguet that they went to the Sabbat at about midnight and that the Sabbat was held on a Thursday night. Boguet comments that witches never confess half of what they have done. Boguet learned from confessions all that happens at the Sabbat: Satan appears to them in the shape of a big black man or goat or ram, and they offer him homage by kissing him on the shameful parts behind; following this, they dance in a ring back to back so that they may not be recognised. Clauda Paget confessed that they mask themselves for the same purpose.

The demons join in these dances. Satan sometimes provides music by playing on the flute. After the dancing, the witches couple with each other. Incest is commonly practised; the son does not spare his mother, nor the father his daughter. Children born of such incestuous coupling had their bodies burned after their blood was collected in phials (Boguet, 1590: 55–57).

After these 'foul fleshy pleasures, the witches fall to feasting and banqueting'. Some confessed that there was a great cauldron on the fire from which they all helped themselves to meat. They confessed that salt as a symbol of immortality is held in 'bitter abhorrence by the Devil'. Salt is used in baptism as an antidote against the power of Satan. All witches agree that there is no taste in the food, and they are still as hungry after eating as they were on starting, and it seemed as if they had eaten nothing. Boguet says, 'all this shows how the Devil is always a deceiver' (Boguet, 1590: 58–59).

Having finished the banquet, they render an account of what they have done since the last assembly. The most welcome are those who have caused the most mischief and wickedness. Those who have behaved most humanely are generally beaten by their master. He then urges them to do all the harm they can do: to afflict their neighbours with illnesses, to kill their cattle and to avenge themselves upon their enemies. He gives them power to spoil the fruits of the earth. He makes them take a solemn oath not to lay information against each other. Boguet says that judges should pay great attention to this point. Lastly, they produce hail. Sometimes they say Mass at the Sabbat. The celebrant is clothed in a black cope with no cross on it. Boguet says, 'the hair stands up on my head' in thinking of the way Satan imitates what Jesus did at the Last Supper (Boguet, 1590: 61).

In 1521 three witches were executed who confessed that they had changed themselves into wolves and in that form had killed and eaten several people (Boguet, 1590: 140). It is Boguet's opinion that the change into a wolf is an illusion, that the devil so confuses the witch's imagination that she believes she has been a wolf and killed and eaten people. The devil

> acts in just the same way as when he causes witches to believe firmly that they have been to the Sabbat, although they have really been lying in their beds; and it is likely that the ointment with which they rub themselves only serves to deaden their senses so that they do not awake for a long time.
>
> *(Boguet, 1590: 146)*

There are natural maladies that cause sick people to believe that they are cocks, pigs or oxen. Boguet says that he had seen them go on all fours, but these people claimed that it was impossible for them to turn themselves into wolves, because they had no more ointment (Boguet, 1590: 151).

Boguet described the methods he used to draw the truth from Thievenne Paget: 'After she had remained in prison for three months without confessing at all, she was lodged in a cell next to that of Groz-Jacques, who was one of her accusers'. Groz promised to do his utmost to induce her to confess. And he fulfilled his promise: after Thievenne had been but one night next to him, she confessed that a man told her that he had been to the Sabbat with her and told her particulars of it. Boguet instructs judges follow this practice sometimes (Boguet, 1590: 158).

2.9. The judges' procedures to obtain confessions: harsh therapy

2.9.1. Interrogations

Bodin recommends that the young daughters of suspected witches be arrested, because they frequently have been taken to the Sabbats. 'They will be easy to persuade', Bodin asserts (Bodin, 1580: 177). After arrest, the judge must, as soon as possible, start interrogating the witch, because immediately after arrest, she feels that Satan has abandoned her, and, terrified, she confesses willingly, what torture could not extract from her later.

Bodin recommends judges investigate all the circumstantial evidence by firstly interrogating 'light and humorous matters', such as conjuring tricks. He recommends the judge 'conceal' his desire to know but 'little by little inquire whether their father and mother practised this craft'. After all, there is nothing more common than mothers winning over their daughters and dedicating them to Satan (Bodin, 1580: 177). Secondly, the judge should inquire what region the witch is from and has she moved about? Witches usually move about, Bodin believes. He advises judges to note any 'inconsistencies', to 'repeat many times at different intervals the same line of questioning' and to interrogate without interruption.

Bodin instructs judges to note, during the trial, the manner and composure of the witch because witches 'would not dare to look you directly in the eye'. A witch not crying was also to be taken as circumstantial evidence against her.

2.9.2. Imprisonment

The hardship of prison often impels witches to confess, especially when they are young. Therefore, if a judge cannot draw a confession out of an accused witch, she must be confined in a dark, narrow cell. Every lawful means must be used to induce the accused to tell the truth (Boguet, 1590: 217). Bodin says that the witch must not be left alone in prison, so that Satan does not make her depart from what she has confessed. He warns that some witches later deny what they have confessed under torture and reduce the judges to such confusion that they are obliged to release them from prison. But a witch who has confessed without torture and later denies it ought to be convicted if the confession is supported by other pieces of evidence. And since witches exercise their wickedness on their enemies, a judge is advised to inquire into whether the bewitched person bore any hostility towards the witch and to intensively question the witch about each point of enmity in order to get to the truth (Bodin, 1580: 178).

2.9.3. Deceptive methods

Bodin recommends using deception and fear to extract the truth. He says that one must give the impression of preparing numerous instruments for tormenting them and thereby keep them for some time in fear. Then let 'someone cry out with a dreadful cry' and 'tell the accused that it is the torture being applied' in order to extract the truth. Bodin assures his readers,

> I saw a judge who put on such a dreadful face and terrible voice, threatening hanging if they did not tell the truth, and in this way terrified the accused so much that they confessed immediately, as if they had lost all courage. But this technique only works with timorous people but not with bold ones.
>
> *(Bodin, 1580: 178)*

Boguet says that judges have been known to extract the truth from witches by promising impunity but then putting them to death afterwards anyway. Boguet doubts the morality of this deceptive lie (Boguet, 1590: 218).

Bodin recommends that judges 'appear to have pity on them' and that if the witches do not confess, they must be made to change their clothes and have all their hair shaved off and again undergo interrogation. The reason for stripping and shaving is because witches were believed to carry drugs to ensure silence. Having lost the drug, they think that they will not be able to withstand the torture, so they often tell the truth without torture.

Boguet has, in his 70 articles, codified the statutes and rulings and the methods and regulations to be used in the witch trials in order to extract a confession. Many of Boguet's recommendations are taken from Bodin's *Demon-Mania* (1580). Boguet adds some recommendations of his own. He says that the judge can by himself conduct the trial of witches when there is definite evidence of the fact of witchcraft. Because it is an extraordinary crime, the trial must be conducted in an extraordinary manner. The usual methods cannot be strictly observed, because of the enormity of the crime and because it is committed secretly and at night (Boguet, 1590: 211). Upon arrest, the accused is searched for ointments and powders used in witchcraft. Those whose duty it is to arrest the accused must note the words of the accused, which can be used as direct evidence against her (Boguet, 1590: 212). The prudent judge will base his examination on this and will use every lawful means to induce the accused to tell the truth (Boguet, 1590: 217). It is best for the judge to remain alone with the accused, concealing the clerk and assessors. A witch is generally ashamed to confess before many people and is frightened to see answers being recorded in writing. The accused must be repeatedly brought before the judge for examination.

2.9.4. Forced confessions

Bodin stated that a voluntary confession is necessary in order to convict a witch (Bodin, 1580: 181). Boguet says that a voluntary confession is always of greater weight than one that is forced by torture (Boguet, 1590: 221). A voluntary confession made before interrogation has more effect than one made through interrogation. Therefore, Bodin recommends that the judge sometimes trick the one he is questioning by putting words into her mouth. Bodin believes in this method of obtaining a confession. He says, 'the judge must get the truth by every means that he can imagine' (Bodin, 1580: 191).

The question of how to overcome silence was an important one for the judges. Bodin asks whether one ought to consider the accused as having confessed if she will not answer anything at all. Freud looked at that possibility in the case of Dora. According to Bodin, if there is proof by witnesses, then silence will have the effect of a confession, leading to a conviction. But the judge must first proceed with tortures against the one accused of witchcraft who will not answer anything. If she will not say anything under torture, the crime will be half confessed. One who purposely gives an obscure answer is deemed to have confessed (Bodin, 1580: 192).

Bodin's recommendations can be compared to Freud's, who wrote that the task of the therapist lay in overcoming resistance: 'He does this in the first place by "insisting", by making use of psychical compulsion to direct the patient's attention to the ideational traces of which he is in search' (Freud, 1895d: 353). Freud says if the 'insistence' is not powerful enough, the therapist 'must think of stronger means'. He says 'pressure . . . seems to be the most convenient way of applying suggestion' (Freud, 1895d: 354). But he adds, 'pressure is no more than a trick', but it 'never fails' to induce the patient to confess (Freud, 1895d: 363–368).

Remy says that witches bind themselves by oath to the demon not to betray their companions to the judge, however exquisitely they might be tortured. Therefore, they keep silent. And therefore, witches are continuously 'being constrained to an unwilling confession by dint of questionings and torture' (Remy, 1595: 62). Amulets worn by witches, to ensure their silence under torture, often hinder the judges from extracting the truth (Remy, 1595: 107). Remy says that when preparing the instruments of torture in order to extract a confession from Barbe Gilet at her trial in Huecourt in September 1587, she spoke as follows:

> What madness it is to suppose that you can extract a confession from me by force! For if I wished I could easily stultify your utmost attempts by means of the power which is at my command to endure every torture. But I gladly spare you all that trouble.

Françoise Hacquart of Ville (1591) confessed to Judge Remy that to free herself from molestation, she abandoned to the demon her daughter Jana when she was as yet scarcely seven years old. Remy continues, 'there have been many others within my memory led away at a tender age by their parents to sin whom, since they seemed to be already capable of guilt, we have sentenced to be stripped and beaten with rods' (Remy, 1595: 94).

To confirm the proof of some witches' confessions, Bodin says that one must link them with the confessions of other witches, because the actions of the devil are always consistent. This is why one finds that the confessions of witches in Germany, Italy, France, Spain and the ancient Greeks and Romans are similar (Bodin, 1580: 194). Bodin says that when a witch confesses and later denies, one must concentrate on the first confession and proceed to pass sentence.

At Remy's trials, witches confessed that they were forced against their wish to kiss the demon's posterior after he had changed himself into a hideous, stinking billy goat (Remy, 1595:66). Some witches confessed that they changed themselves into a dog or a wolf to attack people, but Remy says that 'such transformations are magical portents and glamours, which have the form but not the reality of their appearances. . . . They mistake the hallucinations of their fancy for the truth' because the demon confuses or deludes their imagination. 'So fruitful is the imagination, once it becomes diseased, of absurd and unheard-of ideas; and for this reason, Plato called it the Mistress of Phantoms' (Remy, 1595: 111).

Demons also delude the sight of those whom they will (Remy, 1595: 175). By false deception, they implant shapes and colours in the imagination and cause witches to fancy that they see visions (Remy, 1595: 177). Remy says that there was one witch 'whom I pressed so hard in respect of the evidence given against her that she was left with no loophole for evasion or escape'. She was about to make 'a clean breast of all her crimes' when suddenly she said that she could see her little master fiercely threatening her with hands clawed like a crab and that he seemed to be on the point of flying at her. Remy could not see him, because it was obviously a hallucination, but he encouraged her until she confessed (Remy, 1595: 174).

Remy says that the witches' tolerance of the harsh therapy can proceed from physical hardness or mental determination. A highly approved method was to bind the witch hand and foot and throw her into a pool of cold water: 'if she swims out unharmed, her guilt is said to be proved; but if she sinks she is said to be innocent' (Remy, 1595: 169). Remy finds justification for the ordeal by water and even the red-hot iron and burning coals by drawing attention to the fact that they were formerly practised by Christians and before that by Moses, who ordered a bitter drink be given to women who were suspected of adultery. Chapter five of the Book of Numbers, which Remy draws on, describes the procedure to be followed if a man becomes suspicious that his wife has been unfaithful by adultery. The priest mixes earth from the floor of the Tent with holy water, curses it and makes her drink it. If she has committed adultery, the drink will cause her great pain; her stomach shall swell up; and her genital organs shall shrink. If she is innocent, she will not be harmed and will be able to bear children. The husband shall be free of guilt (Numbers 5:12–31). Remy, from his moral high ground, adds,

> such outlandish trials are prohibited and forbidden to Christians. And we are clearly taught in the Gospel to leave these secret and hidden things to Him . . . and not to delve or pry into them further than is demanded by the due execution of justice; that is, voluntary or extorted confession of prisoners justly convicted by the clear testimony of credible witnesses.
>
> *(Remy, 1595: 170)*

Bodin says that all the crimes of witches, established by confession, by witnesses or by factual evidence, are punishable by death. But Bodin admits that the difficulty often lies solely in the proof, and judges find themselves hampered only by that. Those who cannot be condemned to death must receive the lash or the galleys. But Bodin recommends handing down 'the death sentence if the presumptions are strong'. It is sufficient to have strong presumptions to impose corporal punishment: beatings, amputations, brandings, life imprisonment, fines or confiscations.

2.10. Presumptions in witch trials

When the three necessary proofs are lacking (concrete fact, sound witnesses and voluntary confession), Bodin recommends that judges proceed by examining presumptions. If a person is rumoured to be a witch, it must be presumed that she is guilty. If a witch's child is missing, one must presume that the child has been sacrificed to the devil.

> All kinds of wickedness must be presumed normal with witches. . . . If therefore, a witch has been convicted as a witch, she will always be known as a witch and consequently presumed guilty of all the impieties that witches are well known for.
>
> *(Bodin, 1580: 197)*

Bodin asserts that it is a most powerful presumption that when a woman is reputed to be a witch, she is one, and this is enough to sentence her to the question – that is, to torture. Bodin says, 'when it is a question of witches, rumour is almost infallible' (Bodin, 1580: 198). If a witch visits a house, stable or sheepfold of an enemy and shortly afterwards death or illness suddenly strikes, even though the witch was not found in possession of powders and she was not seen casting a spell, it is presumed that she is guilty. When a female suspect is accustomed to making threats, this is a great presumption. And if after threats, death ensues, it is a most powerful presumption. To extract the necessary proof, one must persist. A strong presumption is if the witch bears a mark. In these nocturnal crimes where one cannot get proof, the skilled judge will combine all the presumptions in order to register the truth (Bodin, 1580: 199–202, 209).

We shall see in Part Two of this work how these presumptions parallel Freud's 'circumstantial evidence', which enabled him 'to tear' from Dora 'her secret'. He said, 'Dora no longer denied my supposition, although she still remembered nothing' (Freud, 1905e: 79). In a similar way to that of the judges, Freud used what he called 'constructions' to 'bring what is concealed completely to light'. He pointed to 'Indications that can be inferred from the patient's reaction when we have offered him one of our constructions'. This 'makes it easy for us to arrive at the decision that we are in search of' (Freud, 1937d: 260, 262, 265).

2.11. Warnings to Judges

Bodin issues warnings to lenient judges. He says that the law deems a judge guilty who remits or reduces the penalty; that a judge must be punished 'with confiscation' if he remits or reduces the prescribed penalty; that the punishment includes exile and punishing with the same penalties that the guilty and convicted person would be punished with, as the law states; and that those judges who send witches away acquitted deserve death. Judge Gentil was found in possession of a host and was hanged at Montfaucon for this great superstition. Magistrates must also be investigated if they let witches escape. The first presumption against a magistrate is when he makes a joke of such witchcraft (Bodin, 1580: 216–217).

Bodin asserts that those who let witches escape can be assured that they will be abandoned by God to the mercy of witches. And the country that tolerates them will be struck by plagues, famines and wars. But those who take vengeance against witches will be blessed by God and will bring an end to his wrath. This is why one who is charged and accused of being a witch must never be simply let off unless the calumny of the accuser or informer is clearer than the sun.

As a final warning, Bodin gives the example of

> a woman in the village of Verigny who was charged and accused of many evil spells, but because of the difficulty of proof, was released. Later, I learned from the inhabitants that a countless number of people and livestock had died. She died in April 1579. Since her death, all the inhabitants of Verigny and their livestock have been at peace and no longer die as before.
>
> *(Bodin, 1580: 218)*

Bodin uses this example as proof that when the chief cause is gone, the effects come to an end too.

2.12. A confession made by a witch to Judge Boguet

The Case of Françoise Secretain
The first case presented by Boguet in *An Examen of Witches* (1590) is that of Françoise Secretain. She was accused of casting a spell on an eight-year-old girl, Loyse Maillet, who was thereby possessed of five devils. Françoise Secretain was made prisoner for casting the spell on Loyse, who was 'struck helpless in all her limbs so that she had to go on all-fours; also, she kept twisting her mouth in a very strange manner'. Loyse claimed that, on the previous day, Françoise Secretain had given her 'a crust of bread resembling dung and made her eat it, strictly forbidding her to speak of it or she would kill her and eat her' (Boguet, 1590: 3). Judging from her appearance that she was possessed; her parents took her to the priest. The girl was found to have five devils. Boguet does not provide evidence of this phenomenon.

Judge Boguet, being fully convinced as to what had happened, had Françoise seized and put into prison. For three days of her imprisonment, Françoise refused to confess anything, saying she was innocent of the crime of which she was accused and that they did her great wrong to detain her. Boguet notes, 'to look at her you would have thought she was the best woman in the world'. But the rosary she carried had a defective cross. It was this last fact that furnished the evidence against her. It was further observed that during her examination she could not shed a single tear. For this reason, threats were used towards her. 'The authorities agree that the presumption is heavily against those who are accused of witchcraft when they cannot shed tears' (Boguet, 1590: 119). When Françoise was being examined, she always kept her eyes bent on the ground so that the judge had great difficulty in making her look him in the face. This, Boguet claims, is an indication of the guilt of the accused. He is inclined to believe that they are then consulting with Satan as to the answers they shall give to the questions put to them by the judge.

The following day, Françoise was pressed to tell the truth, but without success. Accordingly, it was decided to shave off her hair and change her garments and to search her to determine whether she had been marked in any way. She was therefore stripped, but no mark was found. No sooner was her hair cut than she grew perturbed and trembled all over her body and at once confessed, adding to her first confessions from day to day (Boguet, 1590: 1–5). Boguet says that it is customary to take precautions against witches and to shave off all their hair when they fall into the hands of justice, in order to draw the truth from them more easily. This is because witches have drugs that they hide in their hair to procure silence. As long as they carry drugs, they will never confess and will feel no pain when they are tortured. Therefore, it is necessary to shave them. Because they conceal these spells in their clothing, they are required to change their clothes. Françoise was stripped to see if there was any mark on her. Boguet says it is permissible to shave the hair off witches and to change their clothes in order to deprive them of their firm faith that they have in their spell, which may be hidden in their hair or their clothing. Also, it is certain that such witches are much more tender and more susceptible to pain than those who are not shaved. More cunning witches have swallowed drugs to deaden their senses, such that 'torture has become almost useless as a means of wresting the truth from them' (Boguet, 1590: 125–127).

Content of Françoise Secretain's confession:

> She confessed that she had wished five devils on Loyse Maillet; that she had given herself to the devil, who at that time had the likeness of a big black man; that the devil had four or five times known her carnally and that his semen was very cold; that she had countless times been to the Sabbat and that she went there on a white staff, which she placed between her legs; that at the Sabbat she had danced and had beaten the water to make hail; that she and Groz-Jacques Bocquet had caused Loys Monneret to die by making her eat a piece of bread that they had dusted with a powder given to them by the devil; that she had caused several cows to die by touching them with her hand or with a wand while saying certain words; and that she was further accused by Groz-Jacques of having changed herself into a wolf.

Reasons for imprisoning Françoise Secretain:

> There was evidence of witchcraft. Although the girl who gave evidence against Françoise was only eight years old, Boguet claims that her testimonies under oath were precise and never varied. Her mother substantiated the fact that Françoise had lodged at their house after having been at first refused. The girl's father and mother said that they had never had any quarrel with Françoise. During her affliction, the girl had always declared that it was no one but that woman who had bewitched her. Boguet asserts that it was the most abominable of all crimes, one which is usually committed at night and always in secret, and that therefore it did not call for such positive proof as would be required in the case of any other crime. Boguet claimed that a witch has the power to send devils into a person's body and that therefore the accusation against her was a possible one – that is, she had wished five devils on Loys Maillet.
>
> *(Boguet, 1590: 6–7)*

In *An Examen of Witches* (1590), Boguet discusses Françoise's confession and examines the possibility of sending demons into the body of another. He says, 'it is no easy matter to determine whether a person has the power to send demons into the body of another' (Boguet, 1590: 8). He refers to Wier (1563), who claims that it is not possible, but Boguet considers that it is possible and that witches usually offer food to the victims whom they wish to possess with the devil. Loyse Maillet claimed that Françoise Secretain used a crust of bread, but Boguet says that the witch most often uses an apple, the means by which Satan tempted Eve. Boguet concludes that Françoise not only caused Loyse to be possessed but also 'acted in this manner toward several children whom she wished to take by force to the Sabbat, and namely towards a twelve year old girl named Christofle of the village of Aranthon' (Boguet, 1590: 11).

Regarding Françoise's confession, that she had given herself to the devil in the likeness of a big black man, Boguet says 'it is very certain' that spirits can assume bodies. To prove his point, he refers to biblical spirits who appeared to Saul (1 Sam. 28); to Ezekiel (Ezek. 8); to Tobias (Tob. 5); to Lot (Gen. 19); and to Joshua (Josh. 5). Boguet writes, 'When the devil tried to tempt Jesus Christ . . . he had the appearance of a man', and 'it was under the shape of a man that he gained' Françoise Secretain. Of the same form was the demon which appeared to Brutus and that which appeared to Cassius after the defeat of Mark Anthony (Boguet, 1590: 11–20). However honoured this poor homeless woman could have felt to be placed among this noble band, it is clear that Boguet had not done his homework, because the three gospels that recount the temptations of Jesus do not state that, in the temptations, Satan or the devil had the appearance of a man.

Boguet asserts, 'Whenever he assumes the form of a man, he is, however, always black, as all witches bear witness'. Boguet uses this as a proof of his evil intent, 'for evil, as Pythagoras said, is symbolised by black' (Boguet, 1590: 20). Françoise

Secretain confessed that the devil had lain with her four or five times and that he was then in the form either of a dog or a cat or a fowl. At this point, Boguet recalls Agrippa's black dog, which Boguet claims was no other than a devil in disguise (Boguet, 1590: 19).

Boguet describes how Satan seduces people: the wicked one, who is so cunning, knows how to choose the times and occasions most favourable to his designs: when people are alone and in despair or misery because of hunger or some disaster that has befallen them. Eve was alone when she was seduced. Françoise Secretain abandoned herself to him because of her misery and poverty. Boguet claims that the devil seduces people by fair promises: to the poor, he offers riches; to the vengeful, he suggests the means to avenge themselves on their enemies. Boguet adds that witches are tempted by the nature of the rewards that they expect from Satan; that the fault lies wholly with the witch who knows that the devil desires nothing but the destruction of the human race; that they are guilty of a crime that is severely vindicated by the law; that they willingly cast themselves into Satan's net; that it is known to happen that Satan speaks through the shameful parts of a woman; and that they can counterfeit sounds like the human voice (Boguet, 1590: 21–23, 28).

Françoise Secretain was stripped that it might be known if she had any mark on her. Marks constitute extremely strong evidence of guilt, 'so much so that when they are joined to other indications, it is lawful to proceed to an immediate condemnation'. Boguet finishes his account of Françoise Secretain:

> I'm sure you will all agree she was worthy of a witch's death by burning. But she was found dead in prison. The devil either kills them or induces them to kill themselves. I have no doubt that the Devil suffocated Françoise Secretain.
>
> *(Boguet, 1590: 130–131)*

Boguet ends his accounts of the trials of witches:

> It stands to reason that, in such trials, we are chiefly faced with matters done secretly and at night, which are not capable of proof save through the mouths of those who have been present at the Sabbat. And therefore, according to common law, in the case of such a horrible and secret crime a less absolute proof is sufficient
>
> *(Boguet, 1590: 209)*

2.13. Voices of dissent against the harsh therapy

Not everyone agreed with the judges. Influential voices, including Dr Jan Wier, spoke out. It was the enlightenment brought by education that finally ended the persecution of witches. Medical men became reluctant to ascribe sickness to diabolical influence. The Swiss Paraclesus (1490–1541) said, 'mental diseases have nothing to do with evil spirits or devils. . . . one should not study how to exorcise the devil but how to cure the insane'. Wier (1563) said,

> The uninformed and unskilful physicians relegate all the incurable diseases, or all the diseases the remedy for which they overlook, to witchcraft. When they do this, they are talking about disease as a blind man talks about colour.

The Church eventually recognised natural causes and effects for phenomena that hitherto had been ascribed to witches and devils. Today, male impotence is recognised as a serious sexual dysfunctional problem; in the medieval and early modern periods, so-called witches were accused of causing male impotence.

Condemnation of the persecution of witches came from many sources. The first successful attempt at stopping the harsh therapy came from Wier. He had travelled in Africa, where he had a good opportunity of studying sorcery before taking up his position as personal physician to William of Cleves. He believed in the devil and in magic but rejected the possibility of witchcraft and compacts with the devil. William of Cleves, following Wier's advice, suppressed all witch prosecutions in his duchy. Regarding the claims in the *Malleus* (1486) that witches make the male organ disappear, Wier (1563) explains that the male genital organs cannot disappear through witchcraft. He said, 'The demon deludes the victim temporarily by "bewitching" him' (Wier, 1563: 332). Wier denies that this could happen through the wishes of the witch. But he points out that these old women can be brought to believe that they themselves have brought about the sexual failure (Wier, 1563: 334). And 20 years after Wier, Meyfart, rector of the Latin School of Colburg, publicly admonished the Dominican inquisitors, authors of the *Malleus*, reminding them that they would be held accountable for every torture of so-called witches when the Day of Judgement came (Carus, 1900: 373).

In England one of the first to condemn the persecution of witches was Reginald Scot in his *Discoverie of Witchcraft* (1584). Scot (1584) uses the word 'discovery' to mean 'uncovering' rather than 'finding'. He was born in 1538 and studied at Oxford before taking up the life of a country gentleman. Although neither he nor any other writer of his time flatly denied the existence of witches, he was scathing in his attack on their persecutors, the judges and the inquisitors. Scot's scornful treatment of the 'absurd and neurotic fantasies' of the judges is an amusing treatment of an otherwise grim tale of humankind's inhumanity to other humans, specifically in this case, to women. On the subject of the witches' confessions, Scot noted that they were easily brought to make 'absurd confessions' of deeds they never did. Those who were accused were the least sufficient of all people to speak for themselves: 'daunted by authority' and 'compelled by fear', they confessed.

Scot (1584) describes the witch as 'old', 'lame' and 'full of wrinkles' who goes 'from doore to doore' begging (Scot, 1584: 4). If 'some of hir neighbors die or fall sicke or some of their children are visited with diseases', they suppose it 'to be the vengeance of witches'. The neighbour believes 'that all their mishaps are brought to passe by the witch'. Scot says that 'evill humors', not witches, are the cause of such diseases (Scot, 1584: 5).

> The witch, on the other side, seeing things sometimes come to passe according to hir wishes . . . being called before a Justice . . . confesseth that she (as a goddess) hath brought such things to passe. Wherein, not onlie she, but the accuser, and also the Justice are fowlie deceived and abused; as being through hir confession and other circumstances persuaded that she hath doone or can do that which is proper onelie to God himselfe.
>
> *(Scot, 1584: 4–5)*

Scot is saying that the witch is convinced that she herself has brought this misfortune to pass and confesses it. So she, her accusers and the justices are all deceived. Scot declares all the claims by the two Dominican authors of the *Malleus* (1486), that witches 'usuallie devoure and eate yong children, . . . can procure . . . taciturnitie and insensibilitie in their torments, . . . can deprive men of their privities[,] . . . to be false and fabulous' (Scot, 1584: 7).

Scot (1584) also believes that women are weak and prone to delusions, but he argues that witchcraft itself is a delusion of the inquisitors and not an actual pact with the devil. Scot, whose book is still today one of the few primary sources for the study of the witch trials, argues for mercy and forbearance towards these women, whose imaginary trafficking with the devil is a sign of mental instability. (Scot, 1584: 30–31). Scot was a direct witness to what he calls the witch mongering in one of witch-hunting's bloodiest eras. Writing of 'poore melancholike women' who 'imagine they are witches', Scot says, 'what is it that they will not imagine, and consequentlie confesse that they can do; speciallie being so earnestlie persuaded thereunto'. They are forced to make what Scot calls 'false confessions' (Scot, 1584: 30–31). Scot denies that witches have power 'to thrust into the mind or conscience of man what it shall please them', but he believes that the devil

> travelleth to seduce man . . . where he placeth himselfe as God in the minds of them that are so credulous, to attribute unto him, or unto witches, that which is onlie in the office, nature, and power of God to accomplish.
>
> *(Scot, 1584: 103)*

Wier, Agrippa, Spee and other defenders of witches are of the same opinion as Scot regarding witches as melancholics. The witch was seen by the judges as not just a malicious woman but also the embodiment of evil. Scot's defence of witches was condemned by King James.

When James of Scotland became King of England, he ordered that copies of Scot's *Discoverie of Witchcraft* (1584) be destroyed, yet towards the end of his reign, the king's views had undergone a considerable change, largely because of the frequency with which cases of possession by devils were found to be counterfeits.

Some children faked possession by the devil, which they blamed on the witch. They said that in the presence of the accused witch, they became subject to uncontrollable fits and convulsions, and they demonstrated this when brought into the presence of the witch (Peel & Southern, 1969: 132). Webster (1677) also refers specifically to the diabolical counterfeiting of possessions: 'Many attribute natural diseases and accidents to witches when in truth there is no such matter at all. Sometimes they counterfeit strange fits and diseases, as vomiting of preternatural and strange things' (Webster, 1677). *The Crucible* (1953) is an example of the cruel witch beliefs that made helpless old women in Salem the victims of wicked children, fatuous officials, ignorant neighbours and mobs.

Webster (1677) wrote,

> Although you should find some confidently confessing that they had made a league with the Devil, and that he hath carnal copulation with them, and that he doth suck upon some parts of their bodies . . . or that they fly through the air. . . . there never hath been any such witch existent.

Webster claimed that the witches were 'under a delusion'. They

> confidently believe that they see, do and suffer many strange, odd and wonderful things, which indeed have no existence, only in their depraved fancies. And yet the confessions of these, though absurd, idle, foolish, false and impossible are taken to be truth.
>
> *(Webster, 1677: in Parrinder, 1969: 133–135)*

Webster is making the point that Freud later made: the witches 'fancy' these things. I again remind the reader of the comparisons Freud drew when he said, 'stories like those of the witches and my patients' (Letter to Fliess on 24 January 1897). Three Jesuit priests, notably Father Spee (1591–1635), made an appeal in *Cautio criminalis*, published anonymously in 1631, to the German authorities regarding their legal proceedings against witches. Spee, as a pastor, had ministered to two hundred people accused of witchcraft, and he told his bishop in Wurzburg that 'of the many witches whom I have prepared for death, not one was guilty'. He wrote in *Cautio criminalis*,

> Judges frequently record that the accused has confessed without torture. I enquired into this and learned that in reality they were tortured, but only in an iron press with sharp-edged channels over the shins. In this they were pressed like a cake, bringing blood and causing intolerable pain, and this is technically called 'without torture', deceiving those who do not understand the phrases of the inquisitors. . . . Treat the heads of the Church, the Judges, myself in the same way as those unfortunate ones; make us undergo the same tortures and you will convict us all as wizards.
>
> *(Carus, 1900: 375–377)*

Spee did not deny the possibility of witchcraft. He merely objected to the abuses and recommended clemency.

Wier, Scot, Spee and Webster are highlighting the harsh treatment by the inquisitors and judges that forced out of the witch a confession of guilt. Spee sums it up when he says, 'If all of us have not confessed ourselves witches, it is because we have not all been tortured' (Trevor-Roper, 1988: 85). It is these apparently valid arguments that make it difficult to work out the meaning of Freud's statement, 'I . . . understand the harsh therapy of the witches' judges'. But these early modern writings are not denying the witches' fantasies and delusions. It is Freud's claim that these fantasies 'were not created under torture but merely squeezed out by it' (Nunberg & Federn, 1967: 123). And because Freud believes in the importance of squeezing out fantasies, he understands the use of harsh therapy to achieve that aim. This is a matter of the ends justifying the means. The inquisitorial approach for the prosecution of witches was finally abolished in the seventeenth century. But has any aspect of an inquisitorial approach in Freud's psychoanalysis filtered through into and survived in psychotherapy today?

Under torture, the witch was induced to confess. But had witchcraft any other basis besides torture? Trevor-Roper (1988) claims that the problem was more complex. Wier, Scot and Spee had noted how easily the witches could be brought to confess that which they never did. But Trevor-Roper (1988) says that after reading Bodin (1580), it was impossible for him to suppose that the confessions were mere fabrications imposed on reluctant victims of torture. Trevor-Roper says that while we acknowledge that the confessions were extracted under torture, 'equally we are obliged to admit their fundamental subjective reality. For every victim whose story is evidently created by torture, there are two or three who genuinely believe in its truth' (Trevor-Roper, 1988: 48). This view of Trevor-Roper's is in line with Heller's view that we discussed earlier and is close to Freud's view. Just as Trevor-Roper was influenced in his views on the harsh therapy by reading Bodin (1580), I am presenting an argument in this book that Freud also read Bodin's and Boguet's works and was influenced by them in his views.

Trevor-Roper (1988) claims that the inquisitors and judges did not create the basic evidence on which they built their system. He says that they found it in the confessions of the reputed witches, and as those confessions seemed genuine to the witches who made them, we can hardly blame the inquisitors for supposing them to be genuine too (Trevor-Roper, 1988: 52). Freud's understanding of the harsh therapy of the witches' judges may be based on the same theory as Trevor-Roper, who is saying that the forced nature of the procedures did not create the confessions of secret crimes that the judges and inquisitors were searching to find. However, we must remember that Trevor-Roper also said that some of the stories were created by the harsh therapy (Trevor-Roper, 1988: 48).

It is possible to believe that the persecutors, the inquisitors and the judges of the defenceless witches were sincere. Judges believed that they were fighting the devil and resisting his campaign against the work of the Church and the chances of salvation for the witches. Freud also believed that he was in contest with demons that inhabit the human heart. This also may throw light on his statement, 'I understand the harsh therapy of the witches' judges'. However, one questions the sincerity of the judges' motives when one considers that in places where the confiscation of witches' property was not allowed, few witches were found.

By the nineteenth century, one ingredient in the witchcraft cases, or what was then called the sexual hysteria cases, had disappeared: the concept of the devil. In the medieval and early modern cases, the illusions of the witches, their accusers and the judges centred on the power of the devil. The inquisitors claimed that the belief in the witches' ability to fly was easily justified by reference to the Bible: had not the devil carried Jesus to the pinnacle of the Temple in Jerusalem? If he could do this to the Son of God, how easy a task it must be for him to arrange the transport of a few willing old hags to the Sabbats, where they gathered to do him homage (Peel & Southern, 1969: 119–120). Regarding incubi and succubi, the idea of these male and female night visitors long preceded witchcraft. Peel & Southern (1969) explain their origins in the erotic dreams of normal young adults:

> Their association with witches serves as another illustration of the rag-bag of ideas that the witch-hunters put together, although the actual corporeal existence of these spirits had been decided as proved by theologians as early as the time of Thomas Aquinas in the thirteenth century
>
> *(Peel & Southern, 1969: 121)*

The authors are obviously referring to Aquinas' literalising the biblical myth in Gen. 6:1–4, of the sons of God having intercourse with the daughters of men.

In 1685 Anton van Dale, a Dutch physician, exposed belief in witchcraft as a priestly fraud. He prepared the way for two reformers, Bekker and Thomasius, who openly denounced witchcraft as a priestly superstition, and they succeeded in abolishing the official prosecution of witches by the authorities of church and state. Bekker was a Dutch cleric, but he was discharged from his Protestant ministry because of his views on the devil (Carus, 1900: 380–383). The voice of reason gradually prevailed, and the belief in witches faded. Christian European thought was coaxed back from the influence of such books as the *Malleus Maleficarum* (1486), *Demon-Mania* (1580), *An Examen of Witches* (1590) and *Demonolatry* (1595) to the saner sentiments of the Canon Episcopi. The fanatical campaigns of the witchhunters were not responsible for the disappearance of witches. What is believed to have dampened their ardour was the forbidding, in 1630, by the Holy Roman Emperor of the appropriation of witches' property.

Agrippa, Spee, Wier, Scot and Webster all agreed that the powers claimed by witches, or ascribed to them, were largely illusions and that they were the hallucinations of melancholic, half-starved old women. These authors argue that the problem should be interpreted by lay science – medicine – not by theology, and the proper cure was not fire but a cure for human insanity. Pomponazzi at the University of Padua declared that those 'possessed by the devil' were merely melancholic.

Had their views prevailed, there would hardly have been any witchcraft delusion or witch trials. The argument brought forward by these anti-inquisition authors against the witch trials was not that witches did not exist, nor even that the pact with Satan was impossible, but that judges erred in their identification of the problem. Did Freud also err in his identification of the aetiology of hysteria?

Wier (1563) claims that these 'poor doting women' who confess – whether through torture or delusion – to being witches have not made any pact with Satan or surrendered to his charms. They are 'melancholic'. When Wier, Spee, Scot and others condemned the witch trials through their writings, they still retained their belief in the kingdom of Satan and its war on humanity by means of demons. According to Trevor-Roper (1988), if the witch craze were to be attacked at its core, the whole concept of the kingdom of Satan would need to be challenged. Neither Wier nor Scot nor Spee did this.

By the end of the seventeenth century, one writer did attempt to challenge the whole idea of Satan's kingdom. This was the Dutch minister of religion Balthasar Bekker, who published *The Enchanted World* (1690). The first two volumes of his controversial work sold four thousand copies in two months and was translated into French, German and English. Bekker struck at the heart of the witch craze by destroying belief in possession by the devil. Trevor-Roper (1988) claims, 'This point was made by Soldan in 1843 and has been repeated ever since' (Trevor-Roper, 1988: 102n.134). Freud's copy of Soldan's book is in Maresfield Gardens Library. Many others who objected to the witch trials merely criticised the validity of the particular methods of obtaining confessions by torture while retaining their belief in witches and the devil (Trevor-Roper, 1988: 10).

2.14. Conclusion

The aim of this chapter has been to examine what Freud referred to as 'the very interesting witch trials' and to do what Freud proposed to do: 'delve into the literature on the subject'. By examining the primary sources on the witch trials, I have tried to clarify and find answers to the questions that Freud raised in his two letters to Fliess on the subject of witches. The main questions were concerning the devil's copulation with witches and why he abused the witches sexually. I have examined the witches' confessions and highlighted the parallels that Freud drew between the witches' confessions extracted under torture and the communications made by his patients in psychic treatment. We have seen that the main difficulty in finding evidence was because their so-called crimes were committed in secret and at night. I have examined the judges' efforts 'to discover the devil's stigmata' in the witches and also how Freud parallels this search with his own search for clues in his patients' stories.

The three judges, Bodin, Boguet and Remy, examined the witches for evidence of their presence at the Sabbat, their journeyings to the Sabbat and their pact with the devil that empowered them to do evil deeds. These judges also considered the possibility of all these happenings taking place in the witches' dreams or active imaginations. Boguet sums up what Bodin and Remy also held about witches: the devil sometimes

> reveals to them in their sleep what happens at the Sabbat so vividly that they think they have been there. . . . But I hold that this never happens except to such as have previously attended in person the witches' assembly.
>
> *(Boguet, 1590: 51)*

We find this claim, made by the judges, in Freud's first shift in his theory on his hysterical patients. The question is, did his delving into the literature on the witch trials influence him? He wrote in *The Interpretation of Dreams* (1900a),

> I had observed that this is precisely what hysterical patients do: alongside what has really happened to them, they unconsciously build up frightening or perverse imaginary events which they construct out of the most innocent and everyday material of their experience.

In the next chapter, we move on to a closer examination of Freud's theories of hysteria.

PART II

CHAPTER 3

FREUD'S PRE-ANALYTIC CASES

3.1. History of hysteria

The term 'hysteria' comes from the Greek word 'hustéra', meaning womb. In ancient Egypt, hysteria, a female disorder, was said to be caused by a wandering womb. Plato believed that when the womb remained barren for too long after puberty, it became distressed and provoked all manner of diseases. The recommended treatment was marriage and pregnancy. Freud noted in his *Autobiographical Study* that 'in deriving hysteria from sexuality', he was 'following up a thought of Plato's' (Freud, 1925d: 24). Plato's diagnosis and recommended treatment of hysteria prevailed for centuries. In medieval times, a new dimension was added. The hysteric or female deviant was believed to form an alliance with the devil for the purposes of witchcraft. The witch's alliance with this 'foreign body' or devil made her a dangerous force.

Freud saw himself, in his work with so-called hysterics, wrestling with this force. He wrote, 'No one who, like me, conjures up the most evil of those half-tamed demons that inhabit the human breast, and seeks to wrestle with them, can expect to come through the struggle unscathed' (Freud, 1905e: 109). Decker says that Freud had a personal phantasy that he was waging a perilous battle with hysterical patients:

> There is evidence to indicate that Freud felt that women in general were a dangerous foe who held men back professionally. Hence, Freud not only shared his medical colleagues' attitude about the professional hazards posed by female hysterical patients but carried within himself a heightened belief in his own personal vulnerability.
>
> *(Decker, 1986: 99)*

Summers, writing of the witches' judges in the introduction to *An Examen of Witches* (1590), said that 'we must always remember the difficulties and hazards these brave men had to face' (Boguet, 1590: xxiv). Remy, one of the most important sixteenth-century judges in the witch trials, quotes Plato. Referring to the 'diseased imagination' of the so-called witches, Remy says, 'So fruitful is the imagination, once it becomes diseased, of absurd and unheard of ideas that, for this reason, Plato called it "the Mistress of Phantoms"'. Remy says that witches often 'mistake the hallucinations of their fancy for the truth' (Remy, 1595: 111). Misogyny played a major role in the depiction of women as deviant and prone to witchcraft. The authors of *Malleus Maleficarum* (1486) represent the male anxiety in the face of the so-called demonic, sexual power of women. They elaborate the Thomistic view of women as intrinsically defective and, later, as prone to demonic alliances: 'When a woman thinks alone, she things evil. . . . through their inordinate passions, they search for, brood over and inflict vengeances, either by witchcraft or by some other means' (Kramer & Sprenger, 1486: 43, 45). Such accusations against women led to their trial as witches. Catherine Clement argues that the witch trials were the precursors of Charcot's famous clinical seances at the Salpêtrière (Bernheimer & Kahane, 1985: 2–4).

Freud studied under Charcot from October 1885 to February 1886 while Charcot was trying to demonstrate the precise correspondence between hysteria and witchcraft. It was in the year of Charcot's death that Freud and Breuer first published their theory of hysteria, and in his obituary to Charcot, Freud noted how their new theory of hysteria merely 'replaced the "demon" of clerical phantasy by a psychological formula' (Freud, 1893f: 22). A London physician, Samuel Wilks, says that the makeup of a woman meant that she was vulnerable to hysteria. He claimed that from 12 or 14 to 18 or 20 years of age, a young girl's whole nervous system becomes so perverted that no circumstance of the most extraordinary kind may not then happen. Their 'behaviour is like that of one possessed of a devil' (Wilks, 1878: 364 in Decker, 1986: 7).

Hysteria was thought by some doctors to be a degenerate disease. Early in the nineteenth century, hysterics – like their counterparts, the witches in the sixteenth and seventeenth centuries – were accused of deviant sexual conduct. Extreme measures, such as clitorectomies and ovariectomies, were advocated in cases of intractable hysteria. Some doctors, including Charcot, thought hysteria was caused by traumatic memories of, for example, railway accidents; hysterics were believed to suffer from reminiscences. Hysteria was defined as a neurosis characterised by physical symptoms that mimic the effects of physical disorders but that are not determined by organic causes. Stadlen has summed up Freud's account of symptoms of hysteria as physical ailments that are not genuine and emotional distress that is not justified (Stadlen, 1989: 200–201). These symptoms of hysteria were supposed to be the symbolic expression of a psychological conflict.

3.2. Aetiology of hysteria

Although it was believed that hysteria was not difficult to identify, its cause was mysterious. Since hysteria was considered to be so rife, its aetiology sparked intense speculation and sometimes bitter disagreements among medical men. Freud hoped to be the first to unravel the mystery of the aetiology of hysteria. There was no agreement on the specific aetiology of hysteria. Speculation continued. Freud claimed, in a letter to Fliess on 26 April 1896, that he had found the solution to a thousand-year-old problem. But had he? What was his momentous discovery – the discovery of the origins of hysteria?

Just as witches were accused of using their 'pact with the devil' as a weapon to injure men, in the same way, because of the continuing patriarchal attitude towards women, hysterics were accused of using their 'illness' as a weapon against the patriarchal power surrounding them. Bernheimer says, 'the doctor from a righteous position of power, the patient from a deviant position of powerlessness' were often in conflict because of 'the cultural presuppositions upheld by both' (Bernheimer & Kahane, 1985: 6). Freud also saw it as an intrapsychic conflict in terms of the patient's resistance to unpleasurable ideas and her defence against their articulation. The interpretation of resistance became Freud's essential analytic tool in the gradual unveiling of the hysterics' unconscious motivation. Bernheimer claims that 'Freud liberated hysterics from the stigma of degeneracy' (Bernheimer & Kahane, 1985: 9).

Doctors, at a loss to know how to treat hysterics, frequently recommended suffocating 'hysterical' women. Other tortures used were inserting tubes into their rectums or threatening 'hysterical' girls with the application of hot irons to their spines. In the case of 'intractable' hysteria, ovariectomies and clitorectomies were performed. The forceful and painful therapies in the mid and late nineteenth century were used because physicians had nothing else to offer to hysterics except an admission of ignorance (Decker, 1986: 102). Freud was in the avant-garde in his discovery of a psychological treatment for his hysterical female patients, and he acted more humanely than most of his colleagues.

While acknowledging this fact, I have argued in an earlier work that Freud did not go as far as he might have gone towards the liberation of oppressed women. I have claimed that Freud, as a transitional figure, stood with one leg in the past insofar as his psychoanalysis is based on a medical model (Duffy, 1996: 63). I am now claiming that it is an inquisitorial model, a witch-hunt model. But Freud opened the door and led the way into new psychological explorations. Freud was breaking new ground in the treatment he proposed for hysteria. His was a more humane approach than the psychiatric treatment of his predecessors. We must remember that Freud entered a world of psychiatry in Vienna in which women who were supposed to be suffering from hysteria were treated by the surgical removal of the clitoris. Freud wanted to find another treatment, but he first needed to discover the specific aetiology of hysteria.

Freud first called his theory of hysteria a 'theory of a foreign body and the splitting of consciousness'. He wrote to Fliess on 17 January 1897, drawing similarities between his theory and the medieval theory of the witches' possession by the devil,

> my brand-new prehistory of hysteria is already known and was published a hundred times over, though several centuries ago. . . . . the medieval theory of

possession held by the ecclesiastical courts was identical with our theory of a foreign body and the splitting of consciousness. . . . Why are their confessions under torture so like the communications made by my patients in psychic treatment?

In *Studies on Hysteria* (1895), Freud explains in his case histories what he means by 'a foreign body and the splitting of consciousness'. He says that in every analysis of a case of hysteria based on sexual traumas, he has found that 'impressions from the pre-sexual period, which produced no effect on the child, attain traumatic power at a later date as memories, when the girl or married woman has acquired an understanding of sexual life' (Freud, 1895d: 133). Freud used a pressure technique for reawakening the forgotten memories of childhood traumas. He explained his fight to overcome the patients' defences: 'We force our way into the internal strata, overcoming resistances all the time'. The forced nature of his therapy, which Freud describes for overcoming the patient's resistance, can be compared to Judge Remy's statement that not a single witch has freed herself from the evils of Satan 'by any other means than either a forced or a spontaneous confession before the Judge' (Remy, 1595: 185).

Freud says that the indispensable condition for acquiring hysteria is when an incompatibility develops between the ego and some idea presented to it (Freud, 1895d: 122). The ego defends itself by repressing the incompatible idea. An effort is made to forget the experience. Freud asserted that the 'forgetting' of memories is often intentional and desired, but the forgetting is only *apparent*. Freud concluded from his success in using his procedure that 'experiences which have played an important pathogenic part . . . are accurately retained in the patient's memory even when they seem to be forgotten'. He required complete confidence in his technique in order to reawaken details of a forgotten experience (Freud, 1895d: 111–112).

Freud claimed that he used this pressure technique successfully for awakening forgotten memories for the treatment of Lucy R. and Elisabeth von R. In his analysis of Miss Lucy R., Freud decided to start from the assumption that his patient had a memory of everything that was of pathogenic significance and that it was only a question of obliging her to communicate it. When the response to his questioning was 'I don't know' he placed his hand on the patient's forehead and said: 'You will think of it under the pressure of my hand'. Freud assured his patient that after pressure she would certainly become aware of what was wanted. Freud says that he had 'extracted' the 'information' that 'was wanted' from Lucy. But it was not what the patient wanted to say; it was what Freud wanted to hear (Freud, 1895d: 111–112). This approach of Freud's to look for 'what was wanted' is unscientific because it makes accurate observation difficult. To have decided in advance what one wants to find makes it difficult to look at things in a disinterested way.

3.3. Elisabeth von R.

Freud's witch-hunt approach is evident in the case of Fräulein Elisabeth von R. She was born in Budapest in 1867. She was 24 when she was referred to Freud by a doctor as a case of hysteria. Freud stated that he 'did not find it easy to arrive at a diagnosis', but he decided 'to assent to the one proposed by his colleague' (Freud, 1895d: 136). Freud said that it was 'the first full-length analysis of a hysteria undertaken by me' (Freud, 1895d: 139). He is presenting the case not for its own intrinsic value but because of the insight it gives into hysterical symptoms (Freud, 1895d: 161).

Freud presupposes that Elisabeth's presenting problem, pains in her legs, are 'hysterical symptoms'. He seems to have physically examined his patient's legs because he said that the muscles were sensitive to pressure (Freud, 1895d: 136). He said,

> The fact that the hyperalgesia mainly affected the muscles gave food for thought. The disorder which is usually responsible for diffuse and local sensitivity to pressure in the muscles is a rheumatic infiltration of those muscles – common chronic muscular rheumatism. . . . Thus, it was probable that an organic change in the muscles of the kind indicated was present.
>
> *(Freud, 1895d: 137–138)*

Freud found an organic explanation for Elisabeth's pains in her legs, yet he proceeded to treat this woman for hysteria. He 'directed' his 'inquiries' to the first appearance of the pains, but he admits that 'in spite of repeated attempts, we failed to trace any psychical cause for the first pains. I thought it safe to assume that they had in fact appeared without any psychical cause and were a mild rheumatic affection'. He said that he 'was able to establish that this organic disorder' was 'the model copied in her later hysteria'. He goes on: 'These pains, being of organic origin, may have persisted for some time' (Freud, 1895d: 147). Freud is saying that in spite of repeated attempts to establish a psychical cause for the first pains in her legs, he failed. He had to admit that they were rheumatic pains. But when the pains returned to her legs for the second time, Freud is claiming that they are not real organic pains; they are merely copying the earlier organic pains and are therefore hysterical pains.

In response to Freud's questions about the pains in her legs, Elisabeth pointed to an earlier long walk lasting half a day. She began her story by telling Freud how she had nursed her father throughout his illness; then she had to concentrate her whole attention on her mother, who had eye trouble. Elisabeth was 'exhausted' from nursing care when she and her mother joined her two older married sisters and their families at a holiday resort. There she went for a long walk – 'in fact a regular tramp lasting half a day'. Elisabeth had been aware of the pains for a few days after the walk but 'they came on violently for the first time after she had had a warm bath' (Freud, 1895d: 142).

Freud recognised that sick nursing, first her father and later her mother, entailed the disturbance of one's physical health arising from interrupted sleep, neglect of one's own person and constant worry. He acknowledged that Elisabeth was 'exhausted' going to the health resort that the pains in her legs followed the long walk, yet he diagnosed the pains as 'hysterical' (Freud, 1895d: 161–162). Freud was aware that Elisabeth had lost a much-loved father and sister and was occupied with the care of her mother, but he finds the 'unhappy story' of this 'proud girl with her longing for love' a 'great disappointment' (Freud, 1895d: 144).

Freud said he found the story she told of her illness 'wearisome' (Freud, 1895d: 139). He saw how 'it was easy' for people to take the view that Elisabeth had first been 'overtired' after the long walk and had then 'caught cold' (Freud, 1895d: 142). Elisabeth 'remembered being very tired and suffering from violent pain when she returned from the walk' (Freud, 1895d: 151). This long walk could have explained the recurrence of rheumatic pains in Elisabeth's legs. Freud admitted that the long walk was 'intimately connected with Elisabeth's pains' (Freud, 1895d: 155), but he was not looking for the origin of her rheumatic pains.

Freud said he found her 'confession' a 'great disappointment' and too 'commonplace' (Freud, 1895d: 144). Why? Freud gives the reason: 'It threw light neither on the causes nor the specific determination of her hysteria' (Freud, 1895d: 144). He complained, 'it was not easy to see' what benefit it was to her to make her confession 'to a stranger who received it with only a moderate sympathy' (Freud, 1895d: 144). Here we find Freud, the psychoanalyst, describing himself as a 'stranger' who had only 'a moderate sympathy' for his patient. Freud is not putting into practice what he wrote in his paper on 'The Psychotherapy of Hysteria', where he compares himself to a 'father-confessor who gives absolution' and continues 'his sympathy and respect after the confession had been made' (Freud, 1895d: 282).

Freud described the technique he used for extracting the necessary 'confession' out of Elisabeth, a confession that would verify his diagnosis of hysteria. First of all, he 'made her lie down and keep her eyes shut' (Freud, 1895d: 139). He said he 'resorted to the device of applying pressure to the head'. After 'insistence', he gradually extracted 'a secret' – a memory of an evening she was accompanied home from a party by a young man during the time she was nursing her father. This was valuable material for Freud because in it he 'could look for the causes of her first hysterical pains' (Freud, 1895d: 146). Freud is now claiming that Elisabeth's first pains in her legs were 'hysterical'. He says that 'the analysis pointed to the occurrence of a conversion of psychical excitation into physical pain' (Freud, 1895d: 147–148).

Freud 'insisted on her continuing her story' (Freud, 1895d: 148). By repeating the pressure and by 'insisting', he eventually extracted the confession he wanted. Elisabeth remarked to him afterwards, 'I could have said it to you the first time', but 'I thought it wasn't what you wanted'. This indicates that Elisabeth was trying to produce 'what was wanted' by Freud. In so far as the patient was producing what Freud wanted or suggested, one can ask, how valuable is the record of these events? In the witch trials, the accused witch frequently produced the confession she knew the judge wanted to hear. The inquisitors and judges found in the stories they extracted from the so-called witches a confirmation of what they were looking for: the witches were in league with the devil.

Judge Remy recorded the trial of Claude Bogart on 30 October 1590 at Porrentruy. She had 'a scar on the top of her forehead'. Remy, suspecting it was 'the mark of the Demon's talon', ordered a pin to be thrust deeply into it and found that 'she felt no pain'. According to Remy, this was proof that the scar had been made by the Demon, but, he says, 'she persisted in denying the truth'. She said that 'her numbness to pain was due to an old blow from a stone', but after pressure and torture, she 'acknowledged that the mark had been made by a Demon'. Remy asserts, 'it seems to me that they are very far from the truth who ascribe this matter to natural causes' (Remy, 1595: 9–10). Remy did not believe the woman's story that the scar was from 'natural causes'. He used pressure until the accused woman confessed what he wanted to hear, which proved her guilt and thus his theory of witchcraft.

Freud's patient told him 'what he wanted' to hear after he had refused to accept that her pains were from an organic cause. She told him that her brother-in-law accompanied her on the long walk. He had wanted to stay with his sick wife, but she persuaded him to go 'because she thought it would give Elisabeth pleasure' (Freud, 1895d: 155). Naturally, Elisabeth remained in his company all through the walk because he had gone on her account and he was the only member of her family on the walk. She said that she recalled dreaming afterwards about 'finding a husband . . . like this brother-in-law of hers' (Freud, 1895d: 156). She also recalled a later thought she had about her brother-in-law after his wife died: 'Now he is free again, and I can be his wife' (Freud, 1895d: 156). Freud had got the confession he wanted. He put it to her: 'So for a long time, you had been in love with your brother-in-law'. Elisabeth rejected this interpretation. 'It was not true', she asserted. She protested to Freud that he 'had talked her into it' (Freud, 1895d: 157).

In a memorandum in the Freud Archives in the Freud Museum, London, Elisabeth von R.'s daughter says that her mother 'described Freud as "just a young, bearded nerve specialist they sent me to". He had tried "to persuade me that I was in love with my brother-in-law, but that wasn't really so"'. This was first reported by Peter Gay (Gay, 1988: 72). In spite of her vehement protestations, Freud 'probed' to discover more. He claimed that 'her love for her brother-in-law was present in her consciousness like a foreign body' (Freud, 1895d: 165). He tried to persuade her that this 'foreign body' was present within her just as the judges in the witch trials tried to persuade the so-called witches that they were possessed by the devil. Freud made this parallel in a letter to Fliess on 17 January 1897, when he wrote that, 'the medieval theory of possession held by the ecclesiastical courts was identical with our theory of a foreign body and the splitting of consciousness'. Freud claimed that Elisabeth repressed the 'foreign body' causing the conversion into physical pains in her legs. He claimed that this process took place 'at the cost of a psychical abnormality' (Freud, 1895d: 166).

Freud admitted that he discussed Elisabeth's disclosures with her mother, and Elisabeth was indignant with him 'for having betrayed her secret' and stated that she 'would have nothing more to do with him' (Freud, 1895d: 160).

3.4. Katharina

Freud wrote to Fliess on 20 August 1893, 'Recently I was consulted by the daughter of the innkeeper on the Rax; it was a nice case for me'. Freud is referring to

Katharina of the *Studies on Hysteria* (1895d). This is the case of an 18-year-old girl whose father had tried to seduce her, and in one interview, she seems to have been helped. When Freud was on a mountain climb in the Alps during the summer vacation of 1893, an 18-year-old girl, Katharina, came to him complaining that her nerves were bad. One of Katharina's presenting problems was, 'I get so out of breath'. Freud's ensuing question, 'What is it like when you get "out of breath"?' is an example of Freud at his best as a psychoanalyst (Freud, 1895d: 126). He was attending to the girl's statement. Freud made other phenomenological interventions in this case. When Katharina tells him that she caught her father 'with a girl', Freud says, 'What's this story about a girl? Won't you tell me all about it?' Freud's attentive listening and questioning draws a story of her father 'carrying on' with her cousin Franziska: 'he was lying on her' (Freud, 1895d: 127–128).

Not all of Freud's interventions in the Katharina case were phenomenological. Freud also used the power of suggestion in this case. His dogmatic statement 'I'll tell you how I think you got your attacks' shows Freud using suggestion (Freud, 1895d: 127). Katharina describes how, two days after seeing her father having intercourse with her cousin, she was 'sick without stopping for three days' (Freud, 1895d: 129). Freud dogmatically states, 'I believe that means that when you looked into the room you felt disgusted' (Freud, 1895d: 129). Katharina did not say she felt disgusted. Freud is suggesting to her that she felt disgust. It is tempting to accept statements from a doctor she trusts, so her response to Freud's suggestion is, 'Yes, I'm sure I felt disgusted, but disgusted at what? . . . If only I knew what it was I felt disgusted at!' It is clear that Katharina is caught up in reflecting on Freud's suggestion. Freud is seeing Katharina's vomiting as a hysterical symptom, and therefore, he is suggesting that disgust is the normal moral response she should have. We shall see later, in discussing the 'Dora' case, how Freud's attitude to Dora's 'disgust' is different; he describes Dora's disgust at Herr K.'s sexually molesting her as pathognomonic of hysteria.

Katharina tells Freud how her father had tried to seduce her on two occasions. Once, when she was 14 years old, she woke up suddenly one night 'feeling his body' in the bed (Freud, 1895d: 130). She jumped up, ran to the door and stood there until he gave up and went to sleep himself. She did not recognise the attack as a sexual one at the time. Later, Katharina had to defend herself against her father again in an inn where he was drunk. She spoke of another set of memories of her father's interest in Franziska. She seems not to have understood these experiences until she caught her father having intercourse with her cousin Franziska.

At the end of what Freud calls her confession, he again makes a dogmatic statement to her:

> I know now what it was you thought when you looked into the room. You thought: "Now he's doing with her what he wanted to do with me that night and those other times". That was what you were disgusted at, because you remembered the feeling when you woke up in the night and felt his body.
>
> *(Freud, 1895d: 131)*

Katharina did not validate Freud's pontificating. She responded, 'It may well be . . . that that was what I thought' (Freud, 1895d: 131). By telling Katharina that he knows what her thoughts were when she was 16, Freud is presenting himself as infallible. He told her that when she saw her father having intercourse with Franziska, she 'remembered the feeling' when she herself woke up in the night and felt her father's body. Freud questioned her: 'What part of his body was it that you felt that night?' Even though Katharina did not give him a 'definite answer', Freud fantasised 'what the tactile sensation was'.

This short case history, which Freud calls a 'conversation' (Freud, 1895d: 133), shows Freud at his best when he is least intrusive: 'What is it like when you get out of breath?' and 'What's this story about a girl? Won't you tell me all about it?' It also shows Freud at his worst when he is pontificating: 'I'll tell you', and 'I know now what it was you thought' (Freud, 1895d: 127). The Katharina case is a pre-analytic work; it is not a seduction theory case, because Katharina remembers the sexual assaults; they are not repressed or forgotten. Freud added a footnote in 1924 presenting his later theory that Katharina 'fell ill' as a result of sexual temptations [Versuchungen], mistranslated as 'attempts' [Versuchen] by Strachey (Stadlen, 1999). Freud is claiming in 1924 that Katharina fell ill because she was tempted to give in to her father's sexual advances. This claim corresponds to his oedipal theory that the father was doing what the daughter really wanted him to do (Freud, 1895d: 134n.2).

Freud considered the cathartic method, which he used in the Katharina case, as quite invaluable in getting rid of hysterical symptoms. He calls it a 'symptomatic' therapy (Freud, 1895d: 264). In the cathartic method, 'the complete consent and complete attention of the patients are needed, but, above all their confidence, since the analysis invariably leads to the disclosure of the most intimate and secret psychical events' (Freud, 1895d: 265).

It is interesting to compare Freud's different treatment for two 18-year-old girls. While there are elements of Freud's dogmatic approach in the Katharina case, we shall see in the Dora case many of Freud's unexamined assumptions about female sexuality. Freud was gentle and sympathetic towards Katharina when she reported that her father had made sexual advances towards her by getting into bed with her and how she 'defended herself' without fully understanding the sexual nature of the advances. Freud believed her instead of judging her as a hysteric, because she did not respond sexually, although he does see her as a 'hysteric'.

However, in Dora's case, as we shall see, after he has abandoned his seduction theory, Freud proceeds in a manner and tone very different from the one he showed with Katharina. He encourages Katharina by showing his interest in her plight: 'What is it you suffer from?' Freud asked. In an effort to understand further how Katharina is experiencing the hammering in her head, he says, 'And don't you feel at all frightened while this is going on?' To draw her out further, he asked, 'Do you know what your attacks come from?' (Freud, 1895d: 126). Freud helps Katharina to verbalise her anxiety when she saw her father in bed with the young girl. Having heard what happened, Freud encouraged Katharina to express how she felt:

'Fräulein Katharina, if you could remember now what was happening in you at the time . . . it would help you' (Freud, 1895d: 128).

Freud's obvious empathy towards the girl helps her to conduct her own personal investigation, which leads her to remember and describe her father's sexual advances to her when he got into bed with her. Freud provides a secure space for Katharina to get in touch with her feelings while telling her story. In Freud's treatment of Katharina, a position of mutual trust and understanding has been reached. Afterwards, Freud wrote, 'I hope this girl, whose sexual sensibility had been injured at such an early age, derived some benefit from our conversation' (Freud, 1895d: 133). Katharina, 'whose nerves are bad', recognises in this approachable 'doctor' a man of authority who will help her (Freud, 1895d: 125).

But it is tempting for an authority figure such as Freud to use the power of suggestion by making dogmatic statements to susceptible people. The appeal of suggestion is enhanced if it emanates from some source of prestige. In the case of Katharina, she approached Freud as the expert, 'Are you a doctor, sir?' Statements by experts usually carry great weight when the magic word 'infallible' is used to back up the statements. Freud said in *Studies of Hysteria*, 'We must . . . represent ourselves as infallible' (Freud, 1895d: 279). Influencing people's minds by suggestion is a deceptive way of working. It was a procedure that was used by the witches' judges. Bodin writes of the confessions of witches that 'sometimes the judge tricks the one he is questioning, and on occasion puts words into his [her] mouth' (Bodin, 1580: 191). Freud also presented his pressure procedures as 'no more than a trick for temporarily taking unawares an ego which is eager for defence' (Freud, 1895d: 277).

3.5. Freud's harsh therapy?

In his letter to Fliess on 6 November 1898, Freud mentions some of the qualities a psychoanalyst is supposed to have: 'one is supposed to be kind, superior, witty, original'. He does not mention the quality of being dogmatic or being capable of influencing minds by suggestion as being suitable qualities for a psychoanalyst. It appears that Freud fell into these two tendencies because he had a preconceived idea of what he was looking for in the 'confessions' of his patients and because of the difficulty he experienced in working with them in a disinterested way.

In Freud's description of his scientific investigation in *Studies of Hysteria* (1895d), he tells us that at the first interview, he asks if they remember what originally occasioned the symptom. He becomes 'insistent' that if they know, it will occur to their minds. Then something does occur to them, or their memory goes a step further. After this, Freud becomes 'still more insistent'; he tells the patient to lie down and deliberately close their eyes in order to concentrate. He considers it possible for the pathogenic groups of ideas to be brought to light by mere 'insistence'. But he explains how insistence works: to 'guess the secret and tell it to the patient straight out' (Freud, 1895d: 281).

Freud is pressing his patient to produce what he wants to hear. He says to his patient, 'you are mistaken; what you are putting forward can have nothing to do with the present subject. We must expect to come upon something else, and this will occur to you under the pressure of my hand' (Freud, 1895d: 293). Freud continues his work by guessing, by compelling the patient to take sides and by enticing the patient into energetic denial, which betray his undoubted better knowledge. Freud defends his guessing game: 'If something turned out as I had foretold, it was invariably proved by a great number of unimpeachable reminiscences that I had done no more than guess right'. And he concludes, '*we are not in a position to force anything on the patient about the things of which he is ostensibly ignorant or to influence the products of the analysis by arousing an expectation*' (Freud, 1895d: 295, italics in the original). Freud does not take into account the possible suggestibility of his patients.

Because of having to 'insist', Freud realised, 'I had to overcome a resistance, the situation led me at once to the theory that *by means of psychical work I had to overcome a psychical force in the patients which was opposed to the pathogenic ideas becoming conscious (being remembered)*' (Freud, 1895d: 268, italics in the original). This psychical force with which he was in contest had played a part in generating the hysterical symptom and was preventing the pathogenic idea from becoming conscious. In saying that he understands the harsh therapy of the witches' judges, Freud seems to be identifying with them in their contest with demons.

Freud considered the patient's 'not knowing' as, in fact, 'not wanting to know'. He saw his task as overcoming this resistance in his patients. He used insistence and 'psychical compulsion' to overcome the resistance (Freud, 1895d: 270). He applied pressure on the patient's forehead. When Freud removed the pressure, he asked, 'as though there were no question of a disappointment', '"What did you see?" or "What occurred to you?"' (Freud, 1895d: 270). The obstacle in the way to accessing the pathogenic idea is, Freud said, the patient's will (Freud, 1895d: 271). He added, 'In every fairly complicated analysis the work is carried on by the repeated, indeed continuous, use of this procedure of pressure on the forehead' (Freud, 1895d: 272).

Freud believed that the memory of the event he was looking for was in the patients' 'unconscious', so he used his new tool, his pressure technique, to squeeze out of the 'unconscious' the memory for which he was looking. This tendency of expecting to find or knowing what he wanted to find made an accurate scientific investigation impossible. It is always difficult to look at things in a disinterested way, but it is the only way to get an honest result.

Freud gives an account of an elderly woman who came to him claiming that her anxiety attacks originated from her use of iodine, which was intended to reduce the swelling in her thyroid gland. Freud here reveals his dogmatism and his ulterior motivation: 'I naturally rejected this derivation and tried to find another instead of it which would harmonize better with my views on the aetiology of the neuroses' (Freud, 1895d: 274). Under the pressure technique, Freud soon acquired the material that fitted in better with his own views and concluded that the anxiety attack had more to do with a repudiation of a sensual impulse than with any contemporary doses of iodine.

Freud says, 'The procedure by pressure is no more than a trick for temporarily taking unawares an ego which is eager for defence' (Freud, 1895d: 278). He adds,

'We must not believe what they say, we must assume, and tell them too, that they have kept something back. . . . We must insist on this, we must repeat the pressure and represent ourselves as infallible' (Freud, 1895d: 279).

Even when patients say to Freud, 'I know what you expect me to answer' or 'you obviously put it into my head', Freud keeps up the pressure, and if they pause, he admits he is suspicious that they are 're-arranging' or 'mutilating' what has occurred to them (Freud, 1895d: 279). If some information is presented as unimportant, Freud claims that this is an indication that it is an important pathogenic recollection (Freud, 1895d: 280). Freud repeats, 'the pressure technique never fails'. He believes that a facial expression with tension and signs of emotion betrays resistance and defence (Freud, 1895d: 281).

In addition to applying pressure in order to find what he is in search of, Freud tells us that he also applies 'suggestion'. He compares this technique to staring into a crystal ball to disassociate the patient's attention from conscious searching and reflecting, 'to free themselves from their intentional thinking and to adopt an attitude of completely objective observation towards the psychical processes taking place in them' (Freud, 1895d: 271). Freud is requiring objectivity on the part of his patients in their assessment of his 'suggestion'.

3.6. Conclusion

In his treatment of hysteria, Freud opened up the way into new psychological explorations. He claimed that each hysterical symptom disappeared when 'the memory of the event by which it was provoked' was squeezed out and when the patient 'described the event' and 'put the affect into words' (Freud, 1896: 337). To overcome the patient's resistance, Freud used 'pressure' or 'force' as his essential analytic tool for squeezing out the patient's secrets. While at times, as in the case of Katharina, Freud showed that he was attentively and empathetically listening, at other times he was 'insisting', 'suggesting', pressing, pontificating. It is Freud's procedure of pressure and force to extract confessions that can be compared to the procedures used by the witches' judges, as we saw in Chapter 2.

CHAPTER 4
THE SEDUCTION THEORY

4.1. Introduction

From 1894 to 1897, no subject so preoccupied Freud's mind as the reality of sexual molestation in childhood. In three papers in 1896, Freud presented his theory of sexual molestation in childhood as the specific aetiology of hysteria; hysterics were victims of sexual molestation in childhood. Freud formally proposed this theory in 1896. On the 21 April 1896, Freud put forward his thesis:

> at the bottom of every case of hysteria, there are one or more occurrences of premature sexual experience, occurrences which belong to the earliest years of childhood but which can be reproduced through the work of psychoanalysis in spite of the intervening decades. I believe that this is an important finding, the discovery of a caput Nili in neuropathology.
>
> *(Freud, 1896c: 203)*

4.2. Three seduction theory papers of 1896

In the first of his three papers on the seduction theory written in 1896, Freud claims to have carried out 'a complete psycho-analysis on thirteen cases of hysteria'. He claims that, 'In none of these cases is an unconscious memory of childhood sexual abuse committed by another person missing' (Freud, 1896a: 152). Freud argues that it is

> precisely because the subject is in his infancy that the precocious sexual excitation produces little or no effect at the time; but its psychical trace is preserved. Later, when at puberty. . . . this unconscious psychical trace is awakened. . . . The memory will operate as though it were a contemporary event.

Freud describes this as 'a posthumous action by a sexual trauma' (Freud, 1896a: 154). Freud suggests that 'This awakening of a sexual memory after puberty . . . forms the only psychological instance of the immediate effect of a memory surpassing that of an actual event' (Freud, 1896a: 154). This, says Freud, 'is bound to produce a pathological psychical effect'. Freud believes that 'this inverse relation between the psychical effect of the memory and of the event contains the reason for the memory remaining unconscious'. It is this unconscious memory of a precocious sexual experience that Freud claims 'is always found as the specific cause of hysteria' (Freud, 1896a: 154).

In Freud's second paper, *Further Remarks on the Neuro-psychoses of Defence*, published on 15 May 1896, he repeats that he has carried out analyses on 13 'cases of hysteria', and he repeats that to cause hysteria, 'these sexual traumas must have occurred in early childhood (before puberty), and their content must consist of an irritation of the genitals (of processes resembling copulation)'. He claims, 'I have found this specific determinant of hysteria – sexual passivity during the pre-sexual period – in every case of hysteria . . . which I have analysed' (Freud, 1896b: 163). Freud adds,

> In every case a number of pathological symptoms, habits and phobias are only to be accounted for by going back to these experiences in childhood, and the logical structure of the neurotic manifestations make it impossible to reject these faithfully preserved memories which emerge from childhood life.
>
> *(Freud, 1896b: 165)*

Freud writes,

> All the experiences and excitations which, in the period of life after puberty, prepare the way for, or precipitate, the outbreak of hysteria, demonstrably have their effect only because they arouse the memory-trace of these traumas in childhood, which do not thereupon become conscious but lead to a release of affect and to repression.
>
> *(Freud, 1896b: 166)*

Freud states that '"Repression" of the memory of a distressing sexual experience which occurs in maturer years is only possible for those in whom that experience can activate the memory-trace of a trauma in childhood' (Freud, 1896b: 166). In the note on this statement, Freud writes, 'an inverted relation of this sort between real experience and memory seems to contain the psychological precondition for the occurrence of a repression' (Freud, 1896b: 167).

In his first two papers written in 1896, Freud is claiming to have carried out complete analyses on 13 cases of hysteria; that these 13 cases of hysteria are all the cases of hysteria that he has analysed; and that in none of these cases was an unconscious memory of childhood sexual abuse committed by another person missing.

Freud's third paper on *The Aetiology of Hysteria* (1896c), published in five instalments beginning on 31 May 1896, was based on a lecture he delivered on 21 April 1896 to the Society for Psychiatry and Neurology in Vienna. He wrote to Fliess on 26 April, five days after delivering the lecture, telling him that it was given 'an icy reception by the asses and a strange evaluation by Krafft-Ebing[, who said], "It sounds like a scientific fairy tale." And this, after one has demonstrated to them the solution of a more-than-thousand-year-old problem'. Freud is here referring to the ancient problem of the aetiology of hysteria. He again wrote about this problem in greater detail nine months later in two letters to Fliess, on 17 and 24 January 1897. In these letters, Freud compares his theory of hysteria to the medieval theory of the possession of witches.

In his lecture on 21 April 1896, Freud insists on the infallibility of his psychoanalytic procedure in the investigation of cases of hysteria: 'Whatever case and whatever symptom we take as our point of departure, in the end we infallibly come to the field of sexual experience'. Freud claims that

> the singling out of the sexual factor in the aetiology of hysteria . . . is supported by the fact that in some eighteen cases of hysteria I have been able to discover this connection in every single symptom, and, where the circumstances allowed, to confirm it with therapeutic success.
>
> *(Freud, 1896c: 199)*

He adds that these 18 cases 'are at the same time all the cases on which I have been able to carry out the work of analysis' (Freud, 1896c: 200). Referring to 'sexual assaults' in childhood, Freud asserts that in all 18 cases, he has 'come to learn of sexual experiences of this kind in childhood' (Freud, 1896c: 207, 208). In his other two 1896 papers, Freud claims to have investigated only 13 cases of hysteria.

In this lecture, Freud presents his theory that hysteria is always a deferred consequence of sexual abuse before puberty, usually by adults. Freud says,

> we have learned that no hysterical symptom can arise from a real [adult] experience alone, but that in every case the memory of early experiences awakened in association to it plays a part in causing the symptom. If – as I believe – this proposition holds good without exception, it furthermore shows us the basis on which a psychological theory of hysteria must be built
>
> *(Freud, 1896c: 197)*

In other words, 'hysterical symptoms can only arise with the co-operation of memories' (Freud, 1896c: 202).

Freud argues that

> The matter is not merely one of the existence of the sexual experiences, but that a psychological precondition enters in as well. The scenes must be

present as unconscious memories; only so long as, and in so far as, they are unconscious are they able to create and maintain hysterical symptoms.

And he asserts that 'Analysis has arrived at the proposition that hysterical symptoms are derivatives of memories which are operating unconsciously' (Freud, 1896c: 211). He considers that 'The period of growth in which second dentition takes place forms the boundary line for hysteria, after which the illness cannot be caused' (Freud, 1896c: 212).

Freud is saying that symptoms can proceed only from unconscious memories of childhood seduction. Therefore, he adds, 'None of the later scenes, in which the symptoms arise, are the effective ones'. But these later scenes must contain a defensive effort against a distressing sexual experience. This, he claims, is what activates the memory trace of the childhood sexual trauma (Freud, 1896c: 213). In other words, Freud is claiming that 'In hysterical people when there is a present-day precipitating cause, the old experiences come into operation in the form of unconscious memories' (Freud, 1896c: 218). On 1 January 1896, Freud sent Draft K. to Fliess, which states: 'Hysteria necessarily presupposes a primary feeling of unpleasure – that is, of a passive nature. The natural sexual passivity of women explains their being more inclined to hysteria'.

4.3. A new procedure: psycho-analysis

Freud insists that 'it would be useless to try to elicit these childhood traumas from a hysteric by questioning him outside psycho-analysis; their traces are never present in conscious memory, only in the symptoms of the illness' (Freud, 1896b: 165–166). It is in the first of Freud's three papers on his seduction theory, *Heredity and the Aetiology of the Neuroses* (1896a), that he announced, 'a new method of psycho-analysis'. This is his first published appearance of the word 'psycho-analysis'. He claims he owes his results to this new method. 'By means of that procedure', he says, 'hysterical symptoms are traced back to their origin'. Travelling backwards into the patient's past, step by step, Freud claims to have 'finally reached the starting-point of the pathological process' (Freud, 1896a: 151). This starting point, Freud claims, is 'the action of an agent which must be accepted as the specific cause of hysteria' (Freud, 1896a: 152). Freud describes the agent as 'an unconscious memory' of 'sexual abuse committed by another person; and the period of life at which this fatal event takes place is earliest youth – the years up to the age of eight to ten, before the child has reached sexual maturity' (Freud, 1896a: 152). A passive sexual experience before puberty, then, is the specific aetiology of hysteria.

Freud claims to be able to get his hysterical patients to 'reproduce' these experiences through psychoanalysis. He says,

> If we have the perseverance to press on with the analysis into early childhood, as far back as a human memory is capable of reaching, we invariably bring the patient to reproduce experiences . . . for which we have been looking.
>
> *(Freud, 1896c: 202–203)*

In this first paper in 1896, we get a glimpse of Freud's new psychoanalytic technique in obtaining 'confessions' from his hysteric patients who were sexually assaulted or seduced in childhood:

> The fact is that these patients never repeat these stories spontaneously, nor do they ever in the course of a treatment suddenly present the physician with the complete recollection of a scene of this kind. One only succeeds in awakening the psychical trace of a precocious sexual event under the most energetic pressure of the analytic procedure, and against an enormous resistance. Moreover, the memory must be extracted from them piece by piece, and while it is being awakened in their consciousness they become the prey to an emotion which it would be hard to counterfeit.
>
> *(Freud, 1896a: 153)*

Freud is saying here that to extract information from his patients, he uses 'the most energetic pressure of the analytic procedure'.

The psychoanalytic technique that Freud uses for 'awakening the psychical trace of a precocious sexual event' bears a striking similarity to the technique that the judges used to extract the truth out of the witches. Bodin urges judges to 'pursue the interrogation . . . without interruption' and to 'intensely question the witch' (Bodin, 1580: 178). To force a confession out of a witch, Bodin even recommends putting 'words into [her] mouth' (Bodin, 1580: 191). Boguet instructs witches' judges to use pressure:

> the Judge must question the accused without interruption and strongly press him, . . . if the accused refuses to answer one question, he must pass on to another, and afterwards go back to the former one, and must repeat the same question again and again.
>
> *(Boguet, 1590: 214)*

This is continued in order 'to induce the witch to confess the truth' (Boguet, 1590: 217).

On 21 April 1896, Freud read a paper on *The Aetiology of Hysteria* at a meeting of the Society of Psychiatry and Neurology in Vienna, in which he said, 'It is not part of my intention today to discuss the difficult technique of this therapeutic procedure'. At the end of his paper, he says that his

> procedure is new and difficult to handle, but it is nevertheless irreplaceable for scientific and therapeutic purposes. . . . The new method of research gives wide access to a new element in the psychical field of events, namely, to processes of thought which have remained unconscious.
>
> *(Freud, 1896c: 220)*

Freud claims in his second paper that 'psycho-analysis' is 'the only method' for 'making conscious what has so far been unconscious' (Freud, 1896b: 164).

In his third paper of 1896, Freud provides answers to the people who will be tempted to ask,

> Is it not very possible either that the physician forces such scenes upon his docile patients, alleging that they are memories, or else that the patients tell the physician things which they have deliberately invented or have imagined and that he accepts those things as true? . . . Doubts about the genuineness of the infantile sexual scenes can, however, be deprived of their force here and now by more than one argument. In the first place, the behaviour of the patients while they are reproducing these infantile experiences is in every respect incompatible with the assumption that the scenes are anything else than a reality which is being felt with distress and reproduced with the greatest reluctance. Before they come for analysis the patients know nothing about these scenes. They are indignant as a rule if we warn them that such scenes are going to emerge. Only the strongest compulsion of the treatment can induce them to embark on a reproduction of them. While they are recalling these infantile experiences to consciousness, they suffer under the most violent sensations, of which they are ashamed and which they try to conceal; and, even after they have gone through them once more in such a convincing manner, they still attempt to withhold belief from them, by emphasizing the fact that, unlike what happens in the case of other forgotten material, they have no feeling of remembering the scenes.
>
> *(Freud, 1896c: 204)*

Freud is saying that before his patients come for analysis, they know nothing of these scenes. Boguet also speaks of a so-called witch, Rollande du Vernois, whom he claimed was possessed by the devil; when he questioned her, she stated, 'that before her imprisonment she did not know that she was possessed'. She continued to deny the accusations while the judge continued to try 'to draw the truth from her' (Boguet, 1590: 195–196). Scot condemns the judges for the 'absurd confessions' extracted out of the witches. He says, 'Note how easily they might be brought to confess that which they never did' (Scot, 1584: 4).

Freud asks, 'Why should patients assure me so emphatically of their unbelief, if what they want to discredit is something which – from whatever motive – they themselves have invented?' He says,

> It is less easy to refute the idea that the doctor forces reminiscences of this sort on the patient, that he influences him by suggestion to imagine and reproduce them. Nevertheless, it appears to me equally untenable. I have never succeeded in forcing on a patient a scene I was expecting to find.
>
> *(Freud, 1896c: 204–205)*

Like the inquisitors in the witch trials, who claimed uniformity of confession as proof of their truth, Freud vouches for the reality of infantile sexual scenes because of 'their uniformity . . . in certain details' (Freud, 1896c: 205). He says, 'Events of this sort strengthen our impression that the patients must really have experienced what they produce under the compulsion of analysis as scenes of their childhood' (Freud, 1896c: 204–205). Freud is saying because their confessions are similar, they must be true. Bodin (1580) makes this same claim:

> to confirm the proof of the witches' confessions, one must link them with the confessions of other witches. For the actions of the Devil are always consistent. . . . This is why one finds that the confessions of witches . . . are similar.
>
> *(Bodin, 1580: 194)*

Peel & Southern in *The Trials of the Lancashire Witches* (1969), writing on the witch trials in Europe, claim that the reason for the similarity of so many of the witches' confessions is that suggestion was used as a form of questioning in which the accused had only to answer yes to the suggestions (Peel & Southern, 1969: 118). The stereotypical questions extracted the information for which the judges were looking. Could it be possible that Freud's suggestions followed the same pattern in order to get his patients 'to reproduce experiences' for which, Freud says, 'we have been looking' (Freud, 1896c: 202–203).

Peel & Southern (1969) claim that 'the ridiculous confessions' of the witches were the result of torturous investigations that 'forced supposed agents of the Devil to assent to anything suggested to them' (Peel & Southern, 1969: 117). Peel & Southern (1969) also say that 'One woman told her confessor that she had been forced eventually to plead guilty and accuse others' (Peel & Southern, 1969: 117). In the witch trials, the interrogators believed they were uncovering the truth. But the witches' confessions do not establish their stories as fact, because of the inquisitorial procedures employed. Parrinder tells us that African women today make the same sort of confession without clear proof that they have actually done the wicked things they confess (Parrinder, 1958: 53). As late as 1925, Freud denies that his procedure is inquisitorial. He says, 'I do not believe even now that I forced the seduction-phantasies on my patients, that I suggested them' (Freud, 1925d: 34).

4.4. Conclusion

On 21 April 1896, Freud announced his theory of hysteria that in literally every case of hysteria there was sexual abuse in childhood. He used a procedure similar to the witches' judges to overcome the 'resistance' of his patients. This entailed the use of force to extract the scenes for which he was looking. By 21 September 1897, Freud revealed to Fliess that he no longer believed in his theory of hysteria. The next chapter will examine Freud's transition to a new theory.

Freud's original theory was that patients came to him having no knowledge of infantile seduction and the knowledge therefore had to be dragged out of them by sheer force of the treatment. In this pressure treatment, Freud sees himself mirroring 'the harsh therapy of the witches' judges'. It was only by using his forceful method that Freud's patients reproduced the scenes that he was looking for. Even then, according to Freud, they denied them as memory. But he considered their denial the decisive proof that they were memory. Freud claimed that the 'No' uttered by the patient signified the desired 'Yes' (Freud, 1905e: 59). Freud was using the patient's insistence that it was not a memory as scientific evidence that it was a memory. This is Freud's major flaw: his obsession with the idea that things are the opposite of what they are. Freud was taking no to mean yes. There is a magical element in Freud's thinking. Has psychoanalysis today the openness and the expertise to investigate a real problem, or is it still operating out of an inquisitorial system?

CHAPTER 5

TRANSITIONAL PERIOD

5.1. Introduction

No sooner had Freud presented his theory of hysteria to the Vienna Psychoanalytic Society on 21 April 1896 than he realised that he had put himself in an uncomfortable situation, not because his new theory was rejected as a 'scientific fairy tale', nor because he was being isolated by the scientific community, but rather because he had got himself into the untenable position of not having the evidence to substantiate his theory. He had claimed in his 1896 papers to have found the 'specific' aetiology of hysteria in 'all' cases of hysteria that he had analysed (Freud, 1896b: 163, 1896c: 200). He claimed, 'I have been able to carry out a complete psychoanalysis in thirteen cases of hysteria', and 'in all eighteen cases' (Freud, 1896c: 152, 207–208).

Freud's private letters to Fliess showed a very different story. After the public presentation of his theory, he admitted repeatedly in private letters to Fliess that, 'not a single case is finished' (17 December 1896); 'I have not yet finished a single case' (7 March 1897); 'I . . . have not finished a single case' (29 March 1897); and 'I shall wait still longer for a treatment to be completed' (16 May 1897). These statements show that Freud was still looking for conclusive evidence to substantiate his seduction theory. He was searching for a 'paternal aetiology'. We shall see how, at the same time, he was searching in the literature on the witch trials for other explanations of hysteria, and he was also about to embark on a damage limitations exercise by writing papers on memory, preparing the ground for the retraction of his seduction theory. By 17 August 1897, Freud was saying that he was 'tormented by grave doubts about my theory of the neuroses', and finally he admits to Fliess on 21 September 1897 that he no longer believes in his theory of hysteria. We shall look first at his efforts to prove his theory by his search for a 'paternal aetiology'.

5.2. 'Habemus papam!'

In his lecture on 21 April 1896 on presenting the original seduction theory, Freud does not mention fathers as the seducers. In *Studies on Hysteria* (1895), Freud had also avoided reporting 'paternal aetiology' in the cases of hysteria that he had analysed. Katharina and Fräulein Rosalia were both assaulted by their fathers, but it was not until 1924 that Freud revealed that the two girls 'fell ill' as a result of sexual attempts on the part of their own fathers – not their uncles, as reported in the case histories (Freud, 1895d: 134n.2, 170n.1). The 'paternal aetiology' developed from autumn 1896 through 1897, as is evident in private letters to Fliess. Freud's father died in the end of October 1896. In his letter to Fliess on 6 December 1896, Freud mentions a case of seduction by a father. On 3 January 1897, he announces victoriously in a letter to Fliess: 'Habemus papam!' literally 'We have a pope!' but Freud is in fact announcing, 'We've got a father!' who is the perpetrator. One of his patients, G. de B., presented Freud with her problems, which he interpreted as fellatio. His procedure is evident in his letter to Fliess:

> When I thrust the explanation at her, she was at first won over; then she committed the folly of questioning the old man himself, who . . . exclaimed indignantly, "Are you implying that I was the one?" . . . She has never felt as well as on the day when I made the disclosure to her.

By admitting that it was he who 'made the disclosure to her' and that he 'thrust the explanation at her', Freud is showing his inquisitorial procedures with his patients.
On 24 January 1897 Freud again writes,

> In hysteria I recognise the pater in the high demands made in love, in the humility in relation to the lover, or in the inability to marry because of unfulfilled ideals. The reason for this is, of course, the height from which the father lowers himself to the child.

On the 8 February 1897, Freud writes to Fliess, 'Unfortunately, my own father was one of these perverts and is responsible for the hysteria of my brother (all of whose symptoms are identifications) and those of several younger sisters. The frequency of this circumstance often makes me wonder'.
On 28 April 1897, Freud writes, 'a lucky chance this morning brought a fresh confirmation of paternal etiology'. He is referring to a young woman's 'confession': 'I can make myself out as bad as I must; but I must spare other people. You must allow me to name no names'. Freud extracted the confession that

> her supposedly otherwise noble and respectable father regularly took her to bed when she was from eight to twelve years old and misused her without penetrating. . . . A sister, six years her senior, . . . confessed to her that she had the same experience with their father.

Freud's procedure by suggestion is again evident when he writes, 'Of course, when I told her that similar and worse things must have happened in her earliest childhood, she could not find it incredible'. Freud is here using a similar procedure to the witches' judges, by suggesting to his patient his own reconstruction of events and thus leading the patient to agree to what he suggested.

At this time in Freud's efforts to get verification for his seduction theory, he is relentlessly pursuing a paternal aetiology. Freud's letters on 6 April, 2 May and 16 May and Drafts L, M and N in 1897 all refer to a new element in the reproduction of scenes in the solution of hysteria: unconscious fantasies that stem from things that children have overheard at an early age and understood only subsequently. In the letter dated 2 May 1897, Freud writes of 'impulses that derive from primal scenes'. This is a reference to his belief that sexual seduction by the father is the source of neuroses. On 22 June 1897, Freud is complaining of a 'period of intellectual paralysis. . . . I believe I am in a cocoon, and God knows what sort of beast will crawl out'. By the 18 August 1897, Freud is telling Fliess that he is 'tormented by grave doubts' about his theory of hysteria. In his next famous letter, on 21 September 1897, Freud confides in Fliess his 'great secret' that has slowly been dawning on him in the last few months: 'I no longer believe in my neurotica' – that is, in his theory of hysteria. He gives his reasons for giving up the seduction theory: first, his lack of evidence from his clinical practice; second, 'the father, not excluding my own, had to be accused of being perverse . . . surely such widespread perversions against children are not very probable'; third, 'the certain insight' that '(the sexual fantasy invariably seizes upon the theme of the parents)'; and finally, he was not even getting the scenes of seduction.

Are these the reasons that led Freud to give up his seduction theory? Freud knew that seduction had to be present in *all* cases of hysteria in order to present his findings as a theory of a 'specific' aetiology. It was precipitous of Freud to claim this result in his lecture on 21 April 1896 before he had actually proved it, because he wrote to Fliess on 7 March and 29 March 1897 – nearly a year after his formal presentation of his theory – 'I have not yet finished a single case', and again, on 18 August 1897, he wrote to Fliess, 'I have finished nothing [and] am . . . tormented by grave doubts about my theory of the neuroses'. From his letters to Fliess at this time, Freud was revealing that he still had got no evidence to back his theory of seduction even though he was making every effort to find evidence of a father as the seducer. During this period, Freud is convinced that these 'devils' or seducers are, in the majority of cases, fathers.

In the socio-sexual culture of late-nineteenth-century Vienna, it was possible for Freud to believe that fathers would exploit their own daughters for sexual gratification, but it was only in private letters to Fliess that Freud was prepared to acknowledge this fact. In the seduction theory, Freud was opening up an interpersonal investigation into a serious social problem that needed to be investigated, but he abandoned his quest. Freud could have admitted his mistake of claiming that 'all' cases of hysteria had their origins in seduction. He could have said that 'some' cases of hysteria showed evidence of seduction and then worked on this serious social problem, but Freud was not prepared to go down this path.

5.3. 'I have ordered the *Malleus Maleficarum'*

While Freud continued to publicly maintain his belief in his theory of sexual molestation in childhood, he searched for other explanations for hysteria. Freud's two letters on witches, which he wrote to Fliess in January 1897, are at the heart of this transitional period in the evolution of Freud's theories. They show his fascination with fantasies. Freud tells Fliess on 17 January 1897 that his 'theory of a foreign body and the splitting of consciousness' – that is, his theory of hysteria is 'identical' to 'the medieval theory of possession' of witches held by the ecclesiastical courts in the medieval period. Our next step, therefore, is to measure in what way they were perceived by Freud as 'identical'. Were the procedures used by Freud in his case histories of hysteria 'identical' to the procedures used in the witch trials? Is there any relationship between the two procedures, and are they related in their interpretations? How did Freud become interested in the medieval witch trials?

While Freud was in Paris studying under Charcot between October 1885 and February 1886, he was exposed to literature on witches who were believed to be possessed by the devil. His letter to Fliess on 24 January 1897 shows his continuing interest in literature on witches and possession. Appendix 2 has the list of books on witches and witch trials that were being translated and prepared for republication in the *Bibliothèque Diabolique* series at the time that Freud was studying under Charcot. This work was sponsored by the School of Charcot. As Appendix 2 shows, the books being prepared for publication included *On the Demon-Mania of Witches* by Bodin (1580) and *An Examen of Witches* by Boguet (1590). Wier's major opus on witch trials, *De Praestigiis Daemonum* (1563), was published in 1885. Freud's reference to Wier in his 1906 letter to the Viennese publisher shows his familiarity with Wier's major opus on witch trials and its significance to him. As well as the books on the witch trials by Bodin, Boguet and Wier, which Freud was familiar with while in Paris, we can assume that Freud read the first most famous medieval publication on witches, *Malleus Maleficarum* (1486), as he proposed to do in his letter to Fliess on 24 January 1897. He wrote, 'I have ordered the *Malleus Maleficarum,* and . . . I shall study it diligently'.

At the time of his saying 'I must delve into' the medieval literature on the witch trials, Freud begins vacillating between the significance of memory and the significance of phantasy, in the stories told by his patients. I am claiming that Freud was influenced to change his theory of hysteria to sexual phantasies as a result of his study of the witch trials. Freud wrote to Fliess on 24 January 1897 about his drawing similarities between the stories of 'the witches and my patients'. In the same letter, Freud was also equating his procedures in the treatment of his hysterical patients with the judges' procedures in the witch trials because he equated the stories of the witches and the stories of his patients. Freud claimed that the problem that both witches and hysterics had was their secret sexual wishes or phantasies, which were cut off from consciousness and repressed and which therefore became pathogenic. These secret sexual wishes or phantasies were in conflict with the reality of the situation in which they lived, and they were therefore repressed. This repressed psychical material is what Freud repeatedly calls a 'foreign body' and what the witches' judges and inquisitors called the 'devil' or 'incubus', who was being driven out just as the 'foreign body' or secret sexual wish was fended off, repressed or driven out of consciousness by the hysteric. In the hysteric, it was converted into somatic symptoms. In the witch, it gained an outlet in her so-called night flights to the Sabbat.

Freud wrote to Fliess on 17 January 1897, 'I must delve into the literature on this subject'. We know that Freud read the literature on witches by Bodin (1580) and Boguet (1590), if not in the *Bibliothèque Diabolique* series, then at least through the *History of the Witch Trials* by W.G. Soldan (1912), which is in the Sigmund Freud Library in Maresfield Gardens, London. Soldan quotes these two authors and Remy profusely in his work on the witch trials. We know also that Freud read Lecky (1865), who also refers to these authors.

Remy (1595) wrote that witches were victims of their own 'evil impulses' (Remy, 1595: 46). He says that there was much controversy and dissention as to whether the witches were bodily present in 'their nocturnal synagogues' or whether they were only 'possessed by some fantastic delusion, and, as happens when the empty mind is filled with dreams at night, merely imagine that they are present' (Remy, 1595: 47). Remy claims to be in agreement with Bodin (1580) when he writes, 'I am quite willing to agree with those who think that such Sabbat meetings at times exist only in dreams'. Witches often are 'merely visited in their sleep by an empty and vain imagination' (Remy, 1595: 47, 51).

This belief that witches sometimes imagine their Sabbat trysts was a matter of great interest to Freud, because he said in his letter on 17 January 1897 to Fliess that his theory on hysterics was identical with the theory on witches. And because he considered the stories of his hysterical patients and the stories of the witches to be identical, he was going to 'delve into the literature on this subject'. Could it be that his own patients, like the witches, were 'possessed by some fantastic delusion'? He told Fliess, 'I have ordered the *Malleus Maleficarum*, and . . . I shall study it diligently'. In the same letter, on 24 January 1897, he asked Fliess to recommend some good reading on the subject of witches. It is clear that Freud is studying this literature on witches with great interest and is trying to interest Fliess in it also, because three months later, on 28 April 1897, he expresses his annoyance with Fliess, who is 'unable to take any pleasure at all in the Middle Ages'.

An obvious change has been taking place in Freud's thinking about hysterics since he presented his seduction theory. On 21 April 1896, Freud had formally presented his theory of seduction. In it he presented seduction as the specific aetiology of hysteria on 21 April 1896. Was his reading the literature on witches' imaginings of sexual orgies with the devil influencing Freud's thinking about hysterics having phantasies of seduction? Remy (1595) records that Jean Bodin in his *Demon-Mania* (1580) had

> vouched for cases where women have manifestly spent the whole night at home, and even in bed with their husbands, and yet on the next morning

> they have confidently recounted many details of the Sabbat at which they have affirmed they were present on the previous night.
>
> *(Remy, 1595: 47)*

These women were kept under observation and seen

> to move spasmodically in their sleep . . . or even to mount upon a chair or some other object and act as if they were spurring a horse to great speed: yet they did not go out of the house, . . . but on awaking . . . told wonderful stories of what they imagined they had done, and were much offended and angry with those who would not believe them.
>
> *(Remy, 1595: 47)*

Remy was in agreement with Bodin (1580) that 'at times' the so-called witches are at the Sabbat, where the devil abuses them sexually, and at other times this happens 'only in dreams', after which the witches tell stories of what they imagined has happened (Remy, 1595: 51). He adds that 'often they are visited in their sleep by an empty and vain imagination' (Remy, 1595: 51). What these authors are saying is that at times the witches are phantasising the sexual seductions by the devil and at other times they are present at Sabbats in reality. It is at least plausible that this reading influenced Freud into thinking that some of his patients' stories were phantasies of seduction.

During the period that Freud was studying the literature on witches, he began writing *The Interpretation of Dreams* (1900a). Freud saw the dream as an escape route for the pathogenic idea, and therefore, its interpretation would throw light on the pathogenic idea: 'The dream . . . is one of the detours by which repression can be evaded' (Freud, 1905e: 15). Freud could see that dreams or phantasies gave an outlet to the witch for her repressions. Witches were considered to be desirous of revenge (Remy, 1595: 4). Freud records an interpretation of one of his own dreams in which he is taking revenge on his father, who had said of his young son when he was seven or eight years old, 'The boy will come to nothing' (Freud, 1900a: 216). His father was reprimanding him for wetting the bedroom floor. In the dream, Freud was making fun of his father by putting the old man in a defenceless position: 'I had to hand him the urinal because he was blind, and I revelled in allusions to my discoveries in connection with the theory of hysteria, of which I felt so proud'.

In a footnote to his dream, Freud refers to hysterical patients who

> alongside what has really happened to them, they unconsciously build up frightful or perverse imaginary events which they construct out of the most innocent and everyday material of their experience. It is to these phantasies that their symptoms are, in the first instance, attached and not to their recollections of real events.
>
> *(Freud, 1900a: 217n.1)*

While Freud is here holding on to their recollections of real events – 'what has really happened to them' – he is moving towards phantasies as the source of hysterical symptoms.

This shift in Freud's thinking can be seen in his letter of 17 January 1897 to Fliess, where Freud is saying that the inquisitors are using harsh therapy – 'pricking with needles' – to find evidence of the witches' secret relationship with the devil. He is saying that 'in a similar situation', his patients 'think of the same old cruel story in fictionalized form'. Freud is drawing comparisons between what the inquisitors were doing with the witches and what he was doing with his patients, whom he calls 'victims'. In other words, both he and the inquisitors were using harsh therapy to draw out their respective stories 'in fictionalized form'. Freud's thoughts are hovering between the stories as fact and the stories as fiction (Freud, 1900a: 216).

In his letter to Fliess on 24 January 1897, Freud is also looking at the judges' harsh therapy again and seems to be suggesting that it could be an act of revenge for the seductions that the judges themselves underwent as children. Freud is referring to seductions in childhood when he writes on 17 January 1897 that the seducers are being disguised in the victims' stories. In this way, Freud is drawing parallels between himself and the judges and between his patients and the witches.

We shall examine further what led Freud down this path. Bernheimer, quite rightly, points out that Freud is drawing a parallel between his patients' stories and the witches' stories 'that casts the seducer in the role of the devil, a casting that, even as it implies moral judgement, simultaneously suggests that the drama might be a delusive psychic creation' (Bernheimer & Kahane, 1985: 13). Freud was using a similar procedure to that of the inquisitors when he said that 'only under the strongest compulsion of the analysis' can this information be squeezed out of his patients.

5.4. 'The old physician, Johann Weier'

I am suggesting that Freud may have been influenced by his readings to change his theory. One author whose writings influenced Freud was Jan Wier (1515–1588). Wier challenged the theories of satanic possession of witches and re-interpreted their symptoms as mental illness. Wier is a vital link between the old demonology and the modern psychological sciences. Cobben, in his book *Jan Wier, Devils, Witches and Magic* (1960), quoted Fruin on witches: 'The famous physician, Wier, was the first to defend unfortunate victims of their imaginings who were further victimised by their contemporaries. He proves to us through his works how tightly the vice of superstition held everyone' (Cobben, 1960: 176). Wier was the first serious opponent of the witch craze. He argued that most of the witches' confessions were shaped by the torturer's suggestions. Szasz (1997) claims that the emphasis of Wier's argument was not on a criticism of the concept of witchcraft nor on a plea for its replacement by that of mental illness but rather on the procedures employed by the inquisitors and judges (Szasz, 1997: 13). But Wier did argue that these women who told stories of sexual orgies with the devil were victims of their imagination, and in that respect, he claimed, they were mentally ill. Wier studied many witch proceedings and confessions, and it became clear to him that these so-called witches were deluded (Wier, 1563: 510).

Wier's humanitarian aim in pleading mental illness was to protect the witches. Swales (1982b) claims that Wier's influence was of crucial significance to Freud's abandonment of the seduction theory. He says,

> it is likely that Freud avoided ever acknowledging the parallel between his own and Weier's achievements because he did not wish to betray that the provocative reversal of the seduction theory had been undertaken largely under Weier's inspiration.
>
> *(Swales, 1982b: 21)*

While I agree with Swales, I am also claiming that Freud was influenced to abandon his seduction theory because of his studying the literature written by the inquisitors and the witches' judges.

The dynamics in the witch trials could be described as collusion, no doubt unconsciously, between the witch and the judge. The witch is handed over by husband or neighbour to the judge. The judge, who was convinced of the reality of the Sabbat and of the nocturnal flights, compelled the witch, through his inquisitorial procedures, to admit to having flown to the Sabbat and copulated with the devil. The trial was a battle between the forces of God and the forces of the devil, and the battle was fought for the witch's soul. A witch who confessed her guilt was considered to have a chance at salvation. The aim of the judge was to save the soul of the witch. The witch cooperated by confessing to whatever crimes of witchcraft that the fertile imagination of the judge created. Phantasies of sexual orgies with the devil fed into the witch's confession. Other witches' judges were influenced by the writings of such eminent judges as Bodin, Remy and Boguet. How the sexual phantasies of both judge and witch were interwoven would be difficult to determine or disentangle.

Freud's study of the literature on witchcraft and his drawing parallels between himself and the inquisitors and judges is evident in his two letters to Fliess in January 1897. Referring to his theory of hysteria, Freud writes, 'the medieval theory of possession held by the ecclesiastical courts is identical with our theory'. He is also drawing parallels between his patients and the witches. He writes about 'stories like those of the witches and of my patients', and he asks, 'Why are their confessions under torture so like the communications made by my patients in psychic treatment?' Part of the content of the witches' stories that Freud is interested in investigating is their account of 'the gold the devil gives' them, which 'regularly turns into excrement', and also the account that 'they are maltreated at night in the most shameful way sexually'. In his letter on 24 January 1897, Freud is drawing parallels between these confessions and the stories told by his patient, Mr. E. who claimed that his nurse 'Louise's money always was excrement'.

5.5. 'If the sister is not one's mother's child'

As well as the literature on witches by the inquisitors and judges Freud also read, at this time, the historical novel *The Judge* (1976) by C.F. Meyer. It is evident from his letters to Fliess that immediately before his August 1898 holiday in Switzerland with his sister-in-law Minna, Freud avidly read novels by C.F. Meyer. He told Fliess on 30 July 1898 that this trip with Minna 'was inspired by your remark that you know very well the land where *Jürg Jenatsch* [a novel by Meyer] takes place'. In his three previous letters to Fliess, he refers to three other novels by Meyer that he had just read in the original German. One of these is *The Judge* (1976), a historical novel about a female judge during the reign of Charlemagne at the end of the eighth century.

The story of *The Judge* (1976) opens in Rome, but it is set mainly in east Switzerland in Graubunden. Meyer weaves in Judge Stemma's dreams, her memories and associations into a story that resembles what Freud calls 'stories like those of the witches and my patients'. The harsh Judge Stemma is described as 'riding all over the mountains and ordering people to be hanged and beheaded' (Meyer, 1976: 182). The guilty believe she is 'omniscient and can see through them' (Meyer, 1976: 177). But Judge Stemma carries her own secret guilt. She was impregnated by her lover before she was given in marriage to a count whom she poisoned because she did not love him.

Judge Stemma has a dream in which the cleric magician Peregrinus, her dead lover and father of her only child, appears to her and accuses her of seducing him 'with a drop of blood'. He says, 'Show me your finger. You still bear the scar' (Meyer, 1976: 191). When she awoke from the dream, she admitted to herself that the 'episode' began 'when the drop of blood had spurted from her finger' (Meyer, 1976: 192). Meyer is presenting the drop of blood on her finger as seductive. This seductive episode finds an echo in Freud's experience with his patients. He wrote to Fliess on 17 January 1897 describing a seduction scene from Eckstein 'where the diabolus sticks needles into her fingers and then places a candy on each drop of blood'. In the same letter, Freud writes about the witches' seduction stories and the inquisitors' pricking with needles.

In Judge Stemma's second dream, the count, her dead husband whom she poisoned, appears to her, but a 'derisive smile played on her darkened face for she knew how helpless the dead were' (Meyer, 1976: 192). The next day, the count's only son, Wulfrin, by an earlier marriage, comes to the castle and falls in love with Palma, Judge Stemma's daughter, whom he believes is also his father's daughter.

Wulfrin struggles with his incestuous desires. He confesses his secret guilty fantasies to Judge Stemma, but 'She could not investigate in this instance, for to do so would have uncovered a buried secret, reconstructed a destroyed fact, and restored a link of events which she had torn out herself' (Meyer, 1976: 213). A lie, her own lie, had made Wulfrin and Palma believe they were brother and sister. Judge Stemma's 'doom was progressing against her' (Meyer, 1976: 214). Guilty feelings were torturing her. She went out in the night and stood accusingly at the count's grave: 'Why do you torture me? . . .The Judex [my father] did not give you a virgin in marriage! I was already carrying the child of another man. It was Palma novella inside me who killed you' (Meyer, 1976: 215).

When she turned around to go back into her castle, her daughter, Palma, was standing behind her. Judge Stemma realised that she 'had now given her secret a mouth and a witness and this witness was her own child' (Meyer, 1976: 215). Her secret was known to Palma. The lively, spirited Palma became ill. Like Freud's Dora, Palma's distress was justified. People said, 'Some magic had deprived the poor child of her reason!' Others said, 'Perhaps she had met a witch'. Judge Stemma tried to bring her to reason, 'It was a dream', she said, 'the illusions you have about that night . . . that hateful dream . . . is now torturing you and killing you'. The judge was trying to seduce Palma by suggesting to her that her experience that night was an illusion of reality. But Palma knew it was a memory. She encouraged her mother: 'Let's confess the truth'. Judge Stemma at first protested, 'all faith in justice would perish'. But for the sake of her child she invited the emperor to come judge her (Meyer, 1976: 218). Emperor Charlemagne arrived. The people were assembled. Judge Stemma addressed Wulfrin first: 'it is true, is it not, if this girl' – she pointed to Palma – 'were not your father's child, not your sister . . . your sacrilege would collapse'? She went on to confess her husband's murder, that she was carrying Palma before she met the count. Wulfrin, the count's son, jumped forward. Palma was not his sister. He was entirely without blame. His fantasies were not incestuous. He could marry Palma (Meyer, 1976: 221).

This story intrigued Freud. It is a story about a strict judge who used harsh therapy but who herself poisoned, invented stories and tried to induce a false memory. It has many of the elements of the medieval and early modern stories of the witch trials. The point Freud makes is that, for the author, the novel serves the purpose of taking revenge on the strict mother who is judged and exposed. The mother is the seducer. Freud says, 'in every single feature it is identical with the romances of revenge and exoneration which my hysterics, if they are boys, invent about their mothers' (Letter to Fliess, 20 June 1898). Freud is saying here that the stories his hysterics are telling him are 'invented'. They are romances of revenge invented about their mothers. They are not real memories.

Freud made a similar point in his 1896 paper, 'I myself am inclined to think that the stories of being assaulted which hysterics so frequently invent may be obsessional fictions which arise from the memory-trace of a childhood trauma' (Freud, 1896b: 164.n1). Freud is saying that the romances that his hysterics invent arise from the memory trace of a childhood trauma. He seems to be saying the same thing in his letter of 17 January 1897: 'the victims think of the same old cruel story in fictionalized form'. Freud is making an important point here also about the inquisitors. He is saying that the inquisitors, in 'pricking' the witches with needles, are acting out their revenge against their mothers. They are 'recalling in this their earliest youth'. Therefore, the 'harsh therapy of the witches' judges' could be seen as an act of revenge arising from the memory trace of their own childhood traumas (Letter to Fliess, 17 January 1897).

Freud also picks up on Wulfrin's incestuous fantasies: 'I desire my sister' (Meyer, 1976: 208). In a letter to Fliess on 20 June 1898, Freud echoes the judge's words to Wulfrin: 'If the sister is not one's mother's child, one is relieved of all blame'. Wulfrin's incestuous fantasies were blameless. His feelings were not incestuous, because his 'sister' was not his father's child. Not only the theme of incestuous practices at the witches' Sabbat but also the incestuous imaginings were part of the confessions that the witches' judges tried to extract from the witches (Boguet, 1590: 55–57). Not incestuous *practices* but incestuous *fantasies* are gaining ground in Freud's thinking about his theory of hysteria at this time.

Freud has finished reading *The Judge* (1976) as he is about to take a member of his household, his sister-in-law Minna, on a holiday in August 1898, and it seems that he is re-creating the family romance of Meyer's novel so that he too can be 'relieved of all blame'. Upon his return from his trip with Minna, he writes, 'It really was glorious. . . . Leprese was for us enchantingly idyllic, . . . remote from all intellectual pursuits. . . . I am at present chiefly occupied with regretting that so much of the vacation is already gone' (Letter to Fliess, 20 August 1898). But Freud has already planned a trip with his wife Martha to Dalmatia, starting at the end of August. Unlike his detailed and enthusiastic descriptions to Fliess of his time spent with Minna and 'the pleasures of our trip', Freud, interestingly, gives no account of his time spent with Martha during their holiday in Dalmatia.

5.6. Memory papers

It is on holiday with Martha in Dalmatia in September 1898 that Freud went on a trip with a Berlin lawyer to Bosnia–Herzegovina. This trip provided Freud with the theme for the first of the series of his memory papers. Stadlen points out, that at this time, Freud was beginning to write a number of memory papers about false memories, distorted memories, substitute memories and screen memories – all perhaps aiming, among other things, to prepare the ground for the retraction of his seduction theory. The key to his seduction theory was memory. Freud needed to be able to explain, when the time was right, why he made the claims in the seduction theory about 'memories' of seduction and why he now no longer believes them (Stadlen Seminar, 16 May 1999).

Freud builds the first in his series of memory papers, his Signorelli analysis, around the trip with the Berlin lawyer. Freud had made 'a brief stay at Trafoi' in the Tyrol on his trip with Minna. He had received a piece of news there about a patient who 'put an end to his life on account of an incurable sexual disorder'. Freud refers to this incident at Trafoi in his Signorelli analysis (Freud, 1901: 40). He claims to have been reminded 'of what I wanted to forget' (Freud, 1901: 40). He says he had repressed the topic of death and sexuality.

Freud saw the sexual dimension in many forms of behaviour that had been thought to be entirely nonsexual. Freud believed, for example, that sexuality played a principal part as a motive for forgetting, even in cases where the topic or the word forgotten had no obvious sexual connotation. Freud is saying that, in the area of sexuality, memory plays tricks. It can be deceptive. He illustrated this in his Signorelli analysis and in his Aliquis analysis, both of which are found in the first two chapters of *The Psychopathology of Everyday Life* (1901). Freud used them as 'paradigmata' for the analysis of forgetting. He claims that when the memory is connected to the emotive topic of sexuality, it becomes confused and creates its own substitute memories that are not the real memories. Stadlen suggests that these analyses appear to be preparing the ground for the retraction of his seduction theory, in which the key is memory (Stadlen Seminar, 16 May 1999).

In the Signorelli analysis, Freud describes how he tried without success to recall the name of the artist who painted the frescos of the 'Four Last Things' – Death, Judgement, Hell and Heaven – in Orvieto Cathedral. This forgetting of the name Signorelli happened while he was travelling in the company of a stranger, a Berlin lawyer, from Ragusa in Dalmatia to Bosnia–Herzegovina. He was talking to the stranger 'about the customs of the Turks living in Bosnia and Herzegovina' (Freud, 1901: 39). Freud told the stranger that if these people bring a man who is ill to the doctor and nothing can be done for him their reply is: 'Herr, . . . If he could be saved, I know you would have saved him'.

Freud wanted to tell a second anecdote about the Turks, which came into his memory, that 'they place a higher value on sexual enjoyment than on anything else, and in the event of sexual disorders they are plunged into a despair which contrasts strangely with their resignation towards the treat of death.' Freud also remembered a story of a colleague's patient who said to him, '*Herr*, you must know that if *that* comes to an end then life is of no value'. We shall see shortly the significance of the word '*Herr*' being connected in Freud's memory with the content of this sentence.

Freud suppressed the memory of the anecdotes about sex and diverted his conversation to the magnificent frescos in Orvieto Cathedral by the artist. . .? Freud forgot the artist's name. The name Signorelli had escaped his memory. He analyses his own forgetting of this proper name, Signorelli, and his replacing it with the names Botticelli and Boltrafio. In his associations with Boltrafio, Freud's thoughts turned to Trafoi, where he had made a brief stay with Minna some weeks ago.

Freud uses a complicated diagram and the translation of the German word '*Herr*' into the Italian 'Signor' in order to explain the influence of a motive for forgetting (Freud, 1901b: 5). He concludes, 'All we have done is . . . to add a motive to the factors that have been recognized all along as being able to bring about the forgetting of a name' (Freud, 1901b: 6). The motive is the repression of a sexual topic. Freud is pointing out the relation between the forgetting of the name Signorelli and the consciously suppressed sexual topic of conversation that immediately preceded it, as well as what he claims is a truly repressed sexual topic that was activated, as it were, by the suppressed sexual anecdote about the Turks: '*Herr* . . . if *that* comes to an end, life is of no value' (Freud, 1901b: 3).

The Aliquis analysis is similar. I referred to the Aliquis analysis in Chapter 1 when writing on the si aliquis canon, in which the Church condemned contraception. In this analysis, Freud is linking revenge, sexuality and memory. Revenge is also a common theme in the witches' trials where the devil tells the witch to take revenge. Boguet says that the devil suggests to the witches the means to avenge themselves on their enemies (Boguet, 1590: 21–23). Though Freud presents the Aliquis analysis as that of a young Jew of academic background who had been on a trip to Italy with a woman, the whole episode is written like Freud's own self-analysis. Swales (1982a) first proposed that the analysis is a secret confession of Freud's travels to Italy with his sister-in-law Minna, which took place during August –September 1900. Freud describes this trip in a letter to Fliess on 14 September 1900. Ten days later, he again writes to Fliess, 'I must, after all take an interest in reality in sexuality, . . . Am slowly writing the *Psychology of Everyday Life*'. It is in that book that Freud gives the account of his Aliquis analysis.

The young Jew of academic background whom Freud allegedly met on a holiday trip had ambitious feelings, which prompted him to vent a regret: because of his race he could not develop his talents or satisfy his needs. He wanted to end his impassioned speech with a line from Virgil: 'Exoriar(e) aliquis nostris ex ossibus ultor' [Arise, someone from my (our) bones as an avenger] (Virgil, 'Aeneid' 1V,625). The young man forgot the word 'aliquis'. Freud proceeded to analyse this forgetting of the word 'aliquis'. The young man started associating: a-liquis . . . liquefying . . . fluidity, Saint Augustine, Saint Januarius and the blood miracle; the blood of St Januarius is kept in a vial in Naples where it liquifies on a particular day; people get excited if the liquefying blood miracle is delayed.

Then the young man says, 'I've suddenly thought of a lady from whom I might easily hear a piece of news that would be very awkward for both of us'. Freud responds, 'That her periods have stopped?' The young man is amazed that Freud could have guessed what was in his mind. Freud explains how the associations – the calendar saints, the blood that starts to flow on a particular day and the disturbance when the event fails to take place – enabled Freud to come to the motive for forgetting the word 'aliquis'. His memory failed him when it was associated with an emotive sexual topic.

Freud is claiming through these two paradigmatic cases that we are not responsible for what we forget because it is our unconscious that forces us to forget. In the last chapter of *The Psychopathology of Everyday Life* (1901), Freud is arguing total 'psychic determinism' in so far as we are not responsible for forgetting; our unconscious forces us to forget. Freud is denying free will and reducing morality to reaction formation. He says that in the Signorelli example, what he wanted to forget was his previous train of thought about 'death and sexuality': not the name of the artist at Orvieto but something beyond his control 'contrived to place itself in an associative connection with his name, so that my act of will missed its target and I forgot *the one thing against my will*, while I wanted to forget *the other thing intentionally*' (Freud, 1901b: 4). Memory was playing tricks, presenting substitute memories.

When Freud comes to retracting the seduction theory, this idea can be applied to his patients' memories. They cannot be trusted as memories.

One element that the Aliquis analysis has in common with the witches and their judge, and Freud and his patients, was revenge. In his dream, Freud wanted vengeance on his father (Freud, 1900a: 216). Freud believed that the witches' judges, through their harsh therapy, were seeking vengeance for childhood traumas. Dora was accused by Freud of seeking revenge, and the witches were accused of 'commonly desiring revenge'.

The quote '*Exoriare aliquis nostris ex ossibus ultor*' from Virgil's 'Aeneid' is calling on someone to arise as an avenger. It is, understandably, expressing a sentiment with which Freud, as a Jew, could identify. Political anti-Semitism was rampant in Freud's lifetime, and he was personally affected by it. One can relate this to the plight of the witch. Freud would have been aware, from his reading of the witch trials, how the hated and hunted witches believed they were being urged by the demon 'to avenge themselves upon their enemies, saying to them: "Avenge yourselves, or you shall die" (Boguet, 1590: 60).

Freud would have also read in the *Malleus* (1486) about the vengeance of witches, 'through their second defect of inordinate passions, they search for, brood over and inflict various vengeances' (Kramer & Sprenger, 1486: 45). It would be easy for Freud, in his social climate, to identify with the witch and cry out, '*Exoriare aliquis nostris ex ossibus ultor*' [Arise, someone from my bones as an avenger] (Virgil, 'Aeneid' IV: 625). But is it from bones or from blood that new life arises?

Like the so-called witches, Freud had every reason, as a Jew, to harbour feelings of revenge. In 1887 a resolution proposed by an artisan group was introduced into the German Parliament in the form of an anti-Semitic bill by Schönerer, who said, 'We will never accept a Jew as a German. . . . we would rather condone . . . intermarriage with Slavs and Latins than ever with Jews'. In the years that Hitler lived in Vienna, Schönerer became one of his heroes. Parliament was being pressured to incorporate anti-Semitism into its programmes.

Another element in both the Signorelli and the Aliquis analysis is infanticide, an accusation that was constantly being made against both Jews and witches. Blood is also an element common in both analysis and in the witches' stories. Stadlen points out that Freud showed an interest in blood symbolism in the two popular Italian myths in Orvieto and Naples (Stadlen, 1997). One belief holds that a corporal on display in Orvieto Cathedral is stained by drops of blood that fell from the consecrated bread at the eucharist celebrated by a priest who had lost faith in the 'real' presence of Christ in the consecrated bread. The other myth concerns a powdery substance held in a vial in Naples. Popular belief among Neapolitans is that this is the dried blood of their patron, Saint Januarius, which liquefies on his feast day and on one other day every year.

5.7. Freud, blood and the witch

An identification with the witch is evident in the accusation of ritual blood sacrifice brought against both Jew and witch. Freud refers to this accusation against the Jews in his Aliquis analysis. The authors of the *Malleus* (1486) say that witch midwives offer newborn children to the devil. They also say that an inquisition was held 'because a certain man had missed his child from the cradle, and finding a congress of women in the night-time, swore that he saw them kill his child and drink its blood' (Kramer & Sprenger, 1486: 66). The blood symbolism found in the Aliquis and the Signorelli analyses is also found in the context of the witches. Both witches and Jews were accused of killing children for their blood. Blood is the central symbol in both analyses.

The witches were accused of killing children in ritual sacrifice at the Sabbats and using their blood. Many centuries later, similar accusations were being made against the Jews. The witch-hunt of the Jews intensified in Vienna in the 1890s, when the Christian Social Party moved into power in Austria. Freud wrote of 'the increasing importance of the effects of the anti-Semitic movement upon our emotional life' (Freud, 1900a: 196). The Jews had worked hard to assimilate, but they were reminded that total assimilation into Austrian life was impossible even for those who had chosen to be baptised into the Christian faith. Token acceptance of the Christian religion did not lessen persecution.

In his adolescence and 20s, Freud experienced strong embarrassment and shame at the actions of some Jews. Otto Weininger, after converting to Protestantism, shot himself. He had written a doctoral dissertation expounding his hatred of Jews and women. He wrote that even the most superior woman was immeasurably lower than the most debased man, just as Judaism was immeasurably beneath even degraded Christianity. He argued that as women lacked souls, so too did Jews. He concluded that Jews were degenerate women. His book was a hit in 1903. It was the talk of Vienna for months.

Decker says that Weininger expressed what many had come to believe: 'that women were an inferior order of being and that all other inferior groups could be compared with women when one was trying to explain the essence of their deficiencies' (Decker, 1986: 37–39). Although Weininger embraced Protestantism, his expressed views on women did not come from Luther but from Aquinas. It is two members of Thomas Aquinas' Dominican order, Sprenger and Kramer, the authors of the *Malleus* who elaborate the Thomistic view of women as intrinsically defective (Kramer & Sprenger, 1486: 44).

In 1882 a Viennese artisan was charged with inciting a crowd against the Jews. The artisan claimed to have information that the Jews committed ritual murder of Christian children to use their blood in the Matzah. He claimed to have read the account of this in a book written by a priest-professor at the University of Vienna. The general population were being fed the medieval myth that Jews killed children to use their blood for religious purposes (Decker, 1986: 35–36). This myth contravenes the biblical ruling on blood taboos, which included foods and was imposed on the Jewish people (Lev. 17:14).

Blood symbolism in the Bible had many meanings. Blood was used to seal covenants (Ex. 24:6–8). The sacredness of blood as life-giving and as expiation was symbolised by pouring out the blood on the altar. 'The life of every living thing is in the blood, and that is why the Lord has told the people of Israel that they shall not eat any meat with blood still in it' (Lev. 17:11, 14). The symbolism of defiling female blood is also found in Leviticus, chapter 18. Female blood was seen as a source of virulent contamination and defilement. Levitical purity laws affected women in particular. Rulings on the impurities caused by female blood (whether of menstruation, childbirth or irregular flows) were part of an 'all-pervasive blood taboo' that covered foods, sacrifice and effected separations of the sexes (Soskice, 1990: 43).

The symbolism of defiling female blood is also found in the gospel story of the healing of the woman with the haemorrhage (Mark 5:24–34). The woman in the story had suffered from severe bleeding for 12 years. Her problem was a constant source of ritual impurity, according to the laws of Leviticus. She had been treated by many doctors; she had spent all her money, but instead of getting better, she got worse. The gospel records that the woman told Jesus 'the whole truth' (Mark 5:33). In responding with compassion to this suffering woman, who was excluded from society because of her ailment, he restored her dignity. This woman, who was both defiling and infertile, is made whole and, presumably, fertile once again after being healed.

Soskice suggests that the pericope revolves around the contagious impurity of women. As a ritually unclean woman who could have defiled a holy man, this woman in the gospel story has acted audaciously according to Levitical law. Jesus addressed the woman with compassion and is not afraid of ritual defilement. The woman in the story can be taken as a symbol of all those who were excluded – pushed to the margins of religion and society. The story has elements of defilement and 'death' and of fecundity and new life. In all three Gospels, this story is set within the context of the story of a dead child, the daughter of Jairus.

Condren (1989) writes,

> Menstruating women were considered particularly potent and maybe even passionate creatures. A story is told of a monk who was advising a young male friend, whose problem was that "desire lay heavy upon the girl, for it is a third part as strong again in women as in men." The monk dealt with her problem by reducing her diet until at her annual testing he pricked her fingers with a needle. When no more blood came out of her hand he told her to "keep on this pittance until thy death". The Celi-De ascetic movement in the eighth and ninth century Ireland, which arose partly in response to the laxity of the earlier monasteries, believed that "excess of blood in the body" was the cause of passion.
>
> *(Condren, 1989: 92)*

Condren (1989) states that the understanding that women menstruated and did not die meant that they obviously had an excess of blood, which made them passionate creatures. Reducing a woman's diet until she suffered amenorrhea was the treatment prescribed for those who wished to be holy. Such women would easily be brought into submission. It was indeed power that was at stake (Condren, 1989:

92–93).The relating of blood and passionate desire may account for the inquisitors pricking with needles to discover the devil's stigmata and for Freud's patient, Eckstein, describing a scene 'where the diabolus sticks needles into her fingers and then places a candy on each drop of blood' (Letter to Fliess, 17 January 1897).

5.8. 'The secret gatherings'

On 24 January 1897, Freud gave his own interpretation to Fliess of the witches "flying" to the Sabbat: 'the broomstick they ride probably is the great Lord Penis'. He compares their 'secret gatherings' at the Sabbat to children at play in the streets.This is an important comparison for Freud. He repeats the comparison 12 years later at a scientific meeting of the Vienna Psychoanalytic Society, on 27 January 1909. After a presentation by Hugo Heller on the history of the devil, Freud adds, 'a few comments on the very interesting witch trials'. He says that in the witch trials, 'perversions play the main role'. He compares 'the proceedings in the witch trials' to 'children's games in a meadow' (Nunberg & Federn, 1967: 123).

In the time in between these two comparative references to children playing games, Freud published his famous *Screen Memories* (1899), which is considered autobiographical and which describes a scene of three children playing in a meadow (Freud, 1899: 311). He says the scene is 'fixed in my memory'.The children can be identified as himself; his slightly older nephew,John; and his younger niece, Pauline. They are picking yellow flowers.The boys 'fall on' the little girl and 'snatch away her flowers. She runs up the meadow in tears' (Freud, 1899: 311). Freud claims that he is projecting his young adult sexual phantasies back into his childhood and making a childhood screen memory out of them. He is claiming that the screen memory is covering up for the later repressed sexual phantasy of 'deflowering' a girl.

In this 1899 memory paper, Freud is again, it seems, preparing the ground for the retraction of his seduction theory.When he writes about the slipping away of repressed phantasies into childhood screen memories, he says, 'you will find the same thing invariably happening in hysterical patients' (Freud, 1899: 317). Freud is going to apply this screen memories concept to his patients and blame them for presenting him with childhood memories of seduction that he, at first, believed. Freud is also going to compare his psychoanalytic procedure to the judges' procedures in the witch trials. He claimed that the infantile elements in the witches' fantasies were not created under torture but merely squeezed out by it' (Nunberg & Federn, 1967: 123). We will see in the next chapter of my work how Freud will claim that the seduction stories that his psychoanalytic method 'squeezed out' of his patients were mere repressed sexual phantasies.

Notably, it is the 'proceedings' in the witch trials that Freud compares to children's games on a meadow. Freud had already, in his 24 January 1897 letter to Fliess, compared his own psychoanalytic procedure to the judges' procedures, by implication, when he calls their proceedings 'therapy'. Chapter 2 of Part 1 of this work showed how cruel their harsh therapy was. Why does this remind Freud of children's games?

In his *Screen Memories* (1899), Freud describes the cruel treatment that the little girl received from the two boys who were playing with her. In his essay 'Infantile Sexuality' (1905d), Freud writes on the 'cruel component of the sexual instinct'. He says,

> cruelty in general comes easily to the childish nature, since the obstacle that brings the instinct for mastery to a halt at another person's pain – namely a capacity for pity – is developed relatively late. . . . It may be assumed that the impulse of cruelty arises from the instinct for mastery. . . . Children who distinguish themselves by special cruelty towards animals and playmates usually give rise to a just suspicion of an intense and precocious sexual activity arising from the erotogenic zones. . . . The connection between the cruel and the erotogenic instincts, thus established in childhood, may prove unbreakable in later life.
>
> *(Freud, 1905d: 193)*

Freud is saying that children are naturally cruel because their capacity for pity is not developed. He suspects that cruel children have engaged in precocious sexual activity, and therefore, these two instincts remain connected to them in later life.

Relating this to the cruelty of the inquisitors and judges, Freud writes to Fliess 'the inquisitors prick with needles . . . not only the victims but also the executioners recalled in this their earliest youth' (17 January 1897). By these statements, Freud seems to be saying that not only were the witches phantasising but the inquisitors were also, and in both, 'perversions play a main role'. This throws more light of what Freud means when he says he understands the 'harsh therapy of the witches' judges'. In both the witches and judges 'the same polymorphously perverse disposition persists'. He says, 'this same disposition to perversion of every kind is a general and fundamental human characteristic' (Freud, 1905d: 191).

5.9. Emma Eckstein

The overlap in Freud's analysis of Emma Eckstein, in his Signorelli analysis and his Aliquis analysis and in the stories of the witches, is in the context of blood and blood symbolism. Emma Eckstein, whose blood flow endangered her life on more than one occasion, was one of Freud's first patients. Masson (1984) tells us that 'the exact nature of her complaints is unknown, but it appears that she suffered from stomach ailments and menstrual problems' (Masson, 1984: 57). Freud believed that sexual problems, and masturbation in particular, played a key role in neuroses. Fliess believed that vaginal problems could be solved by treating the nose, so the alliance between the two men led to the decision to operate on Emma's nose. Fliess operated on Emma's nose early in 1895.

Freud's correspondence with Fliess in the months that followed show the aftermath of the fateful operation: 'Eckstein's condition is still unsatisfactory . . . the day before yesterday she had a massive hemorrhage, probably as a result of expelling a bone chip the size of a heller; there were two bowls full of pus' (4 March 1895). Four days later, Freud wrote to Fliess again giving an account of what happened on 4 March: 'profuse bleeding had started'. Freud called in Dr Rosanes, who, upon examining Emma's nose,

> suddenly pulled at something like a thread, kept on pulling. Before either of us had time to think, at least half a meter of gauze had been removed from the cavity. The next moment came a flood of blood. . . . At the moment the foreign body came out and everything became clear to me. . . . I felt sick. . . . I do not believe it was the blood that overwhelmed me – at the moment strong emotions were welling up in me. So we had done her an injustice; she was not at all abnormal, rather, a piece of iodoform gauze had gotten torn off as you were removing it and stayed in for fourteen days, preventing healing; at the end it tore off and provoked the bleeding.

Freud admits that this 'resulted in endangering her life'. But he hastens to assure Fliess, 'You did it as well as one can do it' (8 March 1895).

In his next letters to Fliess, we see him more and more trying to exculpate Fliess by beginning to turn the blame for the bleeding onto Emma: 'The nervous effects of the incident are starting hysterical attacks at night and similar symptoms' (15 March 1895). Freud is describing her pain and swelling as having an 'unknown origin', even though he admits that 'she almost died' from the haemorrhages, and that 'Gussenbauer and Gersuny believe that she is bleeding from a large vessel – but which one – and on Friday they want to make an incision . . . to see if they can find the source' (20 March 1895).

Yet Freud is claiming that some of Emma's haemorrhages could be 'hysterical attacks'. Freud is beginning to claim that Emma is a hysterical bleeder. Masson (1984) comments that Freud is saying that 'her pains are unreal, and the haemorrhages which may have appeared to come from your operation were in fact psychologically caused – they were hysterical in origin, deriving from repressed wishes not unskilled surgeons' (Masson, 1984: 72).

During the autumn of 1895, Freud wrote *Project for a Scientific Psychology*, in which he described Emma's sexual molestation by a shopkeeper 'when she was a child of eight' (Freud, 1895: 354). In late 1895 Freud is convinced that Emma's unconscious memories of 'Scene 1' are real, and he is prepared to look at the effect that this early sexual trauma had on Emma's later emotional life. In 1896 Freud is taking a stand on the reality of seduction. But his sexual seduction theory received 'an icy reception'. He was already experiencing isolation and hostility. In a letter to Fliess on the 16 March 1896, he wrote, 'I am satisfied with my progress, but am contending with hostility and live in such isolation that one might imagine I had discovered the greatest truths'. After delivering the lecture on *The Aetiology of Hysteria*, he wrote to Fliess on 4 May 1896: 'I am as isolated as you would wish to be. Word was given out to abandon me. . . . My consulting room is empty'. It is in this context that Freud came to the conclusion that Eckstein 'bled out of *longing*'.

Freud turns his investigation into the haemorrhage away from the operation and seeks an explanation for the cause of the bleeding in Emma herself, in her hysterical longings.

In the same letter, Freud explains how he came to the decision that Emma's bleeding is hysterical. He says,

> She described a scene, from the age of fifteen, in which she suddenly began to bleed from the nose when she had the wish to be treated by a certain young doctor. . . . When she saw how affected I was by her first hemorrhage. . . . she experienced this as the realization of an old wish to be loved.

Freud writes that because of 'an unconscious wish to entice' him to the hospital, 'she renewed the bleeding, as an unfailing means of re-arousing my affection'. The tables have been turned on Emma; she is now painted as the seducer.

Having got a confession of what he claims is 'hysterical longing' out of Emma, Freud asks on 17 January 1897, why are the witches' confessions under torture 'so like the communications made by my patients in psychological treatment'? Have the witches *invented* the sexual seductions by the devil out of longing? Freud is struggling with a major problem. In the letter on the witches, he writes to Fliess, 'Eckstein has a scene [that is, remembers] where the diabolus sticks needles into her fingers and then places a candy on each drop of blood'. Emma is associating blood with the devil in a sexual context.

Freud is presenting Emma Eckstein as a hysterical bleeder. He also calls her a tormentor. It is in his efforts to make sense out of Emma's case that Freud has recourse to the witches. On 17 and 24 January 1897, Freud wrote about Emma Eckstein in the context of the witches. Freud is making analogies between what went on for both Emma and the witches. As we saw in Chapter 2, in the literature on witches, it was claimed that the devil sometimes caused the witches to fantasise that they had been copulating with him. Freud writes on 17 January 1897 that Emma has a scene where the 'diabolus' sticks needles into her fingers and then places a candy on each drop of blood. He continues on the theme of witches:

> the inquisitors prick with needles to discover the devil's stigmata and in a similar situation the victims think of the same old cruel story in fictionalized form (helped perhaps by disguises of the seducers). Thus, not only the victims but also the inquisitors recalled in this their earliest youth.

Freud seems to be considering two possibilities here: the prickings could recall seductions 'in their earliest youth' or, on the other hand, the stories of seduction were 'in fictionalized form'. We saw in the story of *The Judge* (1976), which Freud read, how a drop of blood spurting from the girl's finger was considered seductive (Meyer, 1976: 191). Is Emma's story of 'the diabolus' sticking needles in her fingers and placing a candy on each drop of blood a seductive act? Freud is trying to make sense of his patients' stories by examining the witches' stories. He wants to 'delve into the literature on this subject', because, as he is writing and thinking about Emma, he is asking, 'Why are their confessions under torture so like the communications made by my patients in psychic treatment?' The literature on the witches asserts that the devil sometimes caused them to fantasise or imagine that they had been copulating with him, so Freud was beginning to consider that sometimes his patients could be phantasising sexual abuse in infancy.

I am claiming that Freud's study of the witch trials was to affect his thinking in a profound way, causing him to adopt a more sceptical attitude towards memory, first of all in Eckstein's case and then in all his female patients from 1897. Freud had been first looking at Emma's problems as originating in early childhood seduction. He later interpreted the cause of Emma's bleeding as originating in herself. In Emma's case, Freud was examining the consequences of real events and the consequences of 'wish fulfilment' or phantasy. What was enabling Freud to make this shift? The witches may provide the answer. Freud was comparing what he was doing with his psychoanalytic patients with what the witches' judges were doing. What was he claiming he was doing by making this comparison? Do his claims stand up to scrutiny?

Freud had diagnosed Emma as a hysteric long before he erroneously attributed her haemorrhaging to hysterical longing. He told Fliess on 26 April 1896 that Emma's 'episodes of bleeding were hysterical, were occasioned by *longing*'. And on 4 June 1896, he wrote to Fliess, 'There is no doubt that her haemorrhages were due to wishes'. Much has been written on the incriminating gauze that had been drawn out of Emma after the 'bungled operation', but Freud had now drawn out of Emma an incriminating story about her own secret wishes.

Skues (1987) does a critical analysis of Masson's assertion in *The Assault on Truth* (1984), in which Masson attempts to determine the significance of Emma's hysterical bleeding in the development of Freud's theoretical thinking at the time, particularly in his abandonment of the seduction theory. While Skues makes a valid point, which I shall recount shortly, I disagree with the argument he puts up against Masson: 'the high point of the explanation of the haemorrhage as hysterical' was also 'the high point of the seduction theory' (Skues, 1987: 310).

The point that Skues makes regarding Emma's 'hysterical' bleeding is contained in his argument that

> Hysterical symptoms of the kind that Freud diagnosed in Eckstein are on the face of it organic symptoms, but they turn out to have a psychological not an organic cause. This is not to say that Freud's interpretation of the bleeding was not a bad diagnosis, but it is important to note that symptoms are no less real for their being hysterical in origin. Hysterical bleeding is just as real as that which results from physical trauma: the causes are different but again psychological causes are no less real than organic ones.
>
> *(Skues, 1987: 309)*

Skues thus refutes Masson's argument that Freud's shift in his interpretation of the account of seduction from being based in reality to being based in illusory phantasy was occasioned by the Eckstein episode.

Arthur Miller's play *The Crucible* (1953) makes a similar point to Skues's when he links the so-called witches, feared by the Puritans in Salem in 1692, with those suspected of communism who were feared by the US Congress. Witchcraft was purely a delusion, whereas the communist subversion feared in the 1950s was certainly a fact even though its significance was greatly exaggerated. But Miller's point is that when, out of hysterical fear, people overreact to a situation, be it real or imaginary, the consequences are the same. Miller's play was inspired by McCarthyism. Joseph R. McCarthy was appointed chairman of a committee set up in the 1950s in the United States to investigate the activities of any person suspected of being sympathetic to communism. At that time, there was an intense fear that communism might infiltrate the American government. The excessive zeal of the fanatical extremists who, with McCarthy, carried out the investigation was similar to the hysterical fear that surrounded the witch-hunt in Salem in 1692.

In both cases, as in the medieval and early modern witch-hunts and the Nazi atrocities in Germany, fanatical extremist leaders generated fear and hysteria among the ordinary people. A short extract from Miller's play illustrates the point. A young girl, Abigail, is being investigated by the judge to give evidence against a suspected witch, Tituba. Abigail had been sexually abused by John Proctor while she was his wife's servant girl. Tituba was a Barbados slave owned by a Puritan minister, Reverend Parris. Abigail accused Tituba:

> She comes to me every night to go and drink blood. . . . She comes to me while I sleep; she's always making me dream corruptions. Sometimes I wake and find myself standing in the open doorway and not a stitch on my body.

The Reverend Parris threatens Tituba: 'You will confess yourself or I will take you out and whip you to your death, Tituba'. After 'constant questioning' to extract a confession, Tituba warns her threateningly cruel owner that the devil 'bid me kill you'. She confessed how the devil said, 'you work for me, Tituba, and I make you free. I . . . put you high up in the air and you go-ne fly to Barbadoes' (Miller, 1953: 46–48). This is understandably a wishful fantasy or a 'hysterical longing' of Tituba's to escape from her cruel owner into freedom. Were Abigail's unconscious phantasies or dreams built up out of memory traces of earlier sexual abuse by John Proctor?

Freud presented Emma Eckstein as a hysterical bleeder. He also calls her a tormentor. Sinason (1994) describes Emma as a 'self-torturer' and claims satanistic abuse of Emma. She claims that Emma remembers a satanic ritual. She asks, 'Could it be that the bungled operation by Fliess contained within it not a sadistic recognition of those same wishes and processes but an acting out of them?' (Sinason, 1994: 2). Sinason is suggesting that Fliess could have been acting out sadistic wishes and processes in his operation on Emma. In this connection, she is also suggesting how Emma could evoke in Freud 'an understanding of the harsh therapy of the witches' judges'.

Unfortunately, Sinason does not give any evidence to back up her speculation. Showalter (1997) points out that 'Therapists speak of "satanic ritual abuse" rather than "alleged satanic ritual abuse which has never been proven or corroborated". "The result", writes Sherill Mulhern, "is that by the magic of language, ritual abuse suddenly appears"' (Showalter, 1997: 179). When people are reluctant to accept that parents can harm their own children, they use the myth of demonic possession to shift the blame onto satanic ritual abuse.

Sinason (1994) is trying to make sense of Freud's letter to Fliess on 24 January 1897, in which he connects the operation on Emma, the scene about the ritual circumcision of a girl, the secret rituals in a primeval devil religion and the harsh therapy of the witches' judges. Freud says, 'Connecting links abound'. Freud seems to be implying that the so-called witches' Sabbat could be a re-enactment of a primeval devil ritual and then drawing comparisons with Emma, whose bleeding was the secret enacting of her ritualistic longing. While Freud is looking at one theory that the witches' confessions were products of their imagination, he is also looking at the opposing theory that witchcraft is the remnant of 'a primeval devil religion with rites that are carried on secretly'. He is examining the stories of the witches and his patients in the context of a primeval sexual cult, but he never returns to this idea. It has been conclusively proven by many authors that while witches were commonly thought to be part of a secret sexual cult, 'no such cult in fact existed'.

Freud is drawing comparisons between the stories told by the witches, by his patients and by paranoics, 'whose complaints that excrement is put in their food, that they are maltreated at night in the most shameful way sexually'. In this letter, Freud is opening up all possible avenues that will throw further light on his 'brand-new prehistory of hysteria' (Letter to Fliess, 17 January 1897). The literature on witches also shows that the judges were using harsh therapy to squeeze confessions of abuse out of the witches. When Freud says on 24 January 1897 that he 'understands the harsh therapy of the witches' judges', it is difficult to know, at first glance, what exactly he means. One needs to know what his understanding and his interpretation of what was involved in the European witch-hunts of the fifteenth and sixteenth centuries are.

On 27 January 1909, Freud again refers to the witches at a scientific meeting of the Vienna Psychoanalytic Society. He said that the confessions of the witches were not forced on them – that is, 'were not created under torture but merely squeezed out by it' (Nunberg & Federn, 1967: 123). In other words, the harsh therapy may be regrettable, but what actually emerged under torture, Freud is affirming, was symbolically true. Freud believes that the witches were saying what the torturers and inquisitors wanted them to say in order to put an end to the torture *and* were saying it because it corresponded to their psychic reality. Freud seems to be saying that even though the means of eliciting the confessions from the witches was perhaps regrettable, after it came bona fide confessions when symbolically interpreted. This,

Swales suggests, is what Freud is comparing with what he is doing in psychoanalysis (Swales, 1982b: 25).

Freud is justifying the harshness of the methods used by the witches' judges by their results: confessions and admissions of guilt. This is a matter of the end justifying the means. Freud is modelling his newly founded psychoanalysis on a medieval inquisitorial system that used harsh therapy to achieve its aim. Why does Freud model his technique on that used by the witches' judges and inquisitors? Why does he call them identical? The crime that the witches were accused of was performed secretly, in league with an elusive, invisible devil who possessed them. While Freud did not grant reality to the devil, he said that his hysterics also had a 'foreign body'. First, he claimed that this 'foreign body' was in the form of repressed memories, and later, as is evident in the minutes of the Vienna Psychoanalytic Society on 27 January 1909, Freud claimed that the devil 'represents the personification of the unconscious and repressed instincts, of the sexual components' in humankind (Nunberg & Federn, 1967: 122).

On 8 March 1895, Freud had described the 'foreign body' as the half metre of gauze left by mistake in Emma's nose. After it was pulled out, Freud had to flee from the room. On 17 January 1897, the 'foreign body' is no longer a physical reality; it is a delusive psychic creation, a 'devil', a creation by the witch. Freud has recourse to the witch to throw light on the ongoing formulating of his theory of hysteria. Freud speculates about whether the devil's sexual abuse is a phantasy on the part of the witch. Freud is questioning whether the seduction stories told by his patients were true or invented.

A week later, on 24 January 1897, Freud wrote to Fliess once again about witches, blood and the devil in the context of Emma Eckstein's operation. Freud is drawing comparisons between the witches and Emma, who almost bled to death, a near tragedy that Freud blamed on her own perverse wishes. Just as the witches' judges extracted the incriminating confessions out of the witches by their harsh therapy, so too did Freud squeeze out the secret confession out of Emma. Devil, witch, hysteria, blood and sexual imagery are all woven together into a Freudian web that one can 'unpick' only with difficulty, if at all.

5.10. Conclusion

I have shown that because Freud did not have the evidence that he had claimed he had on 21 April 1896, when he presented his theory of sexual molestation in childhood, he continued to search for evidence. He wrote to Fliess on 6 December 1896: 'It seems to me more and more that the essential point of hysteria is that it results from perversion on the part of the seducer, and more and more that heredity is seduction by the father'.

A 'paternal aetiology' would provide the necessary evidence to prove his theory. But he failed to find the necessary evidence. I have shown that, at the same time, he was studying the medieval book the *Malleus* and later literature on witches and witch trials, a study that led him to identify the stories of his patients with the witches' stories and to identify his psychoanalytic procedure with the procedures used by the judges in the witch trials. I have shown how this study first led Freud to the claim that his patients, like the witches, were victims of their imaginations. This enabled Freud to consider his patients' seduction stories as perverse fantasies rather than pure memories. I have shown that as a result of this shift in his thinking, Freud was, during this period, writing papers on memory – substitute memory, false memory, screen memories – that were preparing the ground for the retraction of his seduction theory, which had memory as its key factor. The next chapter will examine Freud's retraction of his seduction theory.

Importantly, although Freud retracted his seduction theory, he never withdrew his belief that *some* cases of hysteria were caused by sexual seduction in childhood.

CHAPTER 6
WHY DID FREUD ABANDON HIS SEDUCTION THEORY?

6.1. Introduction: 'I no longer believe in my neurotica'

Freud had not written any case history to back up his theory of hysteria. He was very aware of this lacuna in his work. In his prefatory remarks to the 'Dora' case, Freud is claiming that in the 'Dora' case, he is bringing forward some of the material on which his seduction theory was based. He wrote,

> No doubt it was awkward that I was obliged to publish the results of my enquiries without there being any possibility of other workers in the field testing and checking them, particularly as those results were of a surprising and by no means gratifying character. But it will be scarcely less awkward now that I am beginning to bring forward some of the material upon which my conclusions were based and make it accessible to the judgement of the world.
>
> *(Freud, 1905e: 7)*

Freud is saying that his investigation of his 'seduction theory' has been carried to a conclusion and that he is now, in the 'Dora' case, making 'accessible to the judgement of the world' some of the material upon which his conclusions were based. This statement of openness appears to be honest but it is obscuring the fact that the 'Dora' case does not back up his 'seduction theory', and it is obscuring the second fact that there had ever been a seduction theory or that he had abandoned it. He told Fliess privately on 21 September 1897, 'I no longer believe in my neurotica'; that is, he no longer believed in his seduction theory. He also said in the same letter, 'Of course I shall not tell it in Dan, nor speak of it in Askelon, in the land of the Philistines'. The 'Philistines' did not hear until 1905 about his abandonment of his seduction theory (Freud, 1905d: 190). Importantly, although Freud abandoned his seduction theory, he never withdrew his belief that *some* cases of hysteria were a deferred consequence of sexual abuse in childhood.

6.2. 'Of course, I shall not tell it in Dan'

Why is Freud not prepared to admit publicly that his seduction theory has not been verified by factual evidence? He could have admitted his mistake and said that seduction played a big role in hysteria, which would have been acceptable while abandoning his theory. But Freud was not prepared to do that. In his 1905d and 1906 papers, he leads us into a maze of sentences about his theory that can mesmerise and deceive. In his 1905d paper, Freud claimed to have reached a new understanding of hysteria. Writing on the effects of seduction in *Three Essays on the Theory of Sexuality* (1905d) Freud states,

> I cannot admit that in my paper on the aetiology of hysteria that I exaggerated the frequency or importance of that influence, though I did not then know that people who remain normal may have had the same experiences in their childhood, and though I consequently overrated the importance of seduction.
>
> *(Freud, 1905d: 190)*

Upon examining this statement, we learn that Freud is saying that he was not trying to exaggerate the frequency or importance of seduction. He is saying that he overrated the importance of seduction because he 'did not then know' that numerous people who experienced seduction remained 'normal'. This appears an honest confession, but it is not honest, because if we look at the 1896c paper, it clearly shows that Freud *did* have this knowledge: 'We have heard and have acknowledged that there are numerous people who have a very clear recollection of infantile sexual experiences and who nevertheless do not suffer from hysteria' (Freud, 1896c: 211). Why is Freud denying in 1905 that he had this knowledge in 1896?

Again in his 1906 paper, he tells us that it was because 'a disproportionately large number of cases in which sexual seduction by an adult or by older children played the chief part in the history of the patient's childhood' that he had 'overestimated the frequency of such events (though in other respects they were not open to doubt)' (Freud, 1906a: 274). This also appears an honest statement, but I have just pointed out that Freud did know in 1896 that 'numerous people who experienced seduction did not become hysterics' (Freud, 1896c: 211). Freud has in brackets 'though in other respects they were not open to doubt'; that is, he is saying that he did not overestimate the importance of seduction. But this is in direct contradiction to what he said in his 1905 paper: 'I . . . overrated the importance of seduction' (Freud, 1905d:190).

By making these equivocal statements in 1905 and 1906, Freud is claiming that he is correcting the 'misunderstandings' under which his theory then laboured. What caused the misunderstanding? Freud is denying that his own wild exaggerating is to blame. He is still claiming that the causes of hysteria 'can be discovered with certainty by psycho-analytic investigation' (Freud, 1905d: 150). Therefore, he is not blaming his inquisitorial procedure of squeezing out of his patients the stories of seduction that he wanted to hear. Instead, he blames 'chance' and 'falsifications made by hysterics in their memories' (Freud, 1906a: 274). 'Chance' sent onto his couch 'a disproportionately large number of cases in which sexual seduction played the chief part in the history of the patient's childhood'. Yet he is claiming that these same patients were presenting 'falsifications' in their memories of childhood seduction. In other words, this 'disproportionately large number of patients in which sexual seduction played the chief part in their childhood' were the same ones who were presenting 'falsifications' in their 'memories'. That exonerates the 'chance' of any blame, so the blame lies solely on the shoulders of his patients.

Freud claimed that what led him to 'correct' his theory was the 'fact' that he could not distinguish between 'falsifications made by hysterics in their memories of childhood and traces of real events' (Freud, 1906a: 274). Freud seems to have forgotten the claim that he made on at least three occasions in *Studies on Hysteria* (1895) – that is, that his pressure technique worked 'infallibly'. He had said in 1895 about applying pressure, 'Only in this manner can we find what we are in search of, but in this manner we shall find it infallibly' (Freud, 1895d: 270). Later, he said, 'we must repeat the pressure and represent ourselves as infallible, till at least we are really told something' (Freud, 1895d: 279). Again, he claimed, 'If we examine with a critical eye the account that the patient has given us without much trouble or resistance, we shall quite infallibly discover gaps and imperfections in it' (Freud, 1895d: 293). And yet Freud's infallible method did not show up in 1896 the 'falsifications' made by his patients. It had led him into 'error', which he admits in 1925.

Freud addresses Fliess on 26 April 1895 as 'Dear magician', in a letter that presents himself also in the role of magician. He again presents himself in the role of magician when he reveals that 'The procedure by pressure is no more than a trick' (Freud, 1895d: 278). Freud is not admitting that his procedure is responsible for the 'falsifications' that he squeezed out of his patients. And because he does not see his inquisitorial procedure as responsible for his mistakes, he continues to use it, as we will see and then examine in detail in the 'Dora' case.

In spite of his claims in *Studies on Hysteria* (1895) that his technique works infallibly, Freud did not recognise at the time that what he squeezed out of his patients was 'false memories'. Freud wrote in his paper 'Screen Memories' (1899) his defence of the genuineness of a childhood memory. He asserted that

> every suppressed phantasy . . . tends to slip away into a childhood scene. But . . . this cannot occur unless there is a memory-trace the content of which offers the phantasy a point of contact – [and] comes, as it were, half way to meet it.
>
> *(Freud, 1899: 318)*

This shows Freud's first shift towards phantasy, where he conceived of the possibility of seduction stories as perverse phantasies rather than pure memories. We examined in Chapter 5 the reasons for this first stage in the reversal of his seduction theory.

In his 1906 paper, we see his second shift from his sexual seduction theory to his theory of phantasies of seduction: 'I have learned to explain a number of phantasies of seduction as attempts at fending off memories of the subject's *own* sexual activity (infantile masturbation)' (Freud, 1906a: 274). Freud said that this new 'clarification' made it necessary to 'modify my view of the mechanism of hysterical symptoms. They were now no longer to be regarded as direct derivatives of the repressed memories' of seduction, but instead, they were derivatives of the patient's own adolescent phantasies, which in turn were 'built up out of and over childhood memories' of their own sexual activity (Freud, 1906a: 274). Freud now claims that the subject's own infantile sexual activity was the most important element in the aetiology of hysteria. The traumatic element – 'the most important of my early mistakes' – had now lost its importance (Freud, 1906a: 274).

This admission by Freud of his 'most important' mistake conceals his real mistake, which he does not admit: the claim that he made about the specific aetiology of hysteria. In his seduction theory, he claimed that hysteria is always, in all cases, a deferred consequence of infantile sexual abuse. Freud fudges over this claim of specific aetiology by saying,

> I ceased also to lay exaggerated stress on the *accidental* influencing of sexuality on which I had sought to thrust the main responsibility for the causation of the illness. . . . I believed at that time – though with reservations – that a passive attitude in these scenes produced a predisposition to hysteria. . . . I was obliged to abandon this view entirely.
>
> *(Freud, 1906a: 275)*

Freud had brought no case of seduction to a satisfactory conclusion which could back up his theory. He then changed his first premise in his argument and this conceals his real mistake.

Freud abandoned his seduction theory of the specific aetiology of hysteria in favour of his new theory of the phantasies of seduction (Freud, 1906a: 275). The real reason why Freud abandoned his seduction theory was because he was making wild generalisations about 'seduction'. And having presented these wild generalisations about seduction as a theory of the aetiology of hysteria he proceeded to try to prove he was right by squeezing out of his patients the stories of seduction he needed to prove his theory.

Freud's abandonment of his seduction theory has been discussed at length by many authors, but what has not been given any consideration is the important question of what led Freud to formulate this hypothesis in the first place. Freud made a wild guess that all hysterics were sexually abused in childhood. He was always trying to make sense of hysteria; he wanted to be the first to discover the solution to a thousand-year-old problem – that is, the discovery of the aetiology of hysteria, 'the discovery of a caput Nili in neuropathology' (Letter to Fliess on 26 April 1896). He wanted to prove that his hypothesis was true, so he insisted with all 'eighteen cases' (Freud, 1896c: 199) or all 'thirteen cases', (Freud, 1896b: 152, 163) – whichever is the correct figure – that they were sexually abused in childhood. It was only by an inquisitorial procedure, the infallible method, that he could achieve his aim. But patients ran away from his harsh therapy, leaving him with no other option but to abandon his hypothesis of sexual seduction as the specific aetiology of hysteria. While Freud is claiming therapeutic success in his 1896 papers, he revealed later to Fliess on 17 December 1896 that 'So far not a single case is finished'.

6.3. Stories 'I . . . forced on them'?

In 1925 Freud wrote of an 'error' into which he fell for a while and 'which might well have had fatal consequences' for the whole of his work. He said,

> Under the influence of the technical procedure which I used at that time, the majority of my patients reproduced, from their childhood, scenes in which they were sexually seduced by some grown-up person. With female patients the part of seducer was almost always assigned to their father. I believed these stores . . . of sexual seduction in childhood. . . . When, however, I was at last obliged to recognise that these scenes of seduction had never taken place, and that they were only phantasies which my patients had made up, which I myself had perhaps forced on them, I was for some time completely at a loss. . . . When I had pulled myself together, I was able to draw the right conclusions from my discovery: namely, that the neurotic symptoms were not related directly to actual events but to wishful phantasies. . . . I do not believe even now that I forced the seduction-phantasies on my patients, that I 'suggested' them. I had in fact stumbled for the first time upon the Oedipus complex . . . which I did not recognise in its disguise of phantasy. . . . When the mistake had been cleared up, the path to the study of the sexual life of children lay open.
>
> *(Freud, 1925d: 33–35)*

In that published statement in 1925, Freud is again claiming that his mistake was that he 'believed these stories . . . of sexual seduction in childhood'. He does not reveal what 'obliged' him to recognise that 'these scenes of seduction had never taken place'. For a solution to that problem, we need to go to his private letters to Fliess. Twice in March 1897, he wrote to Fliess, 'I have not yet finished a single case', and on 21 September, he again writes of 'The continual disappointment in my efforts to bring a single analysis to a real conclusion'. He is not even getting the scenes of seduction: 'the unconscious memory does not break through, so that the secret of childhood experiences is not disclosed'. These revelations to Fliess show that Freud had been claiming results of his investigation before he had actually proven his theory. He could not get the evidence he was looking for from his patients. So he turned to another source.

Freud wrote to Fliess on 24 January 1897 comparing the witches' Sabbat to children' play: 'Their secret gatherings, with dancing and entertainment, can be seen any day in the streets where children play'. In his *Three Essays* (1905d), Freud described children as having a polymorphously perverse disposition. He says that this innately perverse disposition means that they put up little resistance to sexual excesses. Shame, disgust and morality are not innately present. Freud compared children's behaviour at this primitive stage to the 'average uncultivated woman in whom the same polymorphously perverse disposition persists'. If such a woman 'is led on by a clever seducer she will find every sort of perversion to her taste and will retain them as part of her own sexual activities' (Freud, 1905d:191). Freud says that an 'immense number of women who are prostitutes or who must be supposed to have an aptitude for prostitution' retain and exploit this infantile perverse disposition (Freud, 1905d:191). What does Freud think the witches have done with their polymorphously perverse disposition? Dammed it up by excessive repression or persisted in perverse infantilism?

Freud was unable to accept the possibility of so many perverse fathers as is stated in his letter to Fliess on 21 September 1897 and so he pressed on to the discovery of infantile, polymorphously perverse sexuality. In *An Autobiographical Study* (1925d) Freud says,

> I found myself faced by the fact of infantile sexuality. Childhood was looked upon as 'innocent' and free from the lusts of sex, and the fight with the demon of 'sensuality' was not thought to begin until the troubled age of puberty.

Freud's reference to his 'fight with the demon' shows he is still identifying with the medieval and early modern witches' judges in their fight with the demon who possessed the witches. Freud is asserting that 'the sexual function starts at the beginning of life and reveals its presence by important signs even in childhood' (Freud, 1905d: 191).

Freud tried to cover up the fact that he abandoned his original theory that hysteria is always a deferred consequence of sexual abuse before puberty, usually by adults. He says, 'I have never repudiated or abandoned the importance of sexuality and of infantilism'. But his first theory was not a theory of the importance of sexuality or infantilism but rather a 'seduction' theory that he did abandon. He is still not coming out clearly with what his three 1896 papers on the seduction theory was: he says in 1906, 'I have had to abandon a specific aetiology depending on the particular form of the childhood experiences concerned' (Freud, 1906a: 278). But Freud has just written, 'I believed at that time [in 1896] . . . that a passive attitude in these scenes produced a predisposition to hysteria. . . . Later I was obliged to abandon this view entirely' (Freud, 1906a: 275). This clearly states the particular form of childhood experience – 'a passive attitude in these scenes' – that Freud had to eliminate from his 'specific' aetiology of hysteria.

In Freud's psychoanalytic examination of neurotics by his 'infallible' method, he had made an 'error'. He admits in 1925 to 'an error into which I fell for a while and which might well have had fatal consequences for the whole of my work' (Freud, 1925d: 33). It was under the influence of his inquisitorial procedure that his patients produced scenes of being sexually seduced by an adult. Freud admits that perhaps he forced these scenes on them, but he quickly goes on to blame his patients: it was their 'wishful phantasies'. Then he adds, 'I do not believe even now that I forced the seduction-phantasies on my patients' (Freud, 1925d: 34).

In 1906 Freud is certain that his inquisitorial procedure was not to blame. He calls it 'that irreplaceable method of research' that has uncovered a different phenomenon: phantasies. He says, 'the most complicated symptoms are themselves revealed as representing, by means of "conversion", phantasies which have a sexual situation as their subject matter'. Hysteria, he says, 'is concerned *only* with the patient's repressed sexuality' (Freud, 1906a: 278, emphasis mine). Presumably, he means excessively repressed sexuality. What I find contradictory is that Freud goes on to say that 'analysis invariably shows that it is the sexual component of the traumatic experience – a component that is never lacking – which has produced the traumatic result' (Freud, 1906a: 278).

In *New Introductory Lectures on Psychoanalysis* (1933a), Freud compared the opposition to psychoanalysis to a practice in the medieval period when an evildoer, or even an opponent, was put in the pillory and given over to maltreatment by the mob. He compared mob behaviour to the resistance that he had to struggle against in individuals (Freud, 1933a: 170–172). Freud claimed in this paper that his abandonment of the seduction theory came as a result of his female patients bringing him stories of seduction that were untrue. In 1933 Freud is clearly still blaming the patients for his early mistakes.

We need to restate here what the original seduction theory was because Freud's later accounts misstate his original theory. In 1896 Freud stated his original theory regarding the seduction of his patients:

> Before they come for analysis the patients know nothing about these scenes. They are indignant as a rule if we warn them that such scenes are going to emerge. Only the strongest compulsion of the treatment can induce them to embark on a reproduction of them.
>
> *(Freud, 1896c: 204)*

When we compare this 1896 account with his 1933 account of his seduction theory, we see that his later account misleads one to think that people came to him complaining that they had been sexually assaulted and that he at first believed them but now realises they were phantasising. These are his own words in 1933:

In the period in which the main interest was directed to discovering infantile sexual traumas, almost all my women patients told me that they had been seduced by their father. I was driven to recognise in the end that these reports were untrue and so came to understand that hysterical symptoms are derived from phantasies and not from real occurrences. It was only later that I was able to recognise in this phantasy of being seduced by the father the expression of the typical Oedipus complex in women.

(Freud, 1933a: 120)

Freud, in this statement, is misstating his original theory; he is treating his patients as if their memory cannot be trusted. He is blaming his female patients for his seduction theory; they misled him with their 'memories' of seduction.

What Freud does not acknowledge is that it was the inquisitorial procedure he used to extract the 'memories' out of his patients that forced them to produce the scenes that he required in order to substantiate his seduction theory. Freud was suggesting to his patients what to say and leading them into saying what he wanted to hear. Freud had already revealed to Fliess on 21 September 1897 that he had not brought 'a single analysis to a real conclusion' and that his patients were 'running away', so he was not getting 'the complete success on which I had counted'. In his letter to Fliess, he was also blaming his patients for not giving him the scenes of seduction he was so desperately looking for in order to prove his theory: 'Unconscious memory does not break through, so that the secret of childhood experiences is not disclosed'.

Freud, even before he makes known to Fliess that he has abandoned his seduction theory, has already been on the trail of fantasy as a solution to this age-old problem that no one had yet solved. His two January 1897 letters to Fliess show his interest in fantasy; they show the similarities Freud is drawing between the witches and his patients and between his technique and the harsh therapy of the witches' judges. His letters between January 1897 and his famous letter of 21 September 1897 show his increasing interest in fantasy and in the medieval and early modern literature on witches and witch trials.

By September 1897, Freud's 'insight' tells him that 'one cannot distinguish between truth and fiction' in the unconscious, so there was the possibility that 'the sexual fantasy' of the patients was seizing upon the theme of parents. He is ready to drop his theory of sexual seduction in childhood, because, he tells Fliess, 'It seems once again arguable that only later experiences give the impetus to fantasies'. I am claiming that Freud's study of the literature on witches led him to the 'insight' that his patients were fantasising, just as it was claimed that the witches were fantasising sexual seduction by the devil. Freud says in *New Introductory Lectures* (1933a) that he was driven to change his theory of seduction to phantasies of seduction. Is it possible that his reference in this lecture to the practices in the medieval and early modern periods provide us with a clue to what drove him to this 'insight'? I am claiming that Freud drew this 'insight' from his reading about witches. We recall that Freud wrote to Fliess about the medieval book on witches: 'I have ordered the *Malleus Maleficarum*, and . . . I shall study it diligently'. Boguet (1590) had written in *An Examen on Witches* that Satan

> reveals to them in their sleep what happens at the Sabbat so vividly that they think they have been there; and therefore, they can give a marvellously accurate account of it. But I hold that this never happens except to such as have previously attended in person the witches' assembly.
>
> *(Boguet, 1590: 51)*

I believe that Freud's reading of this literature on witches accounts for his first shift towards the 'insight' that the patient's phantasies, mostly produced during puberty, were modelled unconsciously on authentic memories of childhood seduction.

Freud has shifted from memories of seduction to wishful phantasies of being seduced by the father. Not fathers but rather children are perverse. Freud writes,

> And now we find the phantasy of seduction once more in the pre-Oedipus . . . but the seducer is regularly the mother. Here, however, the phantasy touches the ground of reality, for it was really the mother who by her activities over the child's bodily hygiene inevitably stimulated, and perhaps even roused, for the first time, pleasurable sensations in her genitals.
>
> *(Freud, 1933a: 20, 154)*

Then the mother forbids the pleasurable activity to which she herself introduced the child during hygiene. This can turn the girl's powerful attachment to her mother into hostility towards her. In his 1931 paper *Female Sexuality*, Freud writes that 'When the girl turns away from her mother, she also makes over to her father her introduction into sexual life. . . . in phantasies in later years, the father so regularly appears as the sexual seducer' (Freud, 1931: 238). Freud had concluded that whereas the father's seduction was mere phantasy, the mother's seduction 'touches the ground of reality'. Gallop says that Freud has solved his riddle: the mother is the 'source' of sexuality, of perversion, of neuroses. The detective work is complete' (Bernheimer & Kahane, 1985: 212–213).

We shall see in the next chapter that Freud claimed in the 'Dora' case that by his purely psychological technique, he could extract unconscious thoughts from the raw material of the patient's associations (Freud, 1905e: 112). He claimed that he adjusted his views to give an account of the facts that had been observed. He says, 'I take no pride in having avoided speculation' (Freud, 1905e: 112–113). His new theory of hysteria points to nothing other than 'the patient's sexual activity'. He is saying in the 'Dora' case that it is the patient's own premature sexual activity that provides the motive power for every single symptom of hysteria; it is the patient's own sexual function with its excitations that is the foundation of hysteria (Freud, 1905e: 114). Freud blamed the patient for his lack of success when on the 21 September 1897 he told Fliess of his abandonment of the seduction theory. He wrote in the same letter of 'this collapse of everything valuable'.

6.4. Conclusion

I have shown that Freud claimed in his 1905 and 1906 papers not to have knowledge regarding seduction that his 1896 papers show he had. I have shown that Freud's later account of the seduction theory in his 1933 paper is misleading because it does not give a correct account of his original theory.

I have looked at the reasons why Freud abandoned his seduction theory. I have shown that the reasons that Freud gave in his 1905 and 1906 papers were not the real reasons for abandoning his theory. I am claiming that the reasons why Freud gave up his seduction theory are to be found in his private letters to Fliess written between January and September 1897, stating that he had not finished a single case. These revelations to Fliess contradict his claims in his 1896 papers. I am also claiming that Freud's letters to Fliess show that he made the shift in his theory to phantasies as a result of reading about the witches in the medieval and early modern literature written by the witches' judges and inquisitors. Freud wrote in 1925 that the scenes of seduction were 'only phantasies' that 'I myself had perhaps forced on them', but he quickly added, 'I do not believe even now that I forced the seduction – phantasies on my patients, that I "suggested" them' (Freud, 1925d:34). An examination of the 'Dora' case in Chapter 7 will show that Freud did use force to press his patients into confessing what he wanted to hear. In this way, his procedure is similar to the harsh therapy of the witches' judges.

There has been much debate about the seduction theory in recent years. Cioffi started it in 1974, though his work was not acknowledged until Stadlen drew attention to it in the early 1980s. Other significant authors whose work I consulted include Schimek (1987) and Schatzman & Israëls (1993), but I have drawn mostly on Stadlen Seminars (1996–).

CHAPTER 7

THE 'DORA' CASE

7.1. Introduction

Freud presents 'Dora' as his principal paradigm case for his specific aetiology of hysteria. He wrote it to throw light on the 'illness symptoms'. Stadlen asks a fundamental question: 'was the subject of Freud's principal paradigm case for "hysteria" an "hysteric"?' (Stadlen, 1989: 196). Dora was 'handed over' to Freud by her father to 'bring her to reason' (Freud, 1905e: 19, 26). The question raised by Stadlen is highly significant for my hypothesis because it parallels the question on the witches: were the women who were handed over to Judges Bodin, Remy and Boguet witches? A second question is, how did Freud 'treat' Dora? How did he carry out his investigations into Dora's 'illness'? Do his investigations bear any comparisons with the judges' investigations in the witch trials?

7.2. A technique 'completely revolutionized'?

Nowhere else does Freud offer both his theory and his investigatory procedures for our close scrutiny as he does in the 'Dora' case. It is here and only here that Freud's practice and the theory that informed his practice can be examined in depth. In the 'Dora' case, he demonstrates the procedures he uses to extract from Dora the information he needed to back up his new aetiology of hysteria. By the turn of the century, Freud claims to have abandoned the pressure technique described in *Studies on Hysteria* (1895), when in the autumn of 1899 he began his treatment of Dora. He is, of course, referring to pressure with the hand on the patient's forehead that he admitted was 'no more than a trick', (Freud, 1895d: 278), but he had claimed that 'The pressure technique in fact never fails' (Freud, 1895d: 281).

Freud says in *Fragment of an Analysis of a Case of Hysteria* (1905) that he has 'completely revolutionized' his psychoanalytic technique. Referring to his pressure technique, he says, 'I have abandoned this technique, because I found it totally inadequate. . . . I now let the patient . . . choose the subject of the day's work. . . . the new technique is far superior to the old' (Freud, 1905e: 12). But, disappointingly, Freud ends by saying, 'I have in this paper left entirely out of account the technique . . . by whose means alone the pure metal of valuable unconscious thoughts can be extracted from the raw material of the patient's associations' (Freud, 1905e: 112). Freud is here claiming that he can 'extract' unconscious thoughts out of Dora. By using the word 'extract', Freud is indicating that his technique forcibly draws out thoughts despite resistance. The judges similarly used force to extract a confession out of the witch.

Through the 'old' technique, which he had claimed was infallible, Freud used pressure to squeeze out the truth (Freud, 1905e: 270). His 'new' technique uses force to extract the truth. Freud claims he is only dealing with 'the internal structure of a case of hysteria' (Freud, 1905e: 112). He states explicitly here that in Dora he is dealing with 'a case of hysteria'. Did Freud extract from Dora the necessary 'confession' to diagnose her as a hysteric? What 'secrets' did Freud extract out of Dora?

The central scene in the case takes place in Herr K.'s shop when Dora was 'a child of fourteen' (Freud, 1905e: 28). Freud describes the scene:

> Herr K. had made an arrangement with her and his wife that they should meet him one afternoon at his place of business in the principal square of B, so as to have a view of a church festival. He persuaded his wife, however, to stay at home, and sent away his clerks, so that he was alone when the girl arrived. When the time for the procession approached, he asked the girl to wait for him at the door which opened on to the staircase leading to the upper storey, while he pulled down the outside shutters. He then came back and instead of going out by the door, suddenly clasped the girl to him and pressed a kiss upon her lips.
>
> *(Freud, 1905e: 28)*

Freud, in his reporting, distances himself from the scene of the kiss by repeatedly referring to 'the girl' who made this confession to him. By using the word 'confession', Freud is implying guilty activity on Dora's part because he says that she kept the incident a secret until 'her confession' during treatment (Freud, 1905e: 28). Freud is acting like the judges in the witch trials by distancing himself from the person, Dora, to pass judgement on 'the girl', on 'this child of fourteen' from whom he has extracted a secret confession.

What is the crime to which Dora confesses? Freud tells us that in a situation that should 'call up a distinct feeling of excitement', this girl of 14 had 'a violent feeling of disgust' (Freud, 1905e: 28). Therefore, this disgust is, according to Freud, a *reversal of affect*; it is also 'a displacement' from the genitals to the oral orifice. It is this disgust that allows Freud to diagnose and label 'this child of fourteen' as 'entirely and completely hysterical'. Witches confessed to 'disgust' in their sexual relations with the devil (Remy, 1595: 60). Dora is found guilty of not succumbing to a sexual seduction by Herr K. and of feeling disgusted when, according to Freud, she should feel pleasure. When Herr K. pressed a kiss on Dora's lips, Freud determined that

> This was just the situation to call up a distinct feeling of sexual excitement in a girl of fourteen who had never before been approached. But Dora had at that moment a violent feeling of disgust, tore herself free from the man, and hurried past him to the staircase and from there to the street door.
>
> *(Freud, 1905e: 28)*

This, Freud says, is pathognomonic of hysteria.

Stadlen (1989) points out that in making this diagnosis,

> Freud here presents a new – indeed, a highly original – criterion for "hysteria". Freud does not seek to justify it. He simply asserts it. This new criterion appears to be a consequence of the theory of "hysteria" that was to be "substantiated" by the "Dora" case. Once again Freud is caught up in circularity.
>
> *(Stadlen, 1989: 201)*

In the 'Dora' case, Freud proposed to 'substantiate' his earlier views on 'the pathogenesis of hysterical symptoms'. He says,

> if it is true that the causes of hysterical disorders are to be found in the intimacies of the patient's psychosexual life, and that hysterical symptoms are the expression of their most secret and repressed wishes, then the complete elucidation of a case of hysteria is bound to involve the revelation of those intimacies and the betrayal of those secrets.
>
> *(Freud, 1905e: 7–8)*

But it is necessary to point out that the views on the causes of hysterical symptoms that Freud puts forward in the 'Dora' case are not the views he has put forward in 1896, so they are not substantiating his earlier views, but through his circularity of argument, we could be deceived into thinking that they are the same views.

Continuing his reflection on the central scene in the case, Freud says,

> In this scene . . . the behaviour of this child of fourteen was already entirely and completely hysterical. I should without question consider a person hysterical in whom the occasion for sexual excitement elicited feelings that were preponderantly or exclusively unpleasurable; and I should do so whether or not the person was capable of producing somatic symptoms.
>
> *(Freud, 1905e: 28)*

This is Freud's new criteria for defining hysteria. The 'unpleasurable feelings' or feelings of 'disgust' when Herr K. kissed her are what Freud calls the 'symptoms' of Dora's 'hysteria'.

Nelson (1978) points out that there is nothing intrinsic about a kiss that determines its erotic meaning. Such meaning developed in certain societies. The same physical act can have a whole range of different meanings, depending on the context (Nelson, 1978: 26). In the Dora incident in Herr K.'s shop, in that context, the kiss could be felt as exploitative rather than pleasurable. There is no reason for diagnosing Dora as hysterical simply because she felt disgust when Herr K. forcibly kissed her.

Freud's notion of sexuality, in which libido is the one great source of energy, is biologically based. For Freud, there is a given biological 'naturalness' about sexuality. Nelson states that the biological basis of sexuality is genetically given but that our sexuality is not merely biological; we are humans becoming. The process by which we become sexual seems to be less a natural unfolding of biological drives, as Freud sees it, and more a social learning process through which we come to affirm certain sexual meanings in our interaction with significant others (Nelson, 1978: 29). In Freud's account of sexuality, he assumes that the norms that define normality and abnormality are absolutely real and unproblematic. When the married man suddenly clasped 'this child of fourteen' to him and 'pressed a kiss upon her lips', the only normal response for 'this child', as far as Freud is concerned, is a 'feeling of sexual excitement'. Freud diagnosed Dora as 'ill' because she failed to make that response (Freud, 1905e: 28).

If Freud, as he himself acknowledged, failed to 'heal' Dora, one can ask was it because of a misdiagnosis. Dora's presenting problem was her great distress about her father's extramarital affair, Herr K.'s attempts at seducing her, both men's denial of the seduction and their accusations that she was imagining the seduction. Freud acknowledged the accuracy of Dora's perception of the situation. He agrees with Dora about what is going on around her in her interfamilial setting and what people are doing to her. He says, 'I could not, in general, dispute Dora's characterization of her father; . . . it was easy to see that her complaints were justified' (Freud, 1905e: 34). Stadlen points out that Freud, while agreeing with Dora's perceptions, 'regards her as sick because her perceptions upset her. . . . A healthy girl, Freud considered, would not be so upset' (Stadlen, 1989: 200). Freud later redefines the story that Dora tells him about Herr K.'s seduction and her father's affair with Frau K., and he presents it as an intrapsychic problem of Dora's (Freud, 1905e: 86).

Herr K. had been called to account by Dora's father after she reported the scene by the lake when Herr K. made a love proposal to her. In defence, Herr K. accused Dora of perverse sexual interest in her choice of reading material and of having an overactive imagination, and Dora's father decided to believe him rather than his own daughter's version of events, which he called a fantasy. Freud notes Dora's reaction to her father's disbelieving her:

> None of her father's actions seemed to have embittered her so much as his readiness to consider the scene by the lake as a product of her imagination. She was almost beside herself at the idea of its being supposed that she had merely fancied something on that occasion.
>
> *(Freud, 1905e: 46)*

It is not difficult to imagine how Dora feels when her seducer claims innocence and turns her words back on her, blaming her imagination, and, worse still, her father sides with her seducer. She is vainly hoping that Freud will believe her. But he, too, looks beyond her account of seduction, which he believes, and peers into her mind to see if he can find Dora's motivation for 'her passionate repudiation' of her seducer's advances (Freud, 1905e: 46).

Freud does not help Dora work through her emotional distress. He has another agenda, which is similar to the agenda of the judges in the witch trials. Freud wanted to know what was Dora's secret knowledge of sexual matters and what was the source of that knowledge (Freud, 1905e: 62). Freud speculated: was it the governess or her cousin or Frau K. with whom she 'had lived for years on a footing of the closest intimacy'? Is Dora trying to protect the identity of her informer? Did her knowledge come from oral or written sources, from her own 'guilty reading'? (Freud, 1905e: 102). Freud finally ended his speculation by deciding that 'the main source of her knowledge of sexual matters could have been no one but Frau K' (Freud, 1905e: 120n.1). Freud had no evidence for this decision.

We recall Freud's interpretation of Dora's first dream: 'she fled *to* her father because she was afraid of the man who was pursuing her; she summoned up an infantile affection for her father so that he might protect her against her present affection for a stranger' (Freud, 1905e: 86). Freud is saying that Dora is looking for protection against *her own affection* for Herr K. So, it appears that Freud has, through his interpretation of her dream, turned Dora's reproaches against Herr K. into self-reproaches.

What ulterior motive have each of these men in relation to Dora? Herr K. wanted to save himself from the accusation of seduction; Dora's father wanted Freud to 'bring her to reason' because 'she keeps pressing me to break off relations with . . . Frau K. . . . But that I cannot do' (Freud, 1905e: 26). Both men's claims of Dora's alleged sexual phantasies played into Freud's hands: he was already holding his own new theoretical interest in 'infantile germs of perversion', and he wanted to test his new theory on Dora (Freud, 1905e: 113). He says, 'this new case also presents all the difficulties which have since led me to go beyond that theory' (Freud, 1905e: 27). Freud is claiming to have 'gone beyond' his theory of seduction, but in fact, he said to Fliess in a letter on 21 September 1897, 'I no longer believe in my theory of the neuroses'. A sexual seduction is now no longer the 'indispensable prerequisite for the production of a hysterical disorder' (Freud, 1905e: 26–27). Dora, accused of phantasies by two men, is in a similar situation to the witch accused of a 'lustful imagination' (Remy, 1595: 22). Dora is 'handed over' to Freud just as the witch was handed over by her accusers to judges whose own phantasies affected their judgement in the trials. When Dora described the scene in the shop, Freud went on to fantasise his own 'reconstruction of the scene' (Freud, 1905e: 29–30).

Freud's new theory of infantile sexual phantasies is now the 'indispensable prerequisite' for the production of hysteria. Freud says, 'neurotics are dominated by the opposition between reality and phantasy' (Freud, 1905e: 110). The authors of the *Malleus* (1486), as well as Bodin (1580) and Remy (1595), examined the possibility of phantasy in the witches' confessions. In their writings, they discuss the opposition between reality and phantasy in the witches' accounts of their journeyings to the Sabbat and their presence at the Sabbat. Remy (1595) says,

> sometimes they are actually present in person, whereas at other times they are not, but are resting at home in a deep sleep and only imagine that they have gone to the Sabbat, since their senses have been deceived by the Demon who can cause many fancies to creep into the mind of sleepers – fancies which, even after waking, leave the mind convinced of their truth. . . . For so does that crafty one mingles truth with falsehood.
>
> *(Remy, 1595: 60)*

The judges used their inquisitorial approach in their efforts to extract the truth from the witches. Freud used his 'new' technique in the same way to try to extract the truth out of Dora. In his sessions with Dora, Freud saw himself in a contest with 'half-tamed demons' referred to by the witches' judges (Freud, 1905e: 109). He hoped to prove the dominance of phantasy in the aetiology of hysteria, but Dora unexpectedly terminated the treatment, 'thus bringing those hopes to nothing' (Freud, 1905e: 109).

7.3. The betrayals of Dora

Witches were often betrayed by family and friends by being handed over to the judges and inquisitors. Frau K. was guilty of betraying Dora in the same way as the men in Dora's life. Dora's 'sexual researches' with Frau K. had been turned into accusations, and what had been a bond between the two was turned into a weapon by Frau K. She tried to support her husband's accusation by providing him with the innocuous information that Dora had been reading *The Physiology of Love*. When Dora found herself betrayed by Frau K., she recalled an earlier situation with her governess and concluded that Frau K. had used her as a stepping stone to her father (Freud, 1905e: 36–37).

Dora had felt betrayed by her father, who considered the scene by the lake with Herr K. 'a product of her imagination. She was beside herself at the idea of its being supposed that she had merely fancied something on that occasion' (Freud, 1905e: 46, 108). Yet Freud relentlessly persisted in trying to make Dora accept that the hidden object of her desire was Herr K. He asserted, 'I know now . . . that you did fancy that Herr K.'s proposal was serious, and that he would not leave off until you had married him' (Freud, 1905e: 108). Freud said, 'It was justifiable to suspect that there was something concealed' (Freud, 1905e: 46). Suspicion was also enough to convict a witch.

Freud said on the last day of the analysis that Dora 'listened without any of her usual contradictions' (Freud, 1905e: 108). What Freud understood by 'usual contradictions' was Dora's 'resistance', not her reasonable objections to his misinterpretations. Freud tried to overcome Dora's 'resistance' with his questioning and extracting information so that in the end she would succumb to his relentless interrogation. It was in this same way that the judges wore down the witches until they eventually confessed what the inquisitors wanted to hear.

After apparently accepting Dora's version of the scene by the lake, Freud suddenly admits his lack of understanding of Dora: 'Her behaviour must have seemed as incomprehensible to the man after she had left him as to us' (Freud, 1905e: 46). Her behaviour is quite comprehensible to us even without the added knowledge that Herr K. had made a similar speech to his children's governess and had succeeded in seducing her and then spurning her. Herr K.'s proposal must have appeared to Dora as a repetition of his proposal to his children's young governess because he repeated the exact same magic words that he had used to successfully seduce the governess: 'I get nothing out of my own wife' (Freud, 1905e: 26). The words were an insult to Dora. When she described the scene by the lake to Freud, he said to her, 'after all you did not let him finish his speech, and you did not know what he meant to say to you'. But Dora did know, because she had heard the day before how he finished the same speech when he was seducing the governess.

'The only solution for all the parties concerned', Freud worked out, was for Dora to marry Herr K. Freud asks, 'Why did Dora's refusal take such a brutal form, as though she were embittered against him. And how could a girl who was in love feel insulted by a proposal which was made in a manner neither tactless nor offensive?' Dora had every reason to feel embittered. Freud complained that Dora's refusal of Herr K.'s sexual advances was 'brutal', but McCaffrey (1984) says that Freud's handling of Dora's account of the scene of the kiss in the shop could with 'more justice' be called 'brutal' (McCaffrey, 1984: 96).

Like the judges in the witch trials, Freud persisted in his interrogations in order to extract a confession. Speaking to Dora of her 'temptation at L_', he put it to her, 'You took it that he was only waiting till you were grown up enough to be his wife' (Freud, 1905e: 108). Freud is saying, like Dora's father and Herr K. before him, that she is phantasising because she is in love with Herr K. Freud said provocatively to Dora, 'nothing makes you so angry as having it thought that you merely fancied the scene by the lake. I know now that you *did* fancy that Herr K.'s proposals were serious and that he would not leave off until you had married him' (Freud, 1905e: 108). Freud's judgement is not based on evidence. He claimed that marriage would be the only way to reclaim Dora from sexual phantasies to the realities of life. And he depicted Dora as a witch who tried to lure a married man away from his wife in the hopes of permanently destroying the marriage.

7.4. An inquisitorial approach?

Freud says,

> A string of reproaches against other people leads one to suspect the existence of a string of self-reproaches with the same content. All that need be done is to turn each particular reproach on to the speaker himself. There is

something undeniably automatic about this method of defending oneself against a self-reproach by making the same reproach against someone else.

(Freud, 1905e: 35)

Freud set out in Dora's treatment to turn back each particular reproach that Dora made against others onto herself. When Dora brought 'a sound and incontestable train of argument' to Freud that he could not 'attack', he tells us he could only 'suspect the existence of a string of self reproaches with the same content' (Freud, 1905e: 35). He uses each of her reproaches as a weapon that he turns on Dora to prove her guilt. In this way, Freud is repeating the inquisitorial approach of the witches' judges.

It is possible for us to follow Freud's 'witch-hunt' in the 'Dora' case: she complained about her governess being in love with Dora's father. As evidence for her claim, Dora posited that she noticed that when her father was away, the governess had no time for her, but when her father returned, the governess was ready with every sort of service and assistance. Dora concluded that this 'pretended affection for her was really meant for her father'. Freud turned Dora's reproach back on Dora: he informed her that the same inference was to be drawn from her preoccupation with Herr K.'s children: 'she had all these years been in love with Herr K'. But Dora did not assent to this charge (Freud, 1905e: 37). Freud gives no evidence that Dora is not genuinely interested in the children, whereas her reproach against the governess was backed up by evidence and appears to have been justified.

Dora complained that her father did not wish to look too closely into Herr K.'s behaviour towards her for fear of being disturbed in his own love affair with Frau K. Freud retorted that 'Dora herself had done precisely the same thing'. Dora's governess was anxious 'to open her eyes to the nature of her father's relations with Frau K.', but Freud told Dora that 'her silent acquiescence in her father's relations with Frau K.' was because she herself had been at the same time in love with Herr K. (Freud, 1905e: 36–37).

The argument that Dora brought forward that Freud could not contest was that her father handed her over to Herr K. as the price of Herr K.'s tolerating the relations between her father and Frau K. Dora was angry because she was being used as an object for barter, so she argued her case convincingly. A married man could give Dora valuable presents, send her flowers every day and spend all his spare time in her company without her parents registering any concern. Her father was deaf to the call of duty because of his own extramarital affair. Freud agreed that this reproach was justified, but he alleged that Dora's 'sound and incontestable train of argument' against her father was brought forward to cloak her own self-reproaches.

One of Dora's reproaches against her father was that his ill health was only a pretext that he exploited for his own purposes, that he was a malingerer. Freud turned this reproach against Dora with his tu quoque argument: he alleged an ulterior motive for her present 'ill health'; that is, he alleged that Dora's 'present ill health' was motivated by the aim of detaching her father from Frau K., by frightening him with her farewell letter containing a threatened suicide attempt or by awakening his pity or 'at least she would be taking her revenge on him' (Freud, 1905e: 42). Freud says,

> I felt quite convinced that she would recover at once if only her father were to tell her that he had sacrificed Frau K. for the sake of Dora's health. But, I added, I hoped he would not let himself be persuaded to do this, for then she would have learned what a powerful weapon she had in her hands.
>
> *(Freud, 1905e: 42)*

Decker writes that Dr Grey said in a lecture that the hysterical patient 'must be taught day by day . . . by . . . that combination which the French . . . call the iron hand beneath the velvet glove' (Decker, 1986: 99). Freud used that iron hand on Dora to ensure that she would not use the 'powerful weapon she had in her hands' in order to control her father. Freud was determined that Dora would receive no sense of power. He turned the weapon on her: her 'ill health' was motivated to achieve her own aims.

When Dora complained of gastric pains, Freud alleged that she was copying her cousin, who had fallen ill with gastric pains from envy of her younger sister's betrothal bliss. Freud brought forward no evidence to substantiate these serious allegations against Dora. He merely said, 'I will pass over the details which showed how entirely correct all of this was' (Freud, 1905e: 42). All these unproven allegations against Dora mirror the unproven allegations made against the witches. Dora had been turned into a witch, found guilty without any evidence of guilt.

7.5. Literature on Dora

Was Dora a hysteric according to Freud's definition of his theory of hysteria? Almost all the literature written on the 'Dora' case accepts Freud's diagnosis of Dora as a hysteric. The feminist revisionists, Gallop, Ramas and Gearhart, whose articles appear in the book *In Dora's Case* (1985), use the same inquisitional approach in relation to Dora that Freud used as they purport to criticise Freud. They have not questioned Freud's inquisitorial approach or challenged Freud's diagnosis.

While Ramas argues that Freud's analysis of Dora is flawed, 'because it is structured around a fantasy of femininity and female sexuality', she accepts Freud's diagnosis of Dora as a hysteric (Bernheimer & Kahane, 1985: 150). She writes about 'the hysteria of Dora' without examining the basic flaw in the analysis. She merely redefines Dora's 'hysteria' as 'a repudiation of the meaning of heterosexuality' (Bernheimer & Kahane, 1985: 151).

Erikson asks, 'how many of us can follow today without protest Freud's assertion that a healthy girl of fourteen would . . . have considered Mr. K's advances "neither tactless nor offensive"?' (Bernheimer & Kahane, 1985: 49). But he negates this insight by referring, in the next sentence, to the nature and severity of Dora's pathological reaction', which, he says, 'make her the classical hysteric'. He thus accepts without question Freud's diagnosis of hysteria. Kurt O. Schlesinger, following

Erikson's line of reasoning, writes that 'Freud's emphasis on the endopsychic reality . . . and his concomitant de-emphasis of the historical reality . . . might merge, as far as Dora was concerned, with her father's expressed idea of bringing her to reason and dispelling the fantasy' (McCaffrey, 1984: 172).

McCaffrey points out that Freud's 'unearthing of unconscious fantasies, however accurate, bore too close a resemblance to the accusation against her by Herr K. and her father'. Freud, too, was accusing Dora of perverse sexual phantasies. McCaffrey goes on to say, 'Even in some details of the analysis Freud's goals and procedures struck an unfortunate analogy with aspects of Dora's betrayal by her father and her friends' (McCaffrey, 1984: 96).

Freud said that Dora transferred her feelings for Herr K. onto him: 'She took her revenge on me as she wanted to take her revenge on him and deserted me. . . . Thus, she *acted out* an essential part of her recollections and phantasies instead of reproducing it in the treatment' (Freud, 1905e: 119). Freud interpreted the message of Dora's second dream as 'Men are all so detestable that I would rather not marry. This is my revenge' (Freud, 1905e: 120).

Felix Deutsch, a colleague of Freud's, wrote 'A Footnote to Freud's *Fragment of an Analysis of a Case of Hysteria*' (1957), in which he claims that 'At the end of her analytic treatment she had stated unequivocally: "Men are all so detestable that I would rather not marry. This is my revenge". Thus, her marriage had served only to cover up her distaste of men' (Deutsch, 1957: 166). Deutsch's conclusion that 'her marriage had served only to cover up her distaste of men' issues from the fundamentally false premise that Dora said, 'Men are all so detestable'. Dora did not say, 'Men are all so detestable'. Rather, this was Freud's interpretation of her second dream. Deutsch says that 'her death . . . seemed a blessing to those who were close to her' (Deutsch, 1957: 167). He provides no evidence for these allegations. Deutsch's assessment of Dora is based on two interviews in 1922 and on information from an 'informant' who told Deutsch that Dora's husband 'had preferred to die rather than divorce her' and that Dora was 'one of the most repulsive hysterics' (Deutsch, 1957: 167). Again, he provides no evidence for these allegations.

7.6. Female sexuality

Freud's interest in uncovering Dora's sexual secrets is similar to the inquisitors' and judges' intense interest in the so-called witches' sexual orgies at the Sabbat. Dora and the witches are accused of perverse sexual phantasies. The 'Dora' case is unique in the canon of Freud's works in his treatment of female sexuality. His other treatments of female sexuality can be classed as highly theoretical – for example, *Three Essays on the Theory of Sexuality, (1905d)*; *Some Psychical Consequences of the Anatomical Distinction between the Sexes* (1925j); and *Female Sexuality* (1931b).

The case histories in *Studies on Hysteria* (1895d) date from an earlier period of the development of Freud's theories on hysteria. The patient most nearly analogous to Dora was Katharina, who was treated by Freud in a single afternoon's conversation while he was on vacation. Freud admits that he did not succeed in extracting all of Dora's secrets from her. For example, he does not succeed in getting Dora to confess to what he alleges is her most closely guarded secret, her alleged childhood masturbation. Freud had used his new technique, 'this new pathway to knowledge', to try to extract a confession out of Dora that she was a masturbator. Freud believed that there is a fund of knowledge in his patients that is not immediately accessible. This knowledge is in the unconscious. Dora does not appreciate Freud's new pathway to knowledge. She refuses to 'know' what Freud alleges: when she coughs, she is picturing to herself a scene of oral gratification.

In *Three Essays on the Theory of Sexuality* (1905d), Freud wrote that the erotic life of women 'is still veiled in an impenetrable obscurity'. As late as his 1931 essay on *Female Sexuality*, Freud noted that the 'first attachment to the mother seemed to me so difficult to grasp in analysis. . . . Nor have I succeeded in seeing my way through any case completely'. He suspects that 'this phase of attachment to the mother is especially intimately related to the aetiology of hysteria' (Freud, 1905d:151, 1931b: 226–227).

Freud's theories about female sexuality and his attitude towards women are just as problematic as was the attitude of the judges in the medieval and early modern witch trials. The attitude towards women in 1900 Viennese society had a debilitating effect on Dora. She was trapped in a patriarchal society that provided her with few options outside passively accepting marriage and motherhood. Ramas argued that Freud's claim of Dora's love for Herr K. is based on 'an ideological construct developed in defence of a patriarchal phantasy of femininity and female sexuality' (Bernheimer & Kahane, 1985: 150).

Freud was trying to force Dora to fit into the accepted mores of her society, where older married men could have young mistresses. When Dora told Freud that Herr K. had given her a present of an expensive jewel case, Freud remarked, 'Then a return-present would have been very appropriate' (Freud, 1905e: 69). Stadlen states that 'Freud, in recounting the above exchange about the jewel-case, describes without shame how, while responsible as her physician and therapist for the supposedly "ill" Dora, he effectively acted as procurer for Herr K.' (Stadlen, 1989: 202).

This was an intolerable and destructive situation for a young independent adolescent girl like Dora. Freud did not put into practice in this case what he stated at the outset: 'we are obliged to pay as much attention in our case histories to the purely human and social circumstances of our patient as to the somatic data and the symptoms of the disorder' (Freud, 1905e: 18). Freud did not pay adequate attention to Dora's social circumstances: her external reality. He did not explore her reaction to her environment. He concentrated on exploring her alleged internal phantasy world. Enabling Dora to explore and come to terms with her immediate disordered interfamilial environment was not on Freud's agenda.

If we compare Freud's attitude in treating Dora with his attitude towards Katharina, a striking contrast emerges. He is warm and sympathetic towards Katharina. He believed her story. By the time Freud came to treat Dora, he had come to the belief that alleged seductions were not memories but were sometimes phantasies of seduction. Dora was not a complaint patient who would enable him to verify his theory.

Dora recognised herself as a bartered object. After Frau K.'s betrayal, Dora became convinced that Frau K. had been interested in her only because of her father. Dora, having rejected the demeaning role offered to her by these adults, was unable to construct an alternative future role.

Freud failed to help Dora. He was determined to use the case to illustrate his revised theory of hysteria. He wanted to demonstrate that an infantile wish lay behind every dream, and he also wanted to illuminate the path leading to the wish. Dora's case perfectly suited his need to unravel the hidden meaning of the dream that made the world of the unconscious accessible to him. Like the inquisitors Sprenger and Kramer, who wrote *The Hammer of Witches* (1486), Freud seems to be using a hammer to break open the unconscious. His interpretations tell us more about him than they tell us about Dora. Did Freud identify and sympathise with Dora's father? Dora saw Freud primarily because of her father, her betraying father. She had agreed to go to Freud in the hopes that he would understand her angry feelings because of being betrayed by her father. Dora's hopes were not fulfilled.

7.7. Dora's dilemma

Like the witches in the medieval and early modern periods, hysterics in Dora's day were considered to be difficult and exasperating people. Dora was branded a hysteric. She lived in a patriarchal society and in an anti-Semitic world. The roots of Dora's problem in the wider social world and in her own immediate environment were largely overlooked by Freud. Freud was preoccupied with his own agenda, which he believed, if followed, would rid Dora of her hysteria. He wished to put his assumptions to the test and to verify his theory that 'sexual impulses operated normally in the youngest children without any need for outside stimulation' (Freud, 1905d: 128). To support this hypothesis, he wanted to demonstrate that Dora's 'hysteria' had resulted from her own repressed infantile sexuality. He believed that Dora's 'illness' had begun as a result of Dora's own masturbating. Dora could not accept this view.

Were her alleged hysterical symptoms physical manifestations of the anger and assertiveness that a woman in her society was encouraged not to demonstrate openly? Vulnerability was admired in those days as the feminine ideal. Women could express their dissatisfaction through physical illness and thus stay within the confines of appropriate and acceptable feminine behaviour. Also, as a woman and as a Jew, Dora had to cope with the disadvantage and the frustration of being barred from admission to higher education and a career. So, Dora internalised her anger and became aggressive and rebellious. Dora needed someone to listen to her and believe her. Her family and doctors did not help.

Dora was born into a society in which Jews were assimilating into Viennese life, but by the time she came to Freud, it was becoming clear that there were limits to assimilation and that the Jews had raised their hopes in vain. Anti-Semitism was developing. Because of a major influx of Eastern Jews into Vienna, a rally was held by artisans in the year of Dora's birth calling for 'violence against [Jewish] capitalists'. This led to a resolution being passed that called for laws to wipe out the Jews' emancipation and reinstate all the old legal restrictions on Jewish life. This was the world that Dora entered in 1882 and in which she lived during her life in Vienna.

As a Jew and a woman, Dora was labelled doubly deficient. Anti-feminism and anti-Semitism at the turn of the century could fill Dora's personal world with self-doubt and self-loathing. Zweig (1943) described how 'society in those days wished young girls to be silly and untaught, . . . innocent and shy, . . . to be led and informed by a man in marriage without any will of their own' (Zweig, 1943: 78–79 in Decker, 1986: 76). This was Dora's milieu when she first met Freud in Vienna in June 1898 on her way to the lake where Herr K.'s seduction took place.

Five years before Freud treated Dora, he complained of Elisabeth von R. that she had departed from the feminine 'ideal': she was 'greatly discontented with being a girl. She was full of ambitious plans. She wanted to study or have a musical training, and she was indignant at the idea of having to sacrifice her inclinations and her freedom of judgement by marriage' (Freud, 1895d: 140). Conforming to the mores of his society, Freud lacked empathy with these women. Freud's interpretation of Dora's attitude is summed up in his interpretation of her dream: 'Men are all so detestable that I would rather not marry. This is my revenge' (Freud, 1905e: 120). This obviously was not Dora's attitude because she did marry.

Freud failed to express a warm personal interest in Dora in order to get her to stay in treatment even for the sake of his 'theoretical interest' (Freud, 1905e: 109). But a short time before Dora started treatment with Freud, he wrote in a letter to Fliess on 6 November 1898, 'The number of patients is increasing; one is supposed to be kind, superior, witty, original'. In Dora's case, Freud was not kind; he resorted to harsh therapy.

Freud had assumed that Dora's eventual marriage, her surrendering to her love for a man, would have been the reality that would overcome what he called her phantasy life. He shared his contemporaries' notion of women as compliant wives. He saw nothing unacceptable in her father's affair or in a married man's 'love proposal' to Dora when she was 'a child of fourteen' (Freud, 1905e: 28). He accepted these interfamilial entanglements as part of the norm of the social life around him. Arthur Schnitzler, a contemporary of Freud's, exposed the reality of a similar network of interfamilial intrigue in his portrayal of *Miss Else* (Decker, 1986: 109).

Freud recognised the similarity between the medieval world that Schnitzler portrayed in his play and the phenomenon that he was seeing in his work with his patients. He wrote to Schnitzler that 'For many years I have been conscious of the far reaching conformity existing between your opinions and mine on many psychological and erotic problems' (Decker, 1986: 109). Although both men were social critics, they accepted a great deal of the social life of the wealthy bourgeois world around them. It was common practice for the husbands of 'hysterical' women to have mistresses. One of Freud's patients, Frau Cäcilie, whose 'illness' lasted for 30 years, expressed her marital frustration with her lack of independence and her inability to make any alteration in her circumstances. Her husband, Leopold von Lieben, took a mistress, Molly Filtsch, who was eventually accepted by the family circle (Decker, 1986: 109–110).

Freud knew many such families, including Dora's, but he did not address himself to the tangled family relationships in his psychoanalysis with his patients. Freud accepted the position of women in these entanglements, and in this way, he failed to address the root of the problem; or to use his own metaphor, he failed to find the key to unlock the door. Freud wrote to Fliess on 14 October 1900 about Dora, 'a case that has smoothly opened to the existing collection of picklocks'. Freud failed to take into account the importance of the feelings of frustration that these women felt from their confined and sometimes oppressive environment.

Some of the most important women in Dora's life, her governess and Frau K., had used her for their own ends. The sexually dissatisfied men in her life frequently complained about getting nothing from their wives. This calls to mind the many sexually dissatisfied or impotent men in medieval and early modern times who brought their wives before the inquisitors and judges accusing them of being absent from the marriage bed at night or accusing them of making them impotent.

Witches were perceived as dangerous. Dora embodied the dangers that Freud feared from all women: they would handicap his professional life. This danger was based on a phantasy of woman as vengeful and as destroyer or as emasculator of men. It is easy to see the parallel with the minds of the authors of the *Malleus Maleficarum* (1486). A woman's sexuality was a dangerous lure and could ultimately be a trap. This was the theme of the *Malleus Maleficarum* (1486), which Freud had said he would study diligently.

Samuel Wilks, in a lecture on diseases of the nervous system, said of hysterics, 'the behaviour is like that of one possessed of a devil' (Wilks, 1878 in Decker, 1986: 7). Freud shared his medical colleagues' attitude about the professional hazards posed by female hysterical patients. He wrote, 'No one who, like me, conjures up the most evil of those half-tamed demons that inhabit the human breast, and seeks to wrestle with them, can expect to come through the struggle unscathed' (Freud, 1905e: 109). Freud identified his work with the work of the judges in the witch trials, which is described in the introduction to *An Examen of Witches* (1590): 'When we consider the zeal of Jean Bodin, Henry Boguet, Nicholas Remy and Pierre de Lancre we must always remember the difficulties and hazards these brave men had to face ... Their contest with the evil one was hard and long' (Boguet, 1590: xxiv). Judges saw themselves as the 'saviour' of the witch, and Remy, by using the gospel story told by Luke in chapter 13, is comparing himself to Jesus Christ, who 'saved' the possessed woman. Judge Remy saw himself as releasing those bound by demons. Freud also saw himself having a similar mission in treating hysterics.

Freud admitted to Fliess that he did not regard a woman as having the capacity to be a close friend. In his letter to Fliess on 7 August 1901, he wrote, 'In my life, as you know, woman has never replaced the comrade, the friend'. In the same letter, he also refers to Fliess's wife 'working out in a dark compulsion the notion that Breuer once planted in her mind when he told her how lucky she was that I did not live in Berlin and could not interfere with her marriage'. At this stage, Freud's friendship with Fliess was coming to an end. By autumn 1901, Freud had set up another audience: a group of four physicians who met every night in Freud's apartment to discuss psychoanalysis.

Freud, who was eager to demonstrate that hysteria came from Dora's own repressed infantile sexuality and seeking to prove his new theory, ignored the betrayals and seductions that Dora suffered. Instead, he pressed Dora to admit that she was a masturbator, which, he claimed, was the origin of her 'hysteria'.

Madelon Sprengnether writes of 'the coercive quality of Freud's interpretations of Dora': 'On an interpretative level, he subjects her to a process of defloration, impregnation, and parturition in an aggressively oedipal fashion, at the same time that he invalidates her rejection by calling it hysteria'. Sprengnether explains that Freud seems to have accomplished metaphorically with Dora what he could not do to her in reality (Bernheimer & Kahane, 1985: 262–263).

Sprengnether argues that in attributing the phantasy of fellatio to Dora, Freud claims that it is possible to speak to young women about sexual matters 'without doing them harm and without bringing suspicion on himself, so long as . . . he . . . can make them feel convinced that it is unavoidable'. Freud argues, 'A gynaecologist, after all, under the same conditions does not hesitate to make them submit to uncovering every possible part of their body'. Freud had metaphorically undressed and violated Dora, claiming to reveal the 'dirty secrets' he attributes to her: her alleged habit of masturbation and her catarrh. 'Thus, discredited and shamed', Dora is deprived of her power (Bernheimer & Kahane, 1985: 262–264). Freud was acting in a similar way to the judges in the witch trials, who had the witches undressed and searched for secrets. During the trial of the so-called witch Françoise Secretain, Judge Boguet had her stripped and searched for 'secrets' (Boguet, 1590: 2–5, 216). Bodin also required the witch to be stripped in order to force her to yield up her secrets (Bodin, 1580: 112–113).

Freud said he was avoiding the temptation of writing a satire on those who are scandalised by such a therapeutic method. He was defensive about his interrogations of this young woman, Dora, on intimate sexual matters. He said, 'It would be the mark of a singular and perverse prurience to suppose that conversations of this kind are a good means of exciting or of gratifying sexual desires' (Freud, 1905e: 48). He is tempted to attack his critics, who were horrified at his metaphorical undressing of Dora. His laborious protestations of innocence are in stark contrast to his eagerness to tear sexual phantasies and admissions of perverse sexual activities from Dora. His procedures in trying to extract a confession from Dora mirrors the intense interrogations of the witches' judges in their efforts to extract confessions of guilt out of witches.

In his 'postscript' to the 'Dora' case, Freud wrote, 'The symptoms of the disease are nothing else than *the patient's sexual activity*' (Freud, 1905e: 115). He ignored the role of the family in Dora's case. His change of focus from the role of family members to the individual severely limited the effectiveness of psychoanalysis. One can say that in changing the focus from the dysfunctional familial and social environment to the patient's own alleged phantasies and sexual activities, Freud was repeating the thinking of the inquisitors and judges who blamed the witches for their alleged phantasies and sexual orgies with the devil.

In 1912 the chairman of the German League Against Women's Emancipation wrote, 'The modern feminist movement is . . . a foreign body in our national life' (Decker, 1986: 199). The link between anti-Semitism and anti-feminism is undeniable. Both Jews and women were held bound by an unjust system. Phantasies of feminine evil and Jewish evil were rampant. Medieval and early modern witches were the objects of the same sort of phantasies.

Freud had admired Dora's youth and attractiveness, had probed her most secret sexual thoughts and feelings. He ultimately blamed Dora for denying him the victory he had counted on to silence his critics. Freud's determination that Dora should not win over either her father or him was quite marked in that he was aware that she was a 'young woman of very independent judgement, who had grown accustomed to laugh at the efforts of doctors' (Freud, 1905e: 22). He also describes her as a vengeful person (Freud, 1905e: 121). He claimed that Dora took the most effective revenge on him by demonstrating 'the helplessness and incapacity of the physician' (Freud, 1905e: 120). The judges in the witch trials made the same accusations against the witches. Remy (1595) writes that witches were 'commonly desirous of revenge, and so Satan deceives them by promising them a means of avenging themselves when they have been angered by a hurt received' (Remy, 1595: 4). Freud accused Dora of finding satisfaction by taking revenge on the K.s, who had hurt her and also of transferring her feelings of revenge onto him by not allowing him 'the satisfaction of affording her a far more radical cure for her troubles' (Freud, 1905e: 121, 122).

7.8. Conclusion

If Dora was not ill in the way Freud described – as has been proved – then his investigations into 'her flight from life into disease' (Freud, 1905e: 122) bear a precise similarity to the judges' investigations into the witch's flight from life to the Sabbat. Both used harsh therapy to extract the confessions they were looking for from their respective clients/victims.

CONCLUSION

In this book, I set myself the task of trying to make sense of Freud's sentence 'I dream, therefore, of a primeval devil religion with rites that are carried on secretly and understand the harsh therapy of the witches' judges'. I have looked carefully and systematically at the accounts of the witch trials and at the literature that Freud read on the witch trials. I have shown, as far as possible, what Freud meant when he said that he understood the harsh therapy of the witches' judges. I have shown significant features in common between the judges' inquisitorial procedures in treating witches and the partially inquisitorial method used by Freud with his patients between 1892 and 1900. I have therefore achieved what I set out to do.

I have investigated the procedures used by the witches' judges and Freud's methods in detail. My investigation has shown that there is a close structural parallel in the processes used by Freud and the witches' judges. It is not part of my work to investigate the extent to which Freud's inquisitorial approach is used today. However, clarifying what was going on in Freud's psychoanalytic procedures with his patients has raised the following questions:

1 To what extent did Freud continue to use an inquisitorial approach in his psychoanalytic work?
2 To what extent did Freud build an inquisitorial approach into his theory?
3 To what extent are some psychoanalysts and psychotherapists still operating an inquisitorial procedure in their work?

I have asked foundational questions about the origins of the witch-hunts. This led to the discovery of a structural fault in the principal claim made about witches, namely that they copulate with demons. I have shown that this claim was based on a literal interpretation of the pericope Genesis 6:1–4. The literary form of this pericope is myth and when the myth is read literally, its true meaning is lost. The Yahwist writer was *symbolically* presenting the problem of evil. The principal claim about witches copulating with demons was therefore based on a false foundation. The second claim about witches, based on the first claim, was that they had 'seven methods' of doing harm to men sexually, principally by causing impotence (Kramer & Sprenger, 1486: 47). We examined this misogynist misconception of women.

Was the fear of witchcraft symbolic? The forces that shaped the witch-hunts and witch trials, the guilty and vengeful thoughts that people harbour and seek to restrain, needed an outlet. It was also the case that witches, who were for the most part on the lower rungs of the social ladder, needed an outlet for their 'dis-ease', and they expressed it in the only language that was available at that time: their delusions of omnipotence. If the hysterical phenomena of the medieval and early modern witch were a language rather than a devilish delusion, we could say that Freud's paralleling it with his hysteria was apt. Freud was on the way to recognising that hysteria was a language of 'dis-ease' rather than a disease when he used the 'talking cure'. Freud was the first to recognise the value of listening rather than looking at the 'patient'. But as we saw in Part Two, Freud was often listening only to what he wanted to hear. It was most often the 'patient' who was listening to Freud's questionings, suggestions and constructions. Because of this, I have suggested in an earlier work that Freud was a transitional figure (Duffy, 1996)

Because the judges believed that the devil was interfering in the free and open confession of the witch, they administered harsh therapy. In the same way, Freud believed that the patient's resistance was interfering with the free and open confession that would reveal the secrets hidden in the patient's unconscious. He used pressure to force them to give up their resistance. In both the witch and the patient, silence was seen as an indicator of resistance. Freud acknowledged that his unrelenting search for what he wanted to find in the patient's unconscious could be a painful experience for the patient. He said that his treatments, no matter how painful, were undertaken to overcome resistance in order to cure the patient. In this, he was identifying his psychoanalysis with the harsh therapy of the witches' judges, who likewise claimed that their harsh therapy was needed to overcome the demons in order to save the soul of the witch.

Belief in witchcraft served useful purposes for both the witch and the judge. The medieval and early modern women liked to think that they had power to harm those who disempowered them, by thinking them harm. The relief offered by the harsh therapy had the capacity, temporarily, of allaying the male fear of witches and of releasing the impulses and urges of the witches' judges. But the question is, does harsh therapy eliminate or control the elusive forces at work in the human psyche?

Freud (1916) wrote of dreams as a way of releasing wishes for revenge and death wishes:

> These censored wishes appear to rise up out of a positive hell; after they have been interpreted when we are awake, no censorship of them seems to us too severe. But you must not blame the dream itself on account of its evil content.

Do not forget that it performs the innocent and indeed useful function of preserving sleep from disturbance.

(Freud, 1916: 143)

Freud also wrote that these wishes for revenge that rise up out of 'hell', the abode of the devil, 'were not created under torture but merely squeezed out by it'. I have also suggested that Freud believed that this was what the judges were doing in the witch trials, and he saw his work in psychoanalysis as having a similar aim. This, I have suggested, is the explanation for his saying, 'I . . . understand the harsh therapy of the witches judges'. The forced nature of their procedures for squeezing out confessions paralleled Freud's own procedures.

Critically, to examine the historical origins of both the witch trials and the discipline of psychoanalysis by genuine historical research helps to reconstruct what Freud actually did and what the judges and inquisitors actually did in the witch trials. A misplaced loyalty either to the judges and inquisitors or to Freud can prevent a critical examination of what they did. Shielding them from historical scrutiny would be an expression of false loyalty. Although it may be impossible ever to achieve the ideal of recovering history as it actually happened, the most we can hope for is different perspectives on what Freud and the judges actually did. I have presented one perspective.

APPENDIX 1

Charcot demonstrates the physical
symptoms of hysteria in one of his patients

Charcot demonstrates the physical symptoms of hysteria in one of his
patients. Gettyimages

APPENDIX 2

Bibliothèque Diabolique publications

BIBLIOTHÈQUE DIABOLIQUE
(COLLECTION BOURNEVILLE)

I. LE SABBAT DES SORCIERS
Par BOURNEVILLE et TEINTURIER

Brochure in-8, de 40 pages, avec 25 figures dans le texte et une grande planche hors texte. Il a été fait de cet ouvrage un tirage de 500 exemplaires numérotés à la presse; 300 exemplaires sur papier blanc vélin, nos 1 à 300 (épuisé). — 150 exemplaires sur parchemin, nos 301 à 450; Prix: 4 fr. — 50 exemplaires sur Japon, Nos 451 à 500 (épuisé).

II. FRANÇOISE FONTAINE

PROCÈS-VERBAL FAIT POUR DÉLIVRER UNE FILLE POSSÉDÉE PAR LE MALIN ESPRIT A LOUVIERS. Publié d'après le manuscrit original et inédit de la Bibliothèque nationale.
Précédé d'une introduction par B. de Moray. Un volume in-8°, de CIV-99 pages. — Papier vélin, prix: 3 fr. 50. — Papier parchemin, prix: 4 fr. 50. — Papier Japon, prix: 6 fr.

III. JEAN WIER

HISTOIRES, DISPUTES ET DISCOURS DES ILLUSIONS ET IMPOSTURES DES DIABLES, DES MAGICIENS INFAMES, SORCIÈRES ET EMPOISONNEURS, DES ENSORCELÉS ET DÉMONIAQUES ET DE LA GUÉRISON D'ICEUX, par JEAN WIER. Cet ouvrage forme deux beaux volumes de plus de 900 pages, et est orné du portrait de l'auteur gravé au burin. Prix: papier vélin, 15 fr. les deux volumes. — Papier parcheminé (no 1 à 300), prix: 20 fr. les deux volumes. — Papier Japon des manufactures impériales (no 1 à 150), prix: 25 fr. les deux volumes. — N. B. Les prix ci-dessus sont pour les exemplaires pris dans nos bureaux. Pour la France, le le port est de 1 fr. Pour l'étranger, de 2 fr. 50

IV. LA POSSESSION DE JEANNE FERY

RELIGIEUSE PROFESSE DU COUVENT DES SŒURS NOIRES DE LA VILLE DE MONS (1584). Un volume in-8° de 122 pages, avec une préface du Dr BOURNEVILLE. — Papier vélin, prix: 3 fr. — Papier parcheminé, prix: 4 fr. — Papier Japon, prix: 6 fr.

V. SŒUR JEANNE DES ANGES

SUPÉRIEURE DES URSULINES A LOUDUN, XVIIe siècle. Auto-biographie d'une hystérique possédée, d'après le manuscrit inédit de la Bibliothèque de Tours. Annotée et publiée par MM. les Drs G. LEGUÉ et G. DE LA TOURETTE. PRÉFACE DE M. LE PROFESSEUR CHARCOT, MEMBRE DE L'INSTITUT.
Un beau volume in-8 de 330 pages. Papier vélin, prix: 6 fr. — Papier parcheminé, prix: 6 fr. — Papier Japon, prix: 25 fr.

Sous presse : VII. BOGUET : DISCOURS DES SORCIERS.

En préparation : VIII. BODIN : DE LA DÉMONOMANIE.

Note: This is the back page of Book V1 in the series of books on witches that were being republished by the School of Charcot while Freud was studying there. It shows the titles of the books by Judge Boguet and Judge Bodin, who conducted the witch trials.

APPENDIX 3

Baldung-Grien 'The Bewitched Groom' 1544

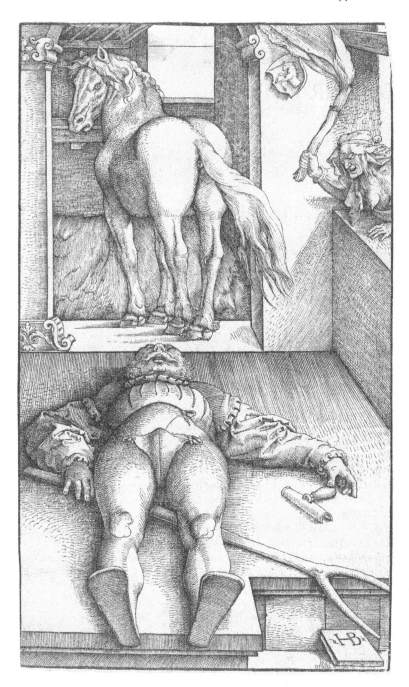

Baldung-Grien is depicting here in 1544 what Bodin (1580) later presumed: 'if the witch was discovered at someone else's . . . stable, and then shortly after, death or illness suddenly struck someone', she was presumed guilty (Bodin, 1580: 199).

BIBLIOGRAPHY

Ady, T. (1655) *A Candle in the Dark*. Calgary, Alberta: Theophania.

Alighieri, D. (1314) *The Divine Comedy*, trans. D.L. Sayers (1949). London: Penguin.

Andreski, S. (1982) 'The Syphilitic Shock' in *Encounter* 52: 7-26.

Appignanesi, L. (1992) *Freud's Women*. London: Weidenfeld and Nicolson.

Balasuriya, T. (1997) *Mary and Human Liberation*. London: Mowbray.

Bernheimer, C. & Kahane, C. (1985) *In Dora's Case: Freud – Hysteria – Feminism*. London: Virago Press Ltd.

Binz, C. (1885) *Doctor Johann Weyer ein rheinischer Arzt der erste Bekämpfer des Hexenwahns*.

Bodin, J. (1580) *De la Demonomanie des Sorciers*, trans. Randy A. Scott (1995). *On the Demon-Mania of Witches*. Toronto: Centre for Reformation & Renaissance Studies.

Boguet, H. (1590) *Discours des Sorciers*, trans. John Rodker (1929). *An Examen of Witches*. Britain: Clay & Sons.

Brown, R.E. (1997) *An Introduction to the New Testament*. London: Doubleday.

Carus, P. (1900) *The History of the Devil and the Idea of Evil from the Earliest Times to the Present Day*. (1974 reprinted) Open Court Pub. Co.

Catechism of the Catholic Church (1994). London: Chapman.

Charcot (School of) (1883–1895) *Bibliothèque Diabolique*. Paris.

Cioffi, F. (1974) 'Was Freud a Liar?' in *The Listener*, 7 February. Also in Cioffi (1998a) 199–204.

Cobben, J.J. (1960) *Jan Wier, Devils, Witches and Magic*, trans. S.A. Prins (1976). Philadelphia, PA: Dorrance & Company.

Cohn, N. (1975) *Europe's Inner Demons: An Inquiry Inspired by the Great Witch-hunt*. London: Heinemann for Sussex University Press.

Condren, C. (1989) *The Serpent and the Goddess: Women, Religion and Power in Celtic Ireland*. San Francisco, CA: Harper & Row.

Decker, H. (1986) *Idols of Perversity: Fantasies of Feminine Evil in Fin-de-Siecle Culture*. Great Clarendon Street, Oxford: Oxford University Press.

Deutsch, F. (1957) 'A Footnote to Freud's "Fragment of an Analysis of a Case of Hysteria"' in *The Psychoanalytic Quarterly*, 28.

Dostoyevsky, F. (1866) *Crime and Punishment*. London: Everyman.

Dostoyevsky, F. (1872) *The Possessed*. London: Everyman.

Douglas, M. (ed.) (1970) *Witchcraft Confessions and Accusations*. London: Tavistock.

Dourley, J. (1981) *The Psyche as Sacrament*. Toronto: Inner City Books.

Duffy, K. (1996) *Freud and Wier: Transitional Figures?* MA Dissertation. Regent's University, London.

Duffy, K. (1999) 'The Harsh Therapy'. PhD Dissertation. Regent's University, London.

Freud, S. (1893f) *Charcot* in SE. 3: 7–24. The Standard Edition of the Complete Psychological Works of Sigmund Freud, trans. James Strachey (24 Vols. London: Vintage 2001) hereinafter cited as SE.

Freud, S. (1950 [1895]) 'Psychopathology' in *Project for a Scientific Psychology* in SE 1: 347–359.

Freud, S. (1895d) With Breuer, J., *Studies on Hysteria* in SE 2.

Freud, S. (1896a) *Heredity and the Aetiology of the Neuroses* in SE 3.

Freud, S. (1896b) *Further Remarks on the Neuro-Psychoses of Defence* in SE 3.

Freud, S. (1896c) *The Aetiology of Hysteria* in SE 3.

Freud, S. (1898b) *The Psychical Mechanism of Forgetfulness* in SE 3.

Freud, S. (1899a) *Screen Memories* in SE 3.

Freud, S. (1900a) *The Interpretation of Dreams* in SE 4

Freud, S. (1901b) *The Psychopathology of Everyday Life* in SE 6.

Freud, S. (1905d) *Three Essays on the Theory of Sexuality* in SE 7.

Freud, S. (1905e) *Fragment of an Analysis of a Case of Hysteria* in SE 7.

Freud, S. (1906a) *My Views on the Part Played by Sexuality in the Aetiology of the Neuroses* in SE 7.

Freud, S. (1906f) 'Contribution to a Questionnaire on Reading' in *Shorter Readings* (1903–1909) in SE 9.

Freud, S. (1912e) *Recommendations to Physicians Practising Psycho-Analysis* in SE 12.

Freud, S. (1914d) *On the History of the Psycho-Analytic Movement* in SE 14.

Freud, S. (1916) *Introductory Lectures on Psycho-Analysis* in SE 15.

Freud, S. (1923d) *A Seventeenth-Century Demonological Neurosis* in SE 19.

Freud, S. (1925d) *An Autobiographical Study* in SE 20.

Freud, S. (1925j) *Some Psychical Consequences of the Anatomical Distinction between the Sexes* in SE 19.

Freud, S. (1931b) *Female Sexuality* in SE 21.

Freud, S. (1933a) *New Introductory Lectures* in SE 22.

Freud, S. (1937) *Moses and Monotheism* in SE 23.

Freud, S. (1937d) *Constructions in Analysis* in SE 23.

Gay, P. (1988) *Freud: A Life for our Time*. London: J.M. Dent & Sons Ltd.

Geis, G. & Bunn, I. (1997) *A Trial of Witches: A Seventeenth Century Witchcraft Prosecution*. London: Routledge.

Guazzo, F.M. (1608) *Compendium Maleficarum*. (trans. 1970). Muller.

Harwick, M. (ed.) (1970) *Witchcraft and Sorcery*. Harmondsworth: Penguin.

Keane, P.S. (1977) *Sexual Morality*. New York: Paulist Press.

Kramer, H. & Sprenger, J. (1486) *Malleus Maleficarum*, trans. Montague Summers. 1971. *The Hammer of Witches*. New York: Dover Books.

Larner, C. (1987) *Witchcraft and Religion: The Politics of Popular Belief*. Oxford: Blackwell.

Lea, H.C. (1907) *History of the Spanish Inquisition*, Vol. 4. London.

Lea, H.C. (1911) *A History of the Inquisition of the Middle Ages*. London. in Parrinder (1958) and Trevor-Roper (1988).

Lecky, W.E.H. (1865) *History of the Rise and Influence of the Spirit of Rationalism in Europe*, Vol. 1. London: Longmans, Green, & Co.

Lecky, W. E. H. (1869). *History of European morals from Augustus to Charlemagne*, Vol. 2. New York, NY, US: D Appleton & Company.

Lohser, B. & Newton, M. (1996) *Unorthodox Freud: The View from the Couch*. London: Guildford Press.

Lyons, E. (1994) *Jesus: Self-portrait by God*. Dublin: Columba Press.

Lyons, E. (1999) Personal communication.

McCaffrey, P. (1984) *Freud and Dora: The Artful Dream*. New Brunswick, NJ: Rutgers University Press.

McFague, S. (1987) *Models of God: Theology for an Ecological Nuclear Age*. London: SCM Press Ltd.

Marwick, F. (ed.) (1970) *Witchcraft and Sorcery*. Harmondsworth: Pelican.

Masson, J.M. (1984) *The Assault on Truth: Freud and Child Sex Abuse*. London: Fontana.

Masson, J.M. (1995) *The Complete Letters of Sigmund Freud to Wilhelm Fliess 1887–1904*. Cambridge, MA, and London: Harvard University Press.

Meier, J.P. (1994) *A Marginal Jew*, Vol. 2. New York: Doubleday.

Meyer, C.F. (1976) 'The Judge' in *The Complete Narrative Prose of Conrad Ferdinand Meyer*, Vol. II, trans. M.W. Sonnenfeld. London: Associated University Press.

Michelet, J. (1862) *La Sorciére: The Witch of the Middle Ages*, English trans. L.J Trotter (1863) London: Simpkin, Marshall. and Co.

Miles, M. (1990) *Carnal Knowing*. London: Burns Oates.

Miller, A. (1953) *The Crucible*. 1992 ed. New York: Heinemann.

Moi, T. (1984) 'Psychoanalysis and Desire: The Case of Dora'. in *Desire*. London: ICA series.

Monter, E.W. (1969) *European Witchcraft*. New York: Wiley & Sons.

Murray, M.A. (1921) *The Witch Cult in Western Europe*. Oxford: Oxford University Press.

Nelson, J.B. (1978) *Embodiment: An Approach to Sexuality & Christian Theology*. Minneapolis, MN: Augsburg.

Nunberg, H. & Federn, E. (1967) *Minutes of the Vienna Psychoanalytic Society*, Vol. 2 (1908–1910). New York: International University Press.

Osborne, H. (ed.) (1970) *The Oxford Companion to Art*. Oxford: Clarendon Press.

Parrinder, G. (1969) *Witchcraft European and African*. London: Faber & Faber.

Peel, E. & Southern, P. (1969) *The Trials of the Lancashire Witches: A Study of Seventeenth Century Witchcraft*. David & Charles: Newton Abbot.

Ranke-Heinemann, U. (1988) *Eunuchs for the Kingdom of Heaven: The Catholic Church and Sexuality*. Harmondsworth: Penguin.

Remy, N. (1595) *Demonolatry*, trans. John Rodker (1930). London.

Roazen, P. (1979) *Freud and His Followers*. London: Penguin.

Roper, T.R. (1988) *The European Witch craze of the Sixteenth and Seventeenth Centuries*. London: Penguin.

Rose, E. (1989) *A Razor for a Goat*. Toronto: University of Toronto Press.

Roskoff, G.G. (1869) *Geschichte des Teufels*. 2 Vols. Leipzig.

Rublack, U. (2015) *The Astronomer and the Witch: Johannes Kepler's Fight for His Mother*. Great Clarendon Street, Oxford: Oxford University Press.

Ruether, R. (1998) *Women and Redemption: A Theological History*. London: SCM Press Ltd.

Russell, J. (1972) *Witchcraft in the Middle Ages*. New York: Cornell University Press.

Scarre, G. (1987) *Witchcraft and Magic in Sixteenth and Seventeenth & Seventeenth Century Europe*. London: Macmillan.

Schatzman, M. (1973) *Soul Murder: Persecution in the Family*. London: Allen.

Schatzman, M. & Israëls, H. (1993) 'The Seduction Theory' in *The History of Psychiatry* 4.

Schimek, J. (1987) 'Fact and Fantasy in the Seduction Theory: A Historical Review' in *The Journal of the American Psychoanalytic Association* 35.

Scot, R. (1584) *The Discoverie of Witchcraft*. New York: Dover (1972).

Shakespeare, W. (1987) *The Tempest*. Great Clarendon Street, Oxford: Oxford University Press.

Showalter, E. (1997) *Hystories: Hysterical Epidemics and Modern Culture*. London: Picador.

Sinason, V. (ed.) (1994) *Treating Survivors of Satanist Abuse*. London: Routledge.

Skues, R. (1987) 'Jeffrey Masson and the assault on Freud', *British Journal of Psychotherapy* 3 (4): 305–14.

Smith, J. (ed.) (1996) *Dictionary of Religion*. London: Harper Collins.

Soldan, W.G. (1843) *Geschichte der Hexenprozesse*. Munich: G. Muller. History of the Witch Trials (trans. 1912).

Solignac, P. (1976) *The Christian Neurosis* (trans. 1982). SCM Press Ltd.

Soskice, J.M. (1990) 'Bound by Blood: Circumcision and Menstrual Taboo' in *After Eve*, ed. J.M. Soskice. London: Marshall Pickering.

Stadlen, A. (1989) 'Was Dora "Ill"?' in *Sigmund Freud: Critical Assessments*, Vol. 2, ed. L. Spurling. London: Routledge.

Stadlen, A. (1994) 'Tell It Not in Dan: The Untold Story of Freud's Seduction theory'. Transcript of an unscripted talk at the Institute of Contemporary Art, London, 19 March.

Stadlen, A. (1997-) 'Freud Centenary' Seminars. Regents University, London.

Stadlen, A. (1999) Personal communication.

Swales, P.J. (1982a) 'Freud, Minna Bernays, and the Conquest of Rome' in *The New American Review*, 1(2/3).

Swales, P.J. (1982b) 'A Fascination with Witches' in *The Sciences*, 22: 21–25. NY Academy of Sciences.

Swales, P.J. (1989 [1982]) 'Freud, Johann Weier, and the Status of Seduction: The Role of the Witch in the Conception of Fantasy' in *Sigmund Freud: Critical Assessments*, Vol. 1: 331–358. ed. L. Spurling. London: Routledge.

Szasz, T.A. (1972) *The Myth of Mental Illness*. London: Paladin.

Szasz, T.A. (1988) *The Myth of Psychotherapy*. Syracuse: Syracuse University Press.

Szasz, T.A. (1997) *The Manufacture of Madness: A Comparative Study of the Inquisition and the Mental Health Movement*. London: Routledge & Kegan Paul.

Trevor-Roper, H.R. The European Witch craze of the Sixteenth and (1988) *Seventeenth Centuries*. London: Penguin.

Ward, I. (ed.) (1993) *Is Psychoanalysis Another Religion: Contemporary Essays on Spirit, Faith and Morality in Psychoanalysis*. London: Freud Museum Publications.

Webster, J. (1677) *Displaying of Supposed Witchcraft*. London: J.M.

Weyer, J. (1563) *De Praestigiis Daemonum, & incantationibus ac Venificiis*, trans. George Mora (1991) *Witches, Devils and Doctors in the Renaissance*. Binghamton, NY: Medieval & Renaissance Texts & Studies.

Wilks, S. (1878) *Lectures on Diseases of the Nervous System*. Philadelphia, PA: Lindsay & Blakiston.

Willems, B.A. (1969) *The Reality of Redemption*. London: Burns & Oates.

Zilboorg, G. (1941) With Henry, G.H. *A History of Medical Psychology*. London: Allen & Unwin.

Zweig, S. (1943) *The World of Yesterday*. New York: Viking.

INDEX

Page numbers in *italics* indicate figures on the corresponding pages.